UNLIKELY PARADISE

UNLIKELY PARADISE

The Life of
FRANCES GAGE

ALAN D. BUTCHER

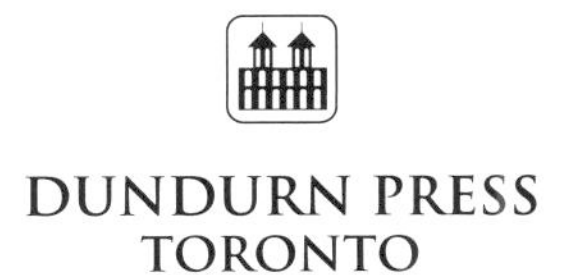

DUNDURN PRESS
TORONTO

Copy Editor: Allison Hirst
Designer: Jennifer Scott
Printer: Friesens

Library and Archives Canada Cataloguing in Publication

Butcher, Alan D
Unlikely paradise : the life of Frances Gage / by Alan D. Butcher.

Includes bibliographical references and index.
ISBN 978-1-55488-423-0

1. Gage, Frances, 1924-. 2. Sculptors--Canada--Biography. I. Title.

NB249.G34B88 2009   730.92   C2009-902454-3

1   2   3   4   5   13   12   11   10   09

 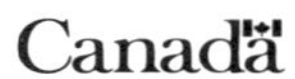 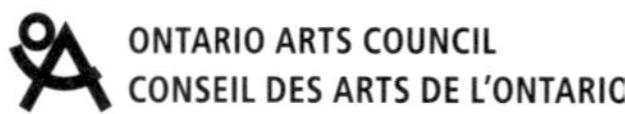

We acknowledge the support of the **Canada Council for the Arts** and the **Ontario Arts Council** for our publishing program. We also acknowledge the financial support of the **Government of Canada** through the **Book Publishing Industry Development Program** and The **Association for the Export of Canadian Books**, and the **Government of Ontario** through the **Ontario Book Publishers Tax Credit program**, and the **Ontario Media Development Corporation**.

Care has been taken to trace the ownership of copyright material used in this book. The author and the publisher welcome any information enabling them to rectify any references or credits in subsequent editions.

J. Kirk Howard, President

Printed and bound in Canada.
www.dundurn.com

Dundurn Press	Gazelle Book Services Limited	Dundurn Press
3 Church Street, Suite 500	White Cross Mills	2250 Military Road
Toronto, Ontario, Canada	High Town, Lancaster, England	Tonawanda, NY
M5E 1M2	LA1 4XS	U.S.A. 14150

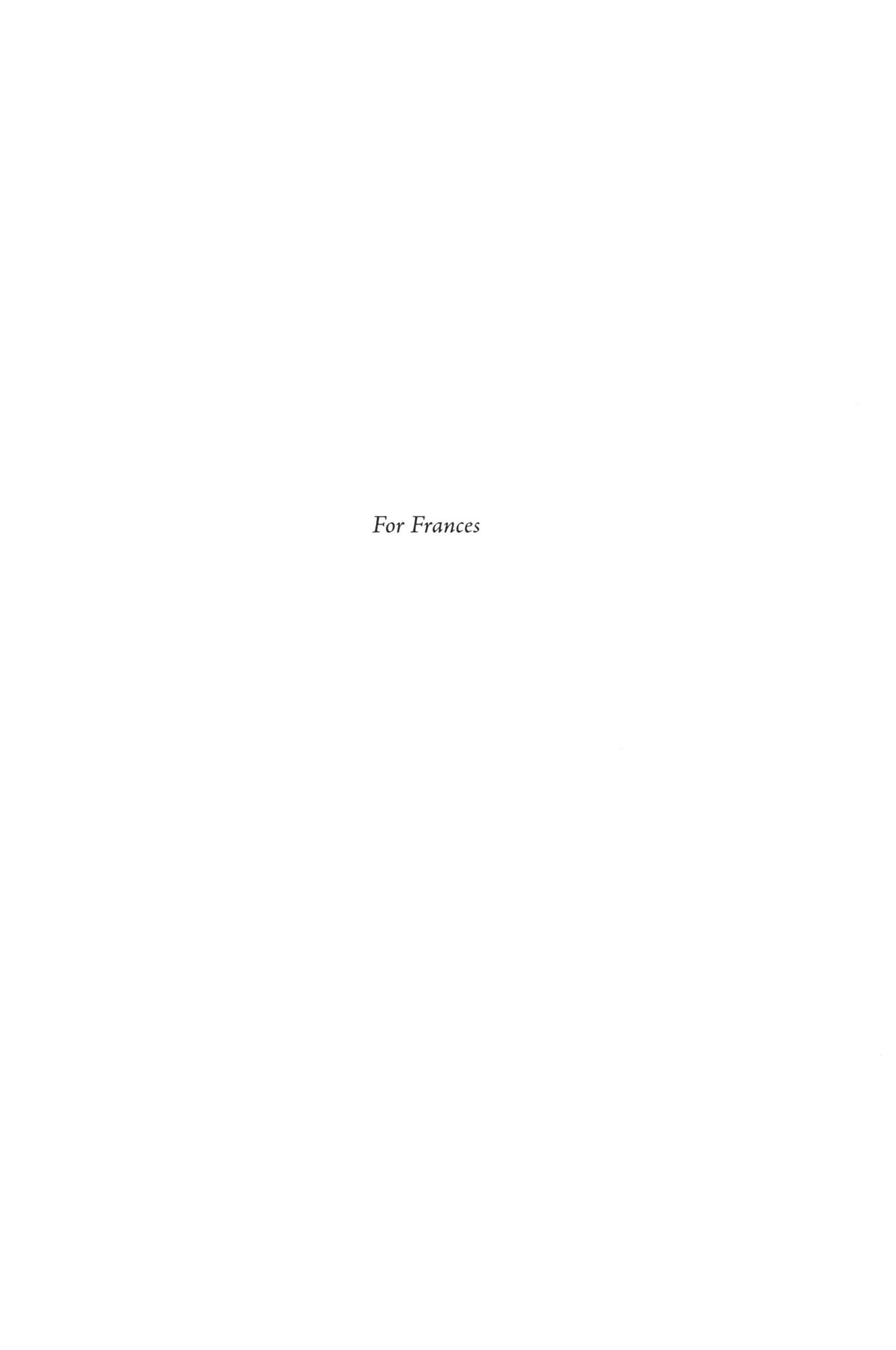

For Frances

CONTENTS

ACKNOWLEDGEMENTS

I WOULD FIRST LIKE TO thank my editor at Dundurn Press, Allison Hirst, without whose keen eye and boundless expertise this book would have been the poorer. Her recommendations and rare common sense made so much difference. In addition, I would particularly like to thank Dorette Carter, curator of the Art Gallery of Northumberland, for her time and the information she provided in what was the first interview for the journey taken in these pages. Marnie Williamson, Frances's classmate during the years at the former Ontario College of Art, added priceless background colour to those early days. Clare MacKay's comments proved invaluable, as did those of Malcolm Wardman.

Rebecca Sisler has been Frances's friend for many years, and her book *Passionate Spirits: A History of the Royal Canadian Academy of Arts* gave me hours of reading enjoyment and, not incidentally, important material for this book.

Repeated proofreading, both by me and by others, has corrected errors and improved many a lazy paragraph. Any that remain are no one's fault but mine. If I have overlooked a source, I apologize, and assure you your contribution is no less appreciated. There will always be errors and oversights in any manuscript. In such cases I must put myself at the mercy of the court of common sense. In many instances the only readily available source of information was my subject herself. To search out and confirm the correct spelling of a name, a name that occurred only once, might often have taken days, if not weeks. May I plead the obvious? There are just so many hours in a day, so many years in a lifetime. If I still stand accused, then I must shrug and accept guilt.

There has been a recent brouhaha over writers who have lied in the writing of biographies. There seems to be a tendency among some to turn to their lawyers when a memoir or biography calls fabrication fact, when every word is not historically true, when every quote is not word for word as uttered by the persons involved. I have not consciously sought lies to stand as truth but as Francis Bacon told us four hundred years ago, anyone undertaking a work such as the one at hand "cannot but meet with many blanks and spaces which he must be forced to fill up out of his own wit and conjecture." I have indeed quoted people as having said this or that as much as half a century ago, and no, I cannot prove their remarks are correct and verbatim. Fifty years is a long time, and those who may have supposedly expressed those views are no longer with us to refute, modify, or confirm them. For literary purposes, I have "quoted" them; quotes, other than those attributed to Frances, are, in most instances, inventions. But all these quotes reflect what the characters *might easily have said* under the circumstances, in words I feel *could have been theirs*, expressing intentions or beliefs they *probably would have held*. In many instances I have fabricated remarks by Frances herself that were never recorded or uttered by her, but these, too, express what I believe she could have said, given the feelings and views expressed in her volumes of correspondence and a half-century of daily records. If you feel I'm wrong in doing this, you are entitled to your opinion, and like Voltaire, I will defend to the death your right to express it.

I have assiduously tried to avoid libel in my own statements and those attributed to others. At one point Frances referred to a confrere as "a prick." Ever on the lookout for offensive material, I deleted it. However,

I am dealing with the life of a human being, with all that implies; an offensive word or phrase may have slipped through the cracks, or indeed I may have used it because I felt it was apropos. If a reader gasps with outrage, I recommend revisiting the "offensive" material; I think you will find, on reflection, I am justified.

The cold January wind sweeps down the darkened alley. At the alley's end, a young woman stands in the doorway of a dilapidated shack. Inside the shack the temperature is below zero, the stove doesn't work, there is no plumbing, a single light bulb hangs from the ceiling, and she barely has a chair to sit on. She has little money and no prospect of earning more. The future is unknown.

She is the happiest woman in the world.

PROLOGUE

THE WOMAN STANDS IN THE doorway of her squalid shack. Already she thinks of it as hers though she took possession only the week before. She will remember that day forever: January 21, 1957.

In front of her, across the patch of overgrown ground, is the three-storey bulk of the Studio Building, built in Toronto more than forty years before by the wealthy painter Lawren Harris for his artist friends, many of whom would later form the famous Group of Seven. The shack had been a tool shed used by the workers during the construction of the building.

Now, standing in the doorway, looking north as the late afternoon shadows creep up the wall of the Studio Building, she shivers. The cold January wind reminds her that February is yet to come, and the shack will grow even colder. The small stove will fight the plain wooden uninsulated walls — and lose. Today it had already taken six hours to coax from it a tenuous Scrooge-like heat that allowed her to remove just one of the many layers of clothing she wore.

But the previous evening, despite the fact that she could see her breath in the arctic air of the shack, she had curled up beside the stove and read a book with deep pleasure. The light from the single bulb had illuminated the paintings of the Group of Seven that hung on the walls, looking down upon her, and she had been happy.

But now, casting her eyes back to the interior of the shack and seeing there the meagre signs of a sculptor's studio, she feels a pang of something deeper than mere concern, rather a real fear of ... what? Disaster? No, not yet. Still ... on the work table there is the model of the small owl. Pretty little thing; it'll be lovely when cast. Yes ... the pang of concern again. When cast. And where, she thought, do I get the money for that casting? It's cast or eat. Okay, not quite as bad as that — yet. She sighs, a sigh that carries an edge of exasperation. There must be thousands, well, hundreds of people in Toronto, in Canada, who would benefit from my work, my talent. I've learned the skills given me by some of the finest sculptors in the world, and my own talents are there, right there in these hands. Isn't that enough? Is it? Have all those years of study been for nothing? The years here in the Ontario College of Art? The years studying in New York, in Paris? All those years? My whole life?

She turns and goes inside, her mind tormented by the shadows of an uncertain future, and the shades of an often unsatisfying past.

| 1 |

THE ARTIST GOES TO SEA

FRANCES HOLDS UP AN OLD photograph. It's small, black and white; the product of a Kodak box camera of the twenties. A child — a baby really — stares out. The rumpled dress, the frills and ribbons, suggest a girl. She looks dishevelled; the clothes seem never to have seen an iron. She appears unhappy, and twists uncomfortably in her grown-up chair. She stares out, a cornered animal.

Frances frowns at the photo. "I've got a funny expression on my face. Father had spanked me because I wouldn't sit still." Her voice takes on a tone of mock outrage. "Thanks a lot!" She tosses the photo on the table. "I think I was a year old, maybe. Hard to tell."

She was born Frances Marie Gage in Windsor, Ontario, on August 22, 1924, the third of four children of Russell Gage (no middle name) and Jean Mildred Collver.

Frances had a brother and two sisters. Robert was the first-born, followed by Marion, Frances, and Barbara. Both Robert and Barbara would eventually fall victim to alcohol dependency. Frances believed that not only genetics led Barbara to alcohol, but that her father's unrelenting attitude, almost of dislike, of constant rejection, was to a great degree responsible.

Marion, on the other hand, was the good little girl, and smart enough to realize that if she sat in the corner and did nothing, she was treated all right, most of the time.

Frances, unfortunately for her, was the adventurous one, the one who got into all the scrapes and ended up on the short end of her father's exasperation with children in general, and Frances in particular.

Frances's cousin Keith Collver was her lifelong friend. In her early years they got into trouble together, regularly. One day her brother had returned home with his pockets full of apples, but like big brothers everywhere, he wouldn't give her any. "If you want some, go and get them yourself," he had said. So she and Keith went off along the highway, two little world travellers, three or four years old, in search of apples. Fortunately word got around, and the adventurers were met along the road by their mothers — with switches. Back home the pair were denied supper and put to bed on bread and milk, which Frances thought was very nice, actually.

Years later, Keith Collver survived the "experimental" Dieppe raid of the Second World War that was mounted in August 1942, during which 6,000 Allied troops — 5,000 of whom were Canadians — landed and suffered losses of 70 percent killed or captured. Keith Collver died in his sixties of bone cancer. Frances never ceased to mourn him.

All her life Frances was drawn to music. Wherever she lived, from basement rooms and cold-water walk-ups, to homes and studios she designed herself, there was always classical music playing softly in the background. Recordings and CBC Radio shared every hour of her life. She travelled widely in Europe, and recitals, symphonies, and musical stage performances were part of every trip. She played the violin in orchestras. She had a fine voice and sang in choirs in New York and Paris as well as Toronto. As a child she sang in the family car during the roadtrips they took together. Her father had a pretty good bass, and her mother a fine contralto. Her brother Bob used to complain that Frances wandered in and out of his tenor parts, but she kept harmonizing, if "harmonizing" is the right term, regardless of his baseless objections.

Like most children, Frances loved every animal, then and forever. Again, like every child, she once brought home a cat. Her father, however, wasn't having any of that. They had a dirt cellar, and the family wasn't about to see a stray cat use the cellar as its litter box. Her parents really didn't like animals that much anyway. Frances was thus faced with one of the first big decisions in her life. She couldn't just throw the cat away; it would probably come back, and her parents would punish her for having deliberately engineered it. So, rather than call the affair a complete loss, she sold the cat to a passerby for a nickel. Hey, a nickel was a lot of money back then. She was now a young titan of the business world. But in those early days, Big Business didn't play an enduring role in her life; within a day or two she would drag home another cat or dog, hoping against all odds to be able to keep this one. When she eventually took control of her own life she was never without a dog and at least one cat, an unbroken series of heartwarming companions down all the years. But in those early days, within her family, her love of animals was a lonely passion.

Her father was five-foot-six, a stocky and powerfully built man. His hair, which he retained until late in life, was blond; all his children were blond. In appearance, Frances took after him; there was never a question of whose child she was. He was a determined, no-nonsense individual, firm in his opinions. As the only male child he had been spoiled by three sisters and became, as a result, unwaveringly self-centred. He was always right, never wrong. He expressed himself bluntly, and did not seem concerned if he offended. Once, when introduced to Russell Gage, a new acquaintance remarked, in the way one parent will with another, "Ah, yes, you belong to Frances." Russell Gage was not the man to let that pass. "No," he said, "Frances belongs to *me*."

When her father was angry he would go out to the barn and beat the horses. This was incomprehensible to Frances. "But," she said, "when you're angry you take it out on whatever you've got, and he took it out on us, as well, when he was frustrated." This behaviour coloured her life. She could never forgive, or forget, such treatment of an animal.

Her brother Robert, though treated as severely as his three sisters, was nevertheless the first-born, The Male. "He was the second coming of Christ," said Frances. "He had the Gage name," she added with a cold smile. Tragically, Robert's only son was killed in a car accident at the age of twenty-seven. "So the name is gone," said Frances. Then her voice rose. "But I've still got it!"

Her paternal grandparents were farmers, and had attempted to raise her father to be a farmer, too. He had no education, other than the basic elementary grade school, but through his own diligence he had rejected farming and become a self-taught engineer. Today, the idea of a self-taught engineer is akin to being a self-taught brain surgeon, but in turn-of-the-century communities it was possible to be self-taught in areas that would be unthinkable now.

Shortly after Frances's birth, he lost his business. He'd had an automobile franchise in partnership with another man. The partner withdrew, taking half the company's funds, and the business collapsed. But Russell Gage was ambitious. He would never be without a job, even during the Depression, and after losing the car dealership, he joined the Ford Motor Company, starting right at the bottom. Later he moved to General Motors and rose to mid-management level as an engineer.

Frances's mother was very Irish: rosy cheeks, bright blue eyes, curly hair. Her disposition was gentle, most of the time, but she could suddenly blow up. If you were smart you learned to recognize the signs. She was a fraction of an inch taller than her husband, and somewhat portly. Her nose had a distinct aquiline cast — the "Celtic beak," as Frances called it. She was a good cook, a characteristic that Frances did not inherit. Her major failing was a lack of self-confidence, again not inherited by Frances, who, despite her many claims to the contrary, never lacked conviction. Her mother's want of self-assurance was not helped by her husband's often blunt assessments. Once, when she remarked, with reference to her cooking methods, that she made up a lot out of her own mind, her husband snorted derisively. "Can't be much left, then, can there?" In assessing her mother, Frances said: "She was just an unhappy woman who spent all her time looking after four kids."

Frances's feelings for her father were reflected in her relations with her paternal grandmother. She did not get along well with Grandma Gage. Once when Frances was a child she had a penny — one of the big pennies that were current in the twenties. She was playing in front of a store, considering how she might invest the penny in some candy, when it accidentally fell from her pocket and a tough kid put his foot on it and wouldn't give it back. She rushed to her Grandma and cried "Help! He won't give me my penny!" Grandma Gage coldly turned her back. "You have to fight your own battles," she said. Frances mourned the loss of her penny and also felt a burning resentment toward her grandma; she had reached out for help and been rejected. In the end, Frances accepted the fact. "She was right. I had to fight my own battles."

Frances claimed that she ran away from home when she was eight or nine years old. It was actually a visit to nearby cousins but, for a little girl, running away is much more exciting than visiting. Anyone can visit; it takes guts to run away.

Frances had cousins who lived on a farm in Ancaster, Ontario, just west of Hamilton. In Frances's eyes the farm was a paradise of horses, cows, ducks, and pets. She loved it. So one day she decided to visit them … and walked. Of course, it took her most of the day because she inevitably met a friendly dog, and studied the petals of a flower, and watched an ant as it hurried along a dirt path; so many important and interesting things. When she neared Ancaster, she spoke to people at various garages and on the street, or homeowners standing in their driveways, and asked where Charlie Gage lived. Ultimately she arrived at the Gage farm.

"Why, hello, Frances!" said Charlie. He looked around. "Where are your parents?"

"In Hamilton." Frances was busy looking for the horses.

Charlie was puzzled. "How did you get here?"

"Walked."

The Gages were horrified, and immediately telephoned the Hamilton Gages. *Uh-oh*, thought Frances, *now I'm in for it.* "But my father didn't say a word. I was gone all day and they hadn't even missed me. That's how treasured I was. Walked all the way," she added with a certain pride.

Uncle Charlie and his wife had two children whom they cherished, a closeness that did not go unremarked by the adventurer from Hamilton. *This is a sappy kind of family*, she thought. *They hug each other.* But this sappy family also had equally beloved animals, and this was something Frances could understand. "I remember when they buried their old horse. They got a big shovel pulled by another horse — a sort of horse-powered backhoe — and they ceremoniously buried the old horse behind the barn, because they loved him so much. They were my kind of people."

Frances's love of animals was firm, enthusiastic, and openly expressed. Beneath the surface, however, there simmered another drive, unrecognized, unformed, but present. And it was growing.

Rebecca Sisler, author of *Passionate Spirits: A History of the Royal Canadian Academy of Arts, 1880–1980*, says that artists spring from every background, and that virtually all exhibit an interest in art from their earliest years. They do not appear to make a conscious choice of art over another profession. They gravitate to art unconsciously, as they would to breathing.

Recognition first came to Frances Gage in the summer of 1932, at the age of eight. On that summer day, Frances was sitting on her front porch working on a mud sculpture. In her critical eye it had a certain merit. When Mr. O'Connor, a neighbour, passed by, his interest was caught by the work-in-progress.

"That sculpture," he said — and the words may have changed the girl's life — "is very good."

Mr. O'Connor took the little sculpture to Sovereign Potteries in Hamilton, where they fired it. But there are times when nothing goes right, and this was one of those times. The clay Frances had used was dirty clay from the nearby creek and it exploded in the company's oven.

But perhaps Mr. O'Connor's sharp eye had seen something in the young sculptor that no one else had seen; maybe he had looked into a little heart and seen what might yet be. Or maybe he was just a nice man who was touched by the expression of loss on the girl's face when he told her of the accident. A few days later, he arrived on Frances's doorstep with a small package of Sovereign Potteries' clay. The real thing! She was beyond words. This was the purest clay, used for fine porcelain.

Mr. O'Connor's considerate gesture made a profound impression on the girl. "I did some marvellous things with that clay," said Frances.

Her father threw them in the furnace.

"One of them was a horse's head," Frances said. "I was very fond of horses. It was one of the things my father threw in the furnace. I found it when I was cleaning out the clinkers. That was one of my chores, sifting the ashes to retrieve unburned coal.

"My mother used to say 'Everything you do is so messy!' My parents were brought up in farming communities where everything had to be tidy and have a reason. No one would ever sit down and do anything that lacked a purpose because there was always something constructive to do. You shelled peas or knitted something for the baby or tilled your soil. Because of my family's background, it was a surprise to them that I would do something as 'silly' as become an artist. But I did it."

Both of Frances's grandmothers may have provided a genetic artistic background. Her father's mother had wanted to be a painter but in those days farmers' wives didn't do what they wanted, they did what the farm, and their husbands, demanded. However, her husband died young, and she took up painting. Her work showed a certain facility, and with professional training she might easily have produced some noteworthy canvases. Frances's grandmother on her mother's side took the literary route, writing poetry. She wrote of her desire to walk in the woods instead of immersing herself in the unending work of the house, animals, and children.

> Away from the fly-sweep, an hour let it rest,
>   the woods are calling me.
> While memory fails where the flies are a pest,
>   the woods are calling me.
> How could I live in the great busy town,
> 'thout the breath of the wildwood and leaves fluttering
>   down,
> The great trees might miss me if I wasn't around,
>   the woods are calling me.[1]

From early days in Hamilton the family moved to Oshawa. Here Frances attended King Street School and ultimately the Oshawa Collegiate and Vocational Institute, where her growing artistic talents were recognized and encouraged by her art teacher, Dorothy Van Luven. Frances graduated from Oshawa Collegiate in 1944, and won the award for Most Outstanding Girl of the School.

Friends indirectly fostered Frances's own artistic inclination. Una Brown Noble, a neighbour and a painter, became a great friend. For two summers, in 1934 and 1935, she took Frances to Algonquin Park, the beautiful nature reserve 145 kilometres north of Oshawa, Ontario. "I don't know why anybody would want to be bothered by a scruffy little kid hanging around all the time," said Frances, "but she did." Una Noble had a small cottage on Canoe Lake, where memories of the painter Tom Thomson's death were still fresh. But Frances's intimate contact with Thomson was still twenty years in the future. As an eleven-year-old girl vacationing with her friend, she spent six to eight weeks in Algonquin Park during those two wonderful summers. It was her first contact with the park, a contact she was later to renew for many years as a counsellor at a summer camp.

Una Noble died of kidney failure at the age of thirty-nine. This was the first big tragedy in Frances's life. Her mother said, "Never

---

1   Laura Kelly Collver. Independently published, posthumously, *circa* 1940.

mind, you'll see her in Heaven." This did little to relieve Frances. "Yeah, but I might be eighty and she'll still be thirty-nine!" she wailed. "What kind of a relationship will we have?!"

Up to this point in her life, Frances felt a lack of what she called "structure." There seemed an absence of organization in her days; all things seemed unplanned, without scope or goals. She felt, not so much a need for someone to tell her what to do and when, but rather recognizable rules to which she might willingly adhere, rules that had a sound reason behind them.

The summer of 1943, the year before she graduated, she worked at odd jobs here and there. But she sensed that nothing had changed; she was drifting, directionless. She worked for a while in the Ontario Parks and Recreation Department and found some of the structure she lacked.

Early in the war, if a young person did well in school they were allowed to work on a farm, so she worked for the Ontario Farm Service for part of that summer. Here, also, she found that structure. She was told to get up at 5:00 a.m., pack her lunch, and go out into the fields. She would return at noon and actually catch an hour's sleep because it was such hard work, but she found it immensely satisfying. Later, she worked for E.D. Smith, grafting, planting, and filling orders for fruit trees, and not incidentally discovering a lifelong passion for trees, plants, and all growing things. She was taught to care for plants, and learned the names of trees; she felt she was learning and doing something useful, both for herself and for others. She was finding new dimensions within herself, and she loved it.

On the heels of self-discovery came a degree of confidence and determination. Germany still controlled Europe, Japanese forces were spreading across the Pacific, and the Normandy landings were still a year away. Frances celebrated her nineteenth birthday that summer, and with that milestone the future opened before her. When she graduated in 1944 she made her decision.

She joined the navy.

| 2 |

A SAILOR'S DAYS AND POLITICAL NIGHTS

BY THE SUMMER OF 1942, the tragedy that was the Battle of Britain had passed, at heartbreaking cost, and England was still there, though standing on the edge of the abyss. The war brought a lack of manpower in many essential areas. The WRCNS, or Women's Royal Canadian Naval Service, was formed to assume the roles men were not available to perform. While many in those years would have looked puzzled if you mentioned the WRCNS, the affectionate sobriquet "Wren" was immediately recognized. Thousands of Canadian women answered the call, and by the time the service was disbanded in August 1946, nearly 7,000 young Wrens had taken over such jobs as sick bay attendant, cook, mail sorter, truck or ambulance driver, radar operator, and, in Frances's case, telegrapher (communications). And these were just a few of the dozens of services provided by the Wrens. The young ladies earned — and earned is the very word; they *earned* their pay — about one-third the money paid their fellow (male) sailors. It was felt, in those misguided days, that it took three women to do the work of one man, an assumption the Wrens quickly disproved.

The Ontario government had provided a school in Galt for the use of the new women's naval service, and by the close of 1942, the initial contingent of Wrens had arrived. In June 1943, the training base was commissioned HMCS *Conestoga*, under the command of the executive officer, Lieutenant H.M. Macdonald, and quickly acquired the nickname "The Stone Frigate."

Marjorie Jordan, one of Frances's old friends and an officer in the Wrens, had persuaded Frances that the navy was the best of the services, and Frances was easily convinced. Marjorie was a very attractive woman, and even more so in her smart uniform.

Life in the navy gave Frances more of the structure she did not see in her life at home. She was never keen about being told what to do, preferring always to do what she felt was right, what she knew was good for her, what she wanted to do. Her first hours in the navy brought a glint of revolt to her eye; anyone who has been part of the military knows that if you seek common sense, you'll not find it there. The military bureaucracy has more rules and regulations than a dog has fleas, and anyone who is prone to do as she pleases and follow the sensible dictates of her own intelligence will quickly find she is in the wrong place.

Frances spent four weeks in HMCS *Conestoga*, undergoing the standard drills and lectures. From there, sixty Wrens were sent to the Canadian Signal School in Saint-Hyacinthe, Quebec, to become visual signallers. Twenty of these, including Frances, then transferred to become TSOs (Telegrapher Special Operator).

During Frances's time in the navy, she was in Intelligence, specifically monitoring Japanese ships and submarines. But she didn't know she was working for the secret service until she was discharged. "We were getting an extra seventy-five cents a day," she said, "and couldn't figure out why." But in 1945, six-bits was six-bits, so you didn't ask questions.

Once, when monitoring a particular frequency, Frances heard a strange and continuous beeping. She and the other Wrens tracked it right across the prairies. They couldn't understand what it was. Eventually they learned it was a weather balloon; one came down over central Canada and the authorities were able to identify it and determine its use. It was Japanese, and had apparently been sent over to test air currents. Some, according to Frances, were armed with small bombs, and all had transmitters and were sending back weather patterns to Japan. "The theory was," said Frances, "they were going to send more powerful bombs and release them in the right place at the right time. Which they didn't, thank goodness!" Frances estimated the balloons were thirty feet in diameter and made of rice paper. "Must have been quite an engineering feat," she said. "I imagine it had ribs and stuff made of bamboo. It seemed beyond belief: a rice paper balloon, borne on air currents, making its way across the Pacific Ocean!"

For the remainder of 1944, until the middle of March 1945, the Wrens' days were an unending series of studies and lectures. There was a rumour that the top fifteen in the upcoming exams would be going to the west coast. The rumour proved true, and Frances was one of the fifteen. They left for Vancouver on May 3, 1945. Frances arrived there on VE Day, then boarded the boat to Victoria — her first "sea" voyage. After five days at HMCS *Givenchy* in Esquimalt, she and her fellow Wrens were sent south to Seattle — Bainbridge Island — on loan to the American navy.

As a child, Frances got into a lot of trouble doing what she wanted to do. As a Wren, not much changed. She was an attractive, blond, twenty-year-old woman, and so was her friend Marnie. American sailors were no slower than Canadian sailors, so, within two days of joining the Canadian Wrens' school in Seattle, she and her friend were invited by an American sailor to tour one of the large warships moored near the navy yard.

When it came time to leave the vessel, the two Wrens stepped ashore in the navy yard — and were promptly arrested. A marine officer seized them and dragged them off to the station.

"How the hell did you get in?" cried the American officer. "A colonel in the U.S. Army can't get into this place without a pass!"

And then he phoned the FBI.

Frances and Marnie looked at each other, at a loss to understand. They had just walked in with their friend, the American sailor, casual as you please, and been given the Grand Tour of the USS *Bunker*

Hill. And here they were, with the officer talking to the FBI guy on the phone.

"Their stories check …" and "Their number on file …" and "At the time they were apprehended …" Frances swallowed. *Apprehended?!*

Finally, another officer came in and said, "How did you people get in?"

Frances, by now more irritated than frightened, looked him coldly in the eye. "We swam in — from Canada."

The officer, Frances thought, appeared to have had "a couple of jars" with his lunch. In any event, he took her response without offence, escorted them to the gate, and let them go.

On July 5, 1945, Frances's group returned to Canada.

In August 1945, the Japanese surrendered, bringing the Second World War to an end, and with the cessation of hostilities, Frances's thoughts turned to the future. Get out or stay in?

A week after the war ended, she celebrated her twenty-first birthday. Her friends gave her a party, and among her gifts were a sketch pad, a pencil, and a portfolio — a subtle hint of things to come. Throughout her time in the navy she had been sketching regularly. She found she had a facility and could capture a likeness easily and quickly.

At this point, her inclination was to leave the navy and take advantage of what was for many servicemen and women the opportunity of a lifetime: A university education, paid for by the Department of Veterans' Affairs.

By mid-September she had made her decision, and submitted her name to the RCN depot, her formal "resignation" from the navy. It was not without the usual advice from many quarters. "Lieutenant Cassidy advised me to take art, but to stay in for awhile," she said. "And after the Victory Loan Show, where I sang, Lieutenant Berlin wanted me to become a torch singer." She laughed, but was thoughtful, too. "Might have been interesting."

Above all, though, was the university education. But in what field? Medical? Her love of animals was strong, and veterinary medicine had its appeal. Music? She was already a competent violinist, she had a good voice, and music had always been in her nature. Art? Her sketching led her to consider drawing or painting; she thought she might become a good portrait artist.

In mid-October she sang at the Givenchy dance. "Dark Eyes" and "Night and Day" went over very well, and once again she saw herself draped over a piano, provocative off-the-shoulder dress, her husky voice lamenting a lost love, with Cole Porter at the keyboard, gazing up at her with a smile as he played the romantic hits of the day: Frances Gage, torch singer.

A long leave allowed Frances to return to home and family for the first time in seven months. Unfortunately, while her time in the navy had opened Frances's mind to the exciting opportunities the world had to offer, nothing much had changed at home. She found that her mother and sister Barbara still didn't get along. "Never did," said Frances. Barbara was the youngest of the family, neglected at best, more often roughly ordered about, to which she responded with the stubbornness inherited from her mother.

"For heaven's sake, girl, haven't you folded those shirts yet?"

"I'll fold them when I get around to it."

"Do it now." (A hard edge to the voice.)

"Later. Can't you see I'm busy?" (Equally hard.)

"Don't you give me that tone, my girl!"

Barbara would respond in kind, and any tranquility the day might have had was lost forever.

"There was the same unyielding nature in both of them," said Frances. "Like a couple of mules. The best thing in the world would have been for Barbara to get away from home. Good for Mother, too." Barbara, barely twenty, was already showing the signs of alcohol addiction, the demon that would torment her for the rest of her life.

On February 27, 1946, though she was technically still a Wren, Frances began a new job. She was hired to work on the development of a new Canadian flag. "I was still in the navy, but I had been doing a lot of drawing and sketching for the past two years, and had shown some of my work to Alan Beddoes, who was a wonderful typographer and an officer in the navy. The result was that I was hired to be the designer. Not so much the actual designer of the flag, but rather working with Alan to render the artwork of each design and determine the final choice among the many designs submitted."

Frances was given a working area in the House of Commons. There she made a panel bearing all the flags of the world, with a small area in the middle where a new Canadian design would be placed, visually affording a quick and easy way of avoiding duplication of, or similarity to, another nation's flag. Design suggestions came from a national contest. Frances took these submissions, drew them to scale, and then placed each in the panel for consideration by Alan Beddoes and herself, and the members of Parliament. They decided yes or no, then moved on to the next submission. "There were some very good ones," she said, "and some that were awful. Twenty years later, when A.Y. Jackson saw the flag we have now, he said it looked like a Japanese dishrag."

During the time she worked on the new flag, she was preoccupied by thoughts of the future. The flag work would not last forever. Veterinary medicine appealed to her. So did art. So did music. And, of course, there was always Frances the torch-singer. She sang at the Valentine party in mid-February, receiving much applause. She had a lovely contralto voice, and was confident that with proper training she could sing professionally. But as a career? Well, Doris Day and Jo Stafford weren't doing too badly. During February she thought about it, but did not forget the other possibilities. Another consideration was the Wrens itself. She could stay in the service and sign on for perhaps twenty years. There were men in the military who were doing just that, planning for a discharge twenty years down the road, with a good pension, only forty years old with twenty years experience in a trade! Get a job and you're looking at two incomes — paycheque and pension. The only thing wrong with that, in her mind, was those twenty long years in the service — not very exciting or satisfying.

Earlier, in February 1946, she had applied to the Ontario Veterinary College at Guelph for particulars on the course. A few days later she received a reply: she was number 361 on their waiting list of veterans. They would look forward to taking her in the fall of 1948. "I was devastated," said Frances. "I knew I simply couldn't wait two years. Now was the time I should be getting my education." Frustrated, depressed, anxious for her future, she didn't know where to turn.

Meanwhile, at "Flag HQ," Frances's "command post" in Ottawa, work on the new Canadian flag was moving ahead and she was buried in the bureaucratic brouhaha that surrounded the flag's development. Her discharge from the navy had come through on the twenty-eighth of February, but because of her work on the flag, a letter was written to the secretary of state, and the discharge was placed in abeyance for another six weeks.

As with all operations in the hands of bureaucracies, work on the flag went beyond the six weeks allotted for its completion, and when Frances's discharge was official, she would be obliged to come back and continue the flag work as a civilian. But until then, most of April was a madhouse of work, changes, delays, more changes, and more work.

On the twenty-third of April, she was on a train to Toronto for a much-appreciated leave, a brief few days with her family. She was twenty-one years old, the war was over, her navy days were over, but looking into her heart she found … nothing. She felt she knew nothing of herself, what she wanted to do with her life, what she *could* do with her life. Just emptiness. A complete blank. She experienced a sense of frustration, and a profound weariness. Study music? Study art? Like a child, she wanted to do both at once, but as a grown-up could decide on neither.

After a few days at home with her family, she was back in Ottawa on the first of May, as a civilian now. Her situation had changed, but it was business as usual in the committee room: Chaos. There were cartons of new flags yet to be examined and evaluated, hundreds of "old" flags that had been tested and found wanting in one way or another, and scores of designs that "seemed to exhibit a certain merit" for which Frances would have to execute the final art for the committee's consideration. By mid-May, she was reproducing what would become the lucky semi-finalists. "Most of them were stupid, though," she said with a long sigh of resignation.

But as sometimes happens in the senseless backing and filling of committee work, a ray of common sense penetrates the clouds of confusion. Someone pauses, and says "Hey, hang on a minute. We've got these flags down to about twelve. How about this: Let's submit them to a group of experts, people who know what they're doing." He then looks around at the committee members, all of whom are frowning, wishing they'd said that. Far away at her drawing board, Frances sighs again. "Should have been done months ago."

But it hadn't been done then, and it wasn't done now. New-born common sense was buried beneath discussions, amendments, meetings, and delays. Bureaucracy was once more ascendant. Disenchantment settled over Frances. "The matter is back in the hands of a bunch of politicians who know nothing about the job. And still it goes on! Even the big shots are getting into the act. The prime minister himself, Mackenzie King, dictated a design to me which he thought was awfully good."

On the seventeenth of June, Alan Beddoes delivered yet another large package to Frances at Flag HQ, the nerve centre of "The Flag Affair." She opened the parcel.

"Twenty-one variations on the red ensign." She marvelled at the consistency of the submissions, the number of treatments that doggedly dwelt on that single theme of the red ensign, at that time the de facto flag of Canada (though historically just the flag of the merchant marine). Frances was somewhat concerned. "I wonder if the ministers are aware that a lot of people don't want to change."

The next day, Alan Beddoes looked in and dropped another parcel on her desk. "More red ensigns," he said, "and, oh, here's a bunch with maple leaves. Not much imagination out there."

Two days later a frazzled Frances plodded up the stairs to the committee room. "Twenty-four more red ensigns, complete with maple leaves, up to the House of Commons. Will this week ever end?"

After four more days of the same monotonous story, she was growing reluctant to show up for work. "Reported in, and got three more designs that must be ready for the day after tomorrow. Don't know how long I can keep my sanity."

The next day: "Two more designs to paint up." After lunch Alan Beddoes looked into her office, hesitantly, and handed her another parcel.

"I don't want to see you!" she cried.

"It's, uh, not many. Maybe … could you do them after supper?"

The following morning she was called into Beddoes's office. He tried to smile bravely. "Hi, Frances!" He shuffled a few papers around on his desk. "There's a few, uh, sort of rush orders to paint …"

"A … few … rush … orders!" She almost stamped her foot. "Do you know? Have you any idea …" she stuttered. "Are you aware that I have yet to be paid for any of this flag business?"

The twenty-second of July was her last day, and she packed her bags and left for home. *As usual,* she thought, with the last shreds of exasperation, *after all this bureaucratic brouhaha, all these weeks of work, it would have been so much easier if they had taken the millions of dollars of taxpayers' money and simply flushed them down the toilet.*

The Great Flag Affair of 1946 was shelved and never heard of again.

To move from the active pointlessness of navy life to the inactive pointlessness of civilian life was not much of a career change, and in the autumn and early winter of 1946, Frances found herself looking for a job, any job, and growing more and more frustrated and hopeless, not to mention poorer and poorer with no source of income. The world seemed filled with jobs that started nowhere, went nowhere, and in that dull progress provided neither the satisfaction nor money to at least make them worth the effort. For Frances, sadness became depression. She was miserable at having missed the entry dates for any kind of educational institution; she still saw university as the only way to go. But she was left with a year to fill before she could try again and, not incidentally, to decide in which field she wanted to study. Her mind still jumped from art to music. Which field to pursue? How? Where? Even with the support of the Department of Veterans' Affairs, she was, as always, concerned about money. The government didn't pay for everything.

For the moment, she was staying with her family in Oshawa, which gave her a roof over her head but also the uncomfortable feeling of not being able to contribute. She had the loner's passion for independence, to be able to pay her own way, to be in a financial position to make her own decisions independent of anything and anyone else.

Two of her acquaintances, Jean and Jim Stafford, had recently been blessed with twins, and Frances agreed to give the parents some help for a period of three months. The pay? Five dollars per week. For a thirteen-hour day. Almost immediately she regretted the move. "God! I felt like — and was treated like — an au pair!" After three weeks, Frances had a serious discussion with the Staffords, and a new schedule was instituted. She would have the same duties, same pay, but the hours were reduced to five hours a day starting at 8:00 a.m. "Wow," said Frances, sarcastically, "my hourly rate more than doubled — seven cents an hour to a princely fifteen cents an hour. For heaven's sake, I knew a fifteen-year-old office boy — a mere gofer — who was making four times that!" And the incredible thing was that the Staffords seemed surprised, even hurt, by Frances's demands for an increase in pay.

During this period, Frances had been talking to the Oshawa YWCA. An offer of work brought the Stafford situation thankfully to an end, and by the last week in October 1946, Frances was working evenings at the YWCA.

Frances was not one to stand around waiting for someone to tell her what to do. From the outset she became involved with many of the YWCA's activities. By January 1947, she was the instructor of the sketching class, running the teen centre, giving lectures to women's groups, and at the same time continuing with her orchestra and choir practices and studying for her chemistry certificate.

Then, on January 20, 1947, there occurred one of those acts, prompted by an inexplicable change in mental state or chemistry, that happens perhaps once or twice in a lifetime. Or was it a rough push from Destiny's impatient hand? On that fateful morning in January, she took a firm grip on her own bootstraps, and pulled. "Okay, that's it. Time to cut the procrastinating and get to work." The next day, she left for Toronto and marched into the office of the registrar of the Ontario College of Art. Later the same day, she sat down with the people from the Department of Veterans' Affairs and made the decision that would change her life.

The following September she would enroll in the four-year program at the Ontario College of Art.

| 3 |

THE FAIRY GODMOTHER

THE DECISION TO ATTEND THE Ontario College of Art
(OCA) only partially solved the problem of Frances's further education.
It would be in the field of art, but as so often happened in Frances's
life, the solution to one problem simply revealed another. She would be
studying art, but which branch? Art is a broad field. Her initial lean-
ings were toward portrait painting, but her first year, Foundation Year,
introduced her to the wide range of disciplines available to her: painting,
yes, in all media, as well as life drawing, architecture, design, lettering,
modelling, costumes, and the entire history of art.

At the beginning of 1947, some eight months before her art studies were due to start, and without consciously considering sculpture as
her chosen field, Frances nevertheless followed her natural inclination.
She began woodcarving, and this occupied much of whatever spare
time she had. In the back of her mind there was always the knowledge
that she would need every dollar for the years at OCA. The Department of Veterans' Affairs would pay the tuition, plus a subsistence of
sixty dollars a month, but she would have to live in Toronto, and there
would be a thousand-and-one minor expenses, day after day, month
after month.

March and April saw Frances pushing ahead with her woodcarving, getting her materials and tools together and producing four dog

portraits. In May, she placed six dog portraits in Ada Mackenzie's gallery in Toronto. These were among her first carving efforts. Later she sent six more dog portrait samples to a sales outlet in Mont Tremblant, Quebec. By the end of September 1947, Frances had seen many of her carvings selling briskly in the two outlets she'd chosen. She produced a wide variety of breeds, among which, perhaps for subtle personal public relations purposes, was a carving of the Alsatian belonging to Ada Mackenzie, the gallery owner. Frances sold the carvings for seventy-five dollars each; the sales outlets sold them for whatever the market would bear.

By the middle of August, Frances was preparing to leave home again, this time for "wild" and "sprawling" mid-century Toronto. The city was not as big and cosmopolitan as Montreal, and it was still seven years away from the inauguration of the first subway system in Canada (and even that would only run between the train station and Eglinton Avenue, a distance of less than seven kilometres). North of Eglinton wasn't quite cattle country, but it was close. And the city was still very much "Toronto the Good." A quarter of a century would pass before the law would allow you to have a drink on your own front porch, and all you could do on a Sunday was wait for Monday.

But to Frances it was the Big City, and she got lost half a dozen times in her house-hunting which took her all over town, without success. She and an ex-navy friend, Marion Cornett, planned to rent an apartment together. Marion had taken a job with the *Telegram*, a Toronto newspaper. She was more familiar with the city and quickly found a place in Rosedale, at 181 Crescent Road. "When I went home to our place in Rosedale, I'd take the streetcar," said Frances. "This was the old streetcar that went up Yonge Street through Hog's Hollow. In those days the streetcar was heated by a coal stove." At some point along the way the conductor would stop and stoke up the stove, then continue up Yonge Street.

"When I went to see the rooms, I was sort of disappointed," said Frances. "They were in the cellar." A basement apartment was all right with Marion because she simply did not care where she lived. But Frances was different. To her a cellar was miserable — people's legs going by the window, the atmosphere damp and unappealing. "My slippers became mouldy under the bed. Horrible." But they had a wonderful landlord, a Mormon. "I heard him one day, hammering a nail. It must have bent or something and he cried 'Oh! That Free Methodist nail!' I guess Free Methodists were about the worst thing he could think of."

The basement apartment was in one of the wonderful old Rosedale mansions which had been "renovated" to accommodate about thirty roomers. The roomers came and went. "There were a bunch of students from Ryerson, and some elderly people down on their luck. They changed all the time.

"And yet, in a way, I liked the basement apartment," said Frances. "We had our own washroom, even though it was a laundry tub. There was a toilet down there. Beautiful old house. I got to know Rosedale very well because I rode around on a bicycle all the time. It was a bit confusing at first; there didn't seem to be a straight street in the whole area. We used to have taxi drivers come and ask us where they were."

Frances was in the Rosedale mansion for all four of her OCA years, first in the basement with Marion, her ex-navy friend. Shortly after moving in together, Marion left to get married, and Frances eventually took a top floor room, smaller but nicer and more convenient.

In that first year, after Marion's departure, Frances was faced with having to carry the full cost of the basement apartment. She approached Marnie Pond, another first-year student at OCA, with the idea of sharing. "Marnie's family came from Simcoe. They knew my relatives there, but not to speak to. Unlike the Ponds, my family was not upper class." Marnie Pond was a strikingly beautiful young woman of eighteen, an only child, fresh from Branksome Hall, an internationally acclaimed and very posh girls' school in upscale Rosedale.

"I would have been delighted to share the apartment with Frances," said Marnie. "At the time I was living with Mrs. Graham, a friend of my father. She had a nice apartment on Bloor Street at St. George. My father came with me to view Frances's rooms."

After a brief introduction to Frances — "How do you do, Mr. Pond." (warm smile) "Nice to meet you." — the gentleman's eye slowly scanned the basement apartment, what Frances herself called "the cellar." He glanced at the washtubs, and the toilet at the end of a dim hallway; saw the legs of passersby through the ground-level window; sensed the mouldy slippers under the bed. And was appalled.

"No," he said to Marnie, "I'd rather you stayed with Mrs. Graham."

"He was horrified," said Frances. "He'd seen the cellar, and the living conditions, which to him must have been primitive in the extreme. He'd absorbed the unabashed bohemian atmosphere, and I'm sure he looked at me — five years older than his daughter, an unknown woman, an artist, *and an ex-sailor!*"

"I had come straight from boarding school to OCA," said Marnie. "I was an only child. My father was very protective."

She did not join Frances.

"At the time, I was kind of mad at her," said Frances, "because she wouldn't share the apartment with me. But more than that, I think it was her father's upper-class attitude that really teed me off. Okay, a bit of ego there, I suppose, but his obvious contempt just irritated me. I imagined him thinking that I had a lot of unmitigated gall to suggest that my ratty cellar might be good enough for his lovely Branksome Hall daughter. But then again, when I thought about it later, I had to feel that maybe, just maybe, he was more than a little bit justified."

Shortly after the brief meeting with Marnie's father, Frances moved to the third floor of the old mansion, to a smaller and less expensive single room, and stayed there for the remainder of her time at OCA. "It was a tiny room. I could stand in the middle and reach anything I wanted. It was so small, almost like a cupboard, so I did all of my work at the school." OCA was open in the evening, and any homework that was required could be done there.

The year 1872 had seen the formation of the Ontario Society of Artists, a group which four years later opened an art school in Toronto.
This school, in 1912, became the Ontario College of Art (OCA). In
1996 the college would see its name changed to the Ontario College of
Art and Design, reflecting its artistic scope and standing as one of the
largest art/design universities in North America. But in 1947, it was
still the earlier OCA when a young woman walked through the front
door: Frances Gage, art-student-to-be.

"The place seemed to be a rabbit warren of stairways and passages
and doorways. It was so confusing. Later we were in the basement.
That's where they put the sculptors because we were so messy and noisy."

Creative pursuits treat rules with the indifference they deserve, and
rules at OCA were observed casually; there were much more important
things to consider, like food. "We always spread papers on the model
stand and had our lunch there. At lunch time in the OCA of 1947, you
didn't see too many knives and forks. We'd cut the bread for sandwiches
with a saw, or whatever was around. Most students brought their own
lunch, though you could, if you wished, and had the money, buy lunch
in the cafeteria. We always made tea, and a lot of the instructors came
and joined us. Will Ogilvie, the drawing instructor, came frequently."

Finances meant that Frances brought her own lunch. "I had the
grant from the Department of Veterans' Affairs. At that time it simply
had to be the best veterans' program in the world! But I still had to do
odd jobs elsewhere when I could. And I did everything, anything that
came along. I worked part-time for a veterinary surgeon on St. Clair
Avenue (Dr. Edith Williams), to learn my animal anatomy. It was very
good practice. Mostly cleaning cages. I also got a job each summer as
a counsellor at a summer camp, Camp Tannamakoon, in Algonquin
Park. I worked there for years."

The first year at OCA was an exciting time. No more "juvenile"
high school art classes; this was the Big Time, the real thing.

"We were in first year together, the same class," said Marnie. "We
became friends, the way one does at school. With the end of the war,

Frances must have found the atmosphere very free after her time in the navy, and I had come straight from boarding school, so we both had the feeling of being cut loose.

"She was not much of an extrovert — there are always lots of those around, among artists, or would-be artists. No, Frances was a serious, hard-working woman. And she was a woman, not a teenager. I was eighteen, she was twenty-three. There were many her age in that year. I think 1947 saw the biggest student roster ever, because so many veterans enrolled.

"Those first days were a very innocent time," said Marnie, "compared to the student life of today. First of all, in the life drawing classes, I had to get used to the idea of drawing a nude model. Not much of a shock to people now, but back then I can remember thinking *How can somebody stand up there like that?* I don't remember if Frances agreed with me." (when asked, Frances, the pragmatic ex-sailor, said, "She can stand up there like that because she's being paid for it.")

At the end of her first year at OCA, Frances was struck by one of her first major illnesses, the first of a long history of medical problems. She spent three months in Toronto's Sunnybrook Hospital battling a serious bout of infectious mononucleosis, a viral disease that attacks the liver. "It was a bad dose and I lost one whole term in my second year at art school, the autumn of 1948, but my wonderful Rosedale landlord kept my room for me. I don't think the medical profession knew very much about mononucleosis in those days. I'd wake up and there'd be four or five doctors in white coats staring down at me, and I'd be thinking *Oh, I'm gonna die!* It took me a long time to get over it. I probably wasn't eating properly, skimping on my food. Students do that. Food was not often a critical matter. We knew we'd live forever."

In Frances's days in art school, when the glass ceiling was made of reinforced concrete, some might wonder if women were really expected to be sculptors. "Just expected to get married," said Frances, "and have children, and look after husbands." But Frances did not encounter any such exclusion, at least not in the art world. Exemplified by art circles such as the Beaver Hall Hill Group in Montreal, and the Julian School in Paris, women had long since assumed a prominent role in the creative world, despite the frowns of the academies.

"The only resistance I found," said Frances, "was in my own family. My father always felt I should be doing something else, and expressed that view in a way that's become a cliché: 'Art is all very fine, my girl, but what are you going to do for a living?' And I don't think I was the only one who encountered that, not where families were concerned."

She felt her instructors at OCA were outstanding. "In Foundation Year, that was first year, there was Arthur Tracy, he was extremely good, particularly with techniques; Carl Schaeffer; Jack Martin; Will Ogilvie was my favourite, he taught drawing.

"And then there was our sculpture teacher, Emanuel Hahn ..."

Emanuel Otto Hahn (1881–1957) was one of the preeminent sculptors in Canada. As head of the sculpture department, he taught at OCA from 1912 to 1951. Among his many works is the design for the Canadian ten-cent Bluenose and twenty-five-cent Caribou coins, still in use after seventy-five years. In 1929, Hahn won the commission for the Adam Beck monument which now stands on the median on University Avenue in Toronto. It was unveiled in 1934.

"The Beck sculpture is a great memorial," said Frances. "Hahn was a wonderful craftsman. He taught me a lot about carving, and how to use tools properly, which was particularly good.

"But Manny Hahn was extremely difficult. He and I just didn't get along, but it wasn't me especially. Though maybe it was — I remember at one of his parties I refused to sit on his lap, and that was that. Crossed off his list forever!" Hahn had stormy encounters with others of the faculty. "Manny was just impossible to deal with. He was in his late sixties and really in his dotage. He retired (Frances's expression was "terminated") in 1951, the year I graduated. He had had life tenure, but he was simply too difficult."

But when is a man all of a piece? Experience teaches us to extend to talent a certain consideration, to accept vagaries of conduct, to see their better sides. Frances herself saw his genius as a sculptor, his imagination; his superior skills that lent her own a breadth she might not have gained. She saw him as once a very good-looking man, though height-challenged, the once-handsome physique now lost to obesity. "I don't think he'd seen his feet for quite a while." His head was round, the nose short, and his temper shorter. "He made his own wine," said Frances, "and had a little jug in his office. In the morning he'd come storming into the studio in a very bad humour. A few moments later he'd come out of his office with little round patches of colour on his cheeks, and he'd be quite jovial."

While Frances recognized that, technically, he taught her a tremendous amount, she would nevertheless hide from him a piece she valued and wanted to develop. "When I was working on something, he would invariably come and tear it all apart and start it all over again. And then, of course, after he did that, the work wasn't mine, was it? And that taught me a very important lesson."

It was a lesson she forgot only once. In later years, Frances was to conduct night-school sculpture classes. Like virtually every artist who was ever born, Frances was constantly concerned about finances. To live creatively, she sculpted; to put bread on the table and pay the rent, she instructed in half a dozen different night-school carving courses in southern Ontario.

During one evening class, a student was having difficulty achieving a certain effect on a clay bust. Frances suggested what might rectify the problem, but the student couldn't seem to grasp the idea. Impatiently the student threw down her tools.

"Well, show me!" she said.

Frances, forgetting for that moment the lesson learned at the hands of Emanuel Hahn, took an instrument and made a slight cut down the side of the bust, then worked for a moment on the planes of the head. "There," she said, happy to have shown the student a valuable sculptural technique.

The student burst into tears. "You've ruined my whole day's work!" she cried.

"And she was right," said Frances. "I mean, even if it's bad, the student has something no one else has. Even if it's second class, it is uniquely theirs and the instructor has no right to go into that person's mind and, you know, sort of shift things around. I never did it again."

Emanuel Hahn had married Elizabeth Wyn Wood (1903–66) in 1926 when he was forty-five and she was twenty-three and one of his students at OCA. Frances met her in the late forties; Wyn Wood was still as lovely then as she was in the beautiful marble portrait Hahn created of her in the year they were married. "She said she married Emanuel thinking it would help her career, but I don't think it did very much.

"I think she was a little suspicious of Emanuel — he was a bit of a womanizer." Frances would sometimes assist Hahn with one of his castings, working with him in his Adelaide Street studio. He and Wyn Wood had adjoining studios. Both were art instructors, he at the Ontario College of Art, she at Toronto's Central Technical School. "Yes, a little suspicious of him. When he was teaching, she would appear around the corner of the studio at the College of Art to see what he was doing. All of a sudden we'd see her look around the corner of the doorway."

The summer after graduation, Frances met Doreen Uren at Tannamakoon, the summer camp where Frances had a part-time job as a counsellor, a post she'd held for the past three years. Doreen had red hair and freckles — the sweet soft-featured, easy-going girl-next-door, whose arms and hands bore the vicious burn scars of a boating accident some years before. But there was determination beneath that sweet exterior; an unrelenting single-mindedness that kept her exercising her arms and hands to retain her piano skills. "Doreen was in her late teens, a superb pianist, and later, an accompanist for the famous singer Lois Marshall.

"Doreen had a funny sense of humour. Well, maybe not so funny. One time at camp she put somebody's bed up in a tree. A lot of people might not think that was funny. I guess it would depend on whose bed it was.

"I had seen Doreen before, but didn't really know her. She was aware that Barbara Howard and I, recently graduated from OCA, were looking for a place in Toronto, and she told us about the possibility of a studio in Mona Bates's house at 519 Jarvis Street."

Mona Bates had been a piano prodigy, giving her first public recital at the age of seven. As a concert pianist she had toured Europe in the early twenties, finally settling in Toronto in 1925 and opening a studio in the Jarvis Street house, an old Massey mansion, where she taught for forty years. Doreen Uren was one of her special students. Through the young girl's recommendation, Frances and Barbara moved into a small ground-floor studio at the Jarvis Street address in the summer of 1951.

The years 1951–53 were hard, both financially and psychologically. There was the initial euphoria after four years at OCA and the excitement of stepping out into the world of art. This was quickly followed by the harsh realities of no job, no money, and no prospects. "I had finished studying at OCA," said Frances, "so there were no more cheques from the Department of Veterans' Affairs. No one was beating a path to my door, and I had no income other than a few dollars in my pocket that I'd put aside from my counselling at summer camp, and any bit of private sculpture tutoring I could scrape together, and a few dollars working part-time for Dr. Williams, the vet." At one point, in the spirit of quid pro quo, Frances painted the entire third floor of the Jarvis Street house in lieu of rent. OCA, too, offered the opportunity to make an extra dollar or two, but sadly just the opportunity. "I taught a night class there for Jacobean Jones, the sculpture instructor who had replaced Emanuel Hahn. It was just for that first winter after I left the school. Jacobean hired me as her assistant. It was never officially recognized, so I never got paid. I was told later that she was notorious for doing that sort of thing."

Frances couldn't understand how she and Barbara Howard existed in the cramped Jarvis Street studio. "We almost murdered each other, trying at one and the same time to both live, and work, in that small place. Our work area was no bigger than the average kitchen. In fact, our work area *was* our kitchen. My stand, that always had a work-in-progress on it, was in front of the sink, and next to me was the gas stove. Behind me were Barbara's workbench, Barbara's easel, and Barbara. She was usually working on a large canvas, often four-by-six feet or bigger. If I were working on a small piece — and even a small sculpture takes up a surprising amount of space — we would literally be working back to back." One of Barbara's works that was hung over Frances's bed actually fell on her one night.

"One of your heavier works," said Frances, rubbing her head.

"Mmm," said Barbara.

"Heavy with significance, a weighty subject," said Frances.

"Mmm," said Barbara again, examining the corner of the canvas that had struck Frances's head, then replacing the painting above Frances's bed.

"I think she was more concerned over the condition of the canvas," said Frances. "But, really, the Jarvis Street studio was just an impossible situation, a crazy idea. But you don't know until you try it."

Frances had always been interested in music — listening, singing, and playing. In the navy she was the Wrens' answer to Édith Piaf, and during her last three years at OCA she played second violin ("very badly") in the University of Toronto's symphony orchestra. There were close ties between the university and the art college, on more than just the academic level, so Frances — holding the view that if you want something, ask for it — went to them and asked to play the violin. "The experience opened my eyes to new dimensions in music. It was a wonderful time, an adventure. It also showed me, once again, that people aren't going to be aware you want something unless you let them know. Most of the time they'll give it to you. Often they'll be delighted you asked." Generations of people who have been in business for themselves have recognized this as the Entrepreneur's Rule Number One.

In the latter part of 1952, Barbara Howard left Jarvis Street for England, and Frances stayed on in the small studio. During this period she was still working for the veterinarian Dr. Edith "Bud" Williams (nicknamed "Bud" for unverified reasons, though the story is that a tiny niece or nephew couldn't pronounce "Edith," which is the way many of us get our nicknames). Williams shared accommodations with her friend Dr. Frieda Fraser on Burlington Crescent just south of St. Clair Avenue. Frieda, a tiny woman, barely a hundred pounds and to a great degree a recluse, was professor of preventive medicine at the University of Toronto.

"I first met Bud just before I went into Sunnybrook Hospital," said Frances. "Ruth Holmes, who taught museum studies at OCA, introduced me. I worked for Bud part-time after school for three years, and continued after graduation while I was living on Jarvis Street."

Dr. Williams was the vet who looked after the cats belonging to Frances Loring and Florence Wyle, known in the art world as "The Girls," two Toronto sculptors already famous for their art, and their parties. "When Frieda and Bud learned that I'd never heard of them, Frieda and her veterinary companion had us all together for dinner, and The Girls invited me over for tea the next day at their studio, an old church on Glenrose Avenue near Mount Pleasant Road and St. Clair Avenue."

In 1913, when The Girls first arrived in Toronto from the United States, they took a studio in the Church/Lombard area, where they lived and worked as sculptors for seven years. In 1920, they moved to the old church on Glenrose and remained there for the rest of their lives.

Frances Gage's first impression of their church was of a large room crammed wall to wall with sculptures, dust, and cats. She had never seen so much sculpture. "It was wonderful!" A.Y. Jackson, a frequent visitor to the church studio, called it "a most colourful place!" He said that in many ways it was the art centre of Toronto. And the parties!

"What wonderful parties they put on!" said Jackson. "Artists, musicians, architects, and writers were proud to be invited to a Loring-Wyle party." Rebecca Sisler, an old friend and fellow sculptor, remembered the regular gatherings when everyone came and mingled among the sculptures (which were) in various stages of completion, and were part of the background."

"Their parties were a legend in Toronto," said Frances. "There was always a 'little bit' to drink. Frances Loring liked her rye whisky. The neighbours, all the members of the Group of Seven, and a lot of other people came. I didn't get in on any of the really wild parties, when The Girls were in their prime. I went to a couple of them later on and helped with catering and giving out drinks, but they weren't as wild in those days. A.Y. Jackson painted a cardboard Christmas tree, and they always put that up in December. Emily Carr was there once, but The Girls were not impressed with her, or she was not impressed with The Girls, one or the other. Pity, because she was such a great woman."

It was through The Girls that Frances met Helen and Charlie Band. Charles Band was a prominent businessman and philanthropist, and former president of the Art Gallery of Ontario. Frances, quite frankly, considered Helen a saint. "They lived in Rosedale, near the Sherbourne subway station. Helen knew The Girls were always short of money, so she arranged for Duguid's, the wonderful Yonge Street butcher, to send The Girls a package of meat twice a week. And these were steaks! I had some myself. Florence Wyle sometimes fed a steak to a neighbour's dog. This big fat dog would come to the window. 'Oh, you poor thing,' she'd say and he'd get a steak."

The Bands had a wonderful collection of works by the Group of Seven. "They also had Emily Carr's *White Church* right inside the front door," said Frances. "Charlie Band knew a lot of the Group of Seven personally."

"Sculpture, in Canada, is something one backs into while viewing paintings."

"I remember a young woman saying that," said Frances. "She was writing a thesis on sculpture." Frances shook her head. "A real winner she must have been."

Frances was not alone in her exasperation. The Girls would repeatedly say to anyone, whether they were listening or not, "For God's sake, *look* at sculpture!" Frances Loring, whose work is most certainly contemporary, nevertheless had a jaundiced view of modern sculpture, and considered much of it "adult kindergarten work."

Academic training formed Loring and Wyle, and at the risk of being considered old-fashioned, they followed the academy's artistic preoccupation with anatomy in their work. Old-fashioned? As Florence Wyle said, "No good work is old-fashioned." Frances Gage agreed. Why should some artists be considered old-fashioned simply because they observe a discipline as basic as anatomy?

Now, in the spring of 1953, came the culmination of the relationship begun by OCA instructor Ruth Holmes's simple introduction of Frances to the vet Edith Williams, followed by Edith's introduction of Frances to the sculptors Loring and Wyle — The Girls — and the subsequent artistic, sculptural, and social relationship forged between Frances and the two sculptors. And thus, finally, to the day when The Girls approached Frieda Fraser on the subject of Frances Gage.

"They spoke to Frieda," said Frances, "pointing out that I had a modest talent as a sculptor, but needed further training. Frieda was quite wealthy, through her own work and family money, and she agreed to finance two years of study for me at the Art Students League in New York City."

And so it happened. Dream-like, New York rose in Frances's mind. Later that year, in the fall of 1953, she turned her steps south, steps on a journey that would take the rest of her life.

The alleyway leading to the street was dark now. The berm rising beside the shack cast the entire area into deep shadow. The late January evening settled over the woman who still stood in the shack's doorway. An icy breeze ruffled the light brown hair across her brow; she felt the cold, and shivered.

Time to go. For a moment a smile touched her face as she glanced inside the door, at this … this appalling shack. This incredible, disreputable, rat-infested … glorious shack.

If I had known, she thought, her mind far away, if I'd known then what I know now. No, it wouldn't have changed anything. Not a thing. I'd do it all again, a hundred times over.

She shook her head. The thoughts of that time … so many years ago it seemed; was it only four?! She smiled again at the memory. Oh the bliss, the unmitigated bloody joy of that time, when New York was just a month away. The unbelievable wonder of it all. And the year in Paris that followed. That priceless time: the excitement, the learning, the exultation when I succeeded; the depression and sense of inadequacy when things went wrong; the challenges; and when I won, the feeling of triumph, almost sublime, of having the world, the whole world, in my hands.

Such wonderful years.

And now?

She pulled her cardigan closer against the cold. Turn off the heater, she thought. Time to go home to bed. Time enough to worry about tomorrow when tomorrow comes.

But, ah — she paused a moment more — those years in New York … in Paris …

$$|\ 4\ |$$

THE AMERICAN DREAM

ON BOARD THE NIGHT TRAIN bound for New York City, Frances gazed out the window and felt slightly miffed that her first sight of the American northeast should be shrouded in darkness. Albany was behind her; ahead, New York. The ambivalence she had felt in Toronto — the security of the known and the insecurity of the new and unknown — was a thing of the past. She felt the excitement of a new life, poised on the threshold of it, boldly knocking on the door.

"I went directly down the Hudson River, which was very exciting, even though I couldn't see anything. Still, the exhilaration was there, and the impatience to arrive, to see this great city." She couldn't afford a sleeper — she wouldn't have been able to sleep anyway — so she sat up all the way, staring out the window. There had been a mix-up at the border, a problem with her visa, but that was eventually resolved. This was an illustration of a problem that Frances encountered throughout her life: she seemed incapable of travelling anywhere without encountering confusion, or getting lost.

"Trains, buses, and boats never seemed to be where they were supposed to be!" On the rare occasion when she caught the right train, she'd end up in the wrong compartment or the wrong seat. Indeed she would often find, in the end, there was simply no such train at all, and in the small hours of the morning, as the cleaners pushed their brooms across the empty station, they would see the solitary figure standing by her suitcase beneath a dim light, waiting for the train that would never come.

By the time she arrived in Grand Central Station she was awed by the incredible size of the city. At a time when Toronto's population was only slightly more than 600 thousand, New York City was home to eight million, and Manhattan Island alone had a population of two million.

Frances took a taxi directly to the YWCA, hoping they would have room for her. They didn't, but they did have a list of people willing to accept roomers, and in this way she met Mrs. Berkovitz.

She was scheduled to see Mrs. Berkovitz the following day, but first things first: "Went to the Art Students League on West 57th Street, just east of 8th Avenue, and registered for Monday. It gave me a strange feeling. The atmosphere was like OCA in Toronto."

Frances stayed overnight in a nearby hotel until she got settled in with Mrs. Berkovitz. "The hotel maids didn't have watches. They opened my door to look at my clock!" *How odd*, she thought. *You'd think in a sophisticated city like New York they'd be able to afford wrist watches.*

A dark and dingy elevator delivered Frances to Mrs. Berkovitz's apartment which was situated on 56th Street, close to 8th Avenue. "It was within easy walking distance of the Art Students League, less than ten minutes. I was a good walker in those days, so I walked back and forth all the time." Frances's room looked out onto a blank brick wall. Not very inspiring. But there were compensations, not the least of which was Mrs. B. herself.

"Mrs. Berkovitz was a real education," said Frances. "She liked to have a non-Jew in the house to turn on the lights on Fridays, because her religion did not permit her to do it. The first night, she took me walking along the East River, and every time I remarked on something she would say 'Honey, dat's New Yoik.' Mrs. Berkovitz was very proud of New York.

"She and her daughter were wonderful," said Frances. "Strangely, Mrs. Berkovitz's chief pleasure was watching Bishop Fulton Sheen on television. This was the first television I had seen. It was a colour set, and Bishop Sheen was splendid in his red robes. She thought that was wonderful entertainment!"

Mrs. Berkovitz's daughter Sondra worked for a Broadway play producer, a Canadian named Whitehead, and it was through Sondra that Frances frequently got press seats for Broadway plays that she never could have otherwise afforded.

"October fourth. First Sunday in New York. All alone. Except for a man who tried to pick me up while I was sketching in the Central Park Zoo." After that brief "romance," she strolled down Fifth Avenue to Central Park South. "While waiting for a traffic light on Fifth Avenue, a toothless old lady gave me her life history." A lifetime in a New York minute.

In the southeast corner of Central Park, facing Fifth Avenue, was the zoo, a favourite sketching place for Frances. "It was wonderful because you could get within a few feet of the animals."

One day she was sitting near the tiger's cage, sketching. The tiger wasn't going anywhere, so it was a good model.

While Frances was drawing, a lady came and stood for a moment near her. She looked over Frances's shoulder. "That's a good likeness," she said.

Frances nodded amicably, though she felt that if you've seen one tiger, you've seen them all. "I've done a lot of cats," said Frances, "but this is my first tiger."

The lady watched for a minute, then went up to the cage and called softly to the tiger, "Mary," and again, "Ma-ry."

"The tiger immediately got up and came over to the bars," said Frances. "It rubbed up against them, and purred! Did you ever hear a tiger purr? Like a vacuum cleaner!"

The lady whispered lovingly to the tiger, then, turning to Frances, she said, "We were in the circus together, but we all have to retire sometime, and she was put here in the zoo." She laughed quietly. "They don't want me to put my hand out and stroke her. Children might get the idea they can, too, and their parents would have heart attacks."

Frances stopped sketching, touched by feelings of sorrow at the passing of a relationship that must have been so close.

The lady turned back to the cage with a sad smile. "I come back here every few days to see her."

"I sat there," said Frances, "and cried, the tears falling on my sketch pad, blurring the image of Mary, the tiger."

Many of the zoo sketches were developed further in the studio of the Art Students League, where John Hovannes, one of her instructors, would pronounce his criticism. "He talks incessantly," said Frances, "but then again he has a lot to talk about." Looking at one of her renditions, he said, "Your transition to freer expression will be slow because of your former training at OCA." *Well*, thought Frances, *so much for you, OCA, my terribly staid and academic alma mater.* But Frances was fortunate in having as her instructors two of the country's most outstanding artists: William Zorach, recognized as the dean of American sculptors; and John Hovannes, a sculptor of striking originality and imagination.

Hovannes's strength lay in his ability to "stretch one's thinking." He challenged his students by giving them tasks that exceeded their abilities. He demanded new thinking, individuality, experimentation. "He was a master carver," said Frances. "I took classes with him in the morning. He was Armenian, and he was wonderful. He talked a lot, and I learned a tremendous amount from him. He was very dapper, very short; he had black, black eyes and black hair. And he never shut up."

William Zorach came originally from Lithuania. He was born Zorach Samovich, but when his family immigrated to the United States in 1891, his father changed Samovich to Finkelstein. When Zorach Finkelstein started school, his teacher arbitrarily changed Zorach to William, and eventually, when the boy became a man, he changed his name to William Zorach, a labyrinthine exercise that must have kept later genealogy students on their toes.

Zorach grew up in a rough area of Cleveland. "Those were the days of a saloon on every corner," he said. "And livery stables. Kids would jump from the upper windows into soft manure piles."

He studied art in Paris, where he met his future wife, Marguerite Thompson, a refined young lady of a wealthy American family and extremely genteel upbringing, who had probably never *seen* a manure pile, would never have uttered the word *manure*, and had certainly never jumped into a pile of it.

"Zorach was very cool at first," said Frances, "until he realized I was serious about sculpture. There were many students who were wealthy and came part-time, then they'd go and play golf, so he was very cool toward me at first." Frances remembered him as often harsh; poor work or indifferent effort earned his contempt.

Frances felt that conditions in the studio were very good. Zorach's views, on the other hand, were not quite so positive. "I found the basement studio at the League very inadequate in earlier days," he said. "It was full of pipes of all sizes going everywhere, and the ceiling was very low. It was wonderful training in how to work under the most adverse conditions."

The classroom in which the students worked was approximately thirty metres long by fifteen metres wide. "Often we had fifteen people working there," Frances remembered. "Doesn't sound like many people, but if everyone was working on a piece, they took up a lot of room." There was a stage for models right in the middle of the room, and the students would be ranged around it. There was a division which separated the working area from the storage of materials, like plaster, equipment, and a great clay bin. The students would scoop out the clay they needed, do their work, then at day's end, cover the work with oilcloth to keep it moist. "Can you believe it? Oilcloth! That was a big problem; it was so stiff. Like trying to fold a steel plate."

Zorach once, on his daily round, paused beside Frances. He glanced over her shoulder, and frowned at the small figure on which Frances had been working. It sat, motionless, almost apologetic, on the stand in front of her. It, too, seemed to wait apprehensively for Zorach's opinion. He continued to frown. "The figure," he said finally, "is good." Frances felt a brief flicker of pleasure. "But," he added, "no punch; it lacks the impact of interpretation."

What does that mean? she thought in panic. *Impact? Interpretation?* She gritted her teeth. She looked at the figure. In agony she saw it had no interpretation at all, none. None! Not a shred of … of … impact. She tore it down in disgust and began again.

She developed a second figure, and anxiously awaited Zorach's criticism. And got it. Taking a tool, he made subtle additions to one side, deletions to another, describing and advising as he worked. Frances sighed. "Now it's more or less a Zorach sculpture. Not quite sure what to do with it now." She gazed at it sadly; the figure gazed back at her. She sighed again. "Still lacks punch."

Despite the negative critiques and the equally negative-leaning results, Frances's tenuous optimism fought back. "I really feel I'm making definite progress in these classes," even though she found the students a frigid group. This would pass quickly; Frances had a natural ability to make friends easily. With time, her address book would become one of the most extensive in North America, a multi-volume work that would rival the telephone book. Yet, paradoxically, her years were filled with frequent periods of desperate loneliness, alone in an empty house, prey to depression and inexplicable despair.

But the joy she found in sculpture inevitably brought the pendulum back. "I am making progress. I know I am." Though she saw the coolness of her fellow students, and her pitifully small circle of friends, at the same time she knew her friends would soon expand in number.

Then the pendulum would swing back again. It's an early mid-October evening, and outside the school all is noise and movement. Groups hurry by; some are students from her studio. One of them waves quickly, "Hi, Frances," and continues on without an invitation to join them. She walks toward Fifth Avenue. She feels isolated, as if the city were empty, a ghost town. In the cool dusk Frances turns at last and walks home alone. "And when I get there the house is still. No one home but me."

Good criticism, and the not-so-good, and sometimes the frankly negative, were a regular part of Frances's day. Yet she was haunted by thoughts of failure. Failure? Negative thinking? If you had seen Frances you would have been surprised. "Surely," you would have said, "you are talking of someone else." Just look at her. She is leaning backward, not quite in challenge, rather as if secure in the correctness of her position on the subject in question. Her feet are slightly apart, planted firmly; her head is back, her smile confident. Why, she's the very picture of self-assurance. You sense immediately that this woman knows what she's talking about, and knows that you know she knows, too. The cynic will say this is classic insecurity: the bluff that hides a lack of belief in herself. And maybe the cynic is right; he's been right before. And yet, she radiates a no-nonsense attitude; she's frank, but not offensive. No deviousness here. Rather, naïveté. And because of this, in the course of her life many will take advantage of her.

Negative criticism of her work often generated self-doubt. She thought back to the previous summer when she stood on the threshold of the great adventure in New York City. She recalled her last days with The Girls, and Frances Loring's parting words: "If you find that it's too overpowering, and you don't want to be a sculptor, it's all right by Florence and me. We'll have work for you when you get back." In the grip of one of her many periods of despair, she thought *What if I should fail?* And, though conscious of melodrama, she would still cry "I must not!"

She recognized that "must not" was easy to say, but not so easy to execute. Work on the morning figure, one that fell within Zorach's instruction, was very slow and discouraging. Frances sighed in exasperation. "Looks like a bowl of porridge." Later the same morning, however, her spirits rose. "Looks better, I think, but lacks *oomph*." The following day: "Zorach's figure pleases me more now." Zorach agreed. "You're doing fine," he said. "Now do some more!"

To take a break from classes, and regain the imagination she sometimes felt she lacked, she turned frequently to the Central Park Zoo — the animals, the broad stretches of greenery, and peace — and there sketched happily for hours. To her surprise and pleasure, she met friends from earlier days in Canada, and strolled through the park with Joan Rowland, well-known classical pianist whom she knew from the Tannamakoon summer camp north of Toronto. She also met Mary King, a friend from her time in the Canadian navy. Mary had been an officer, and Frances had worked with her on a number of artistic projects. They had met again shortly after Frances's arrival in New York. Visits to Mary's home in New Rochelle, just north of New York on Long Island Sound, soon became a haven from the ups and downs of Frances's creative life. It was in October that she spent the first of many wonderful weekends there; days that Frances never forgot. "Those weekends were so good; it was like home. It seemed so far away from New York, but it was only maybe twenty miles or so. And her house was wonderful. Over 250 years old. It was huge, almost a city block long, with a lovely garden. It even had a resident ghost." When the weekend was over, there was the easy drive back in the dawn mist, the East River shrouded in fog.

"I seem always to be either elated or in the depths of despair. This morning Hovannes tried so hard to be helpful." Full marks for Hovannes, but he was still "firmly noncommittal" when it came to her current work. So was she. "Zorach tore my afternoon figure apart and rearranged it." It was one of those days. "I just wish I could get myself straightened out, but he did give me a lesson in observing and drawing." The next day Hovannes spent almost the entire morning working with her on the drawing. "I really think I learned a lot," she said. Then her constant self-doubt rose up. "Can I keep on the right track?"

A few days later, in what seemed to be her perpetual cycle of hope, black despair, and soaring euphoria, she still was able, sometimes, to fling aside all self-doubts. "Inspired this morning! Threw up a life figure that I definitely feel is a step in the right direction!"

Zorach agreed. "Good work, and well carried out! In art," he stressed, "you must not do what someone else thinks is good and right. You must listen, and then make your own decisions as to what is right for *you*."

Hovannes, too, appeared to like what she was doing. "Good day," she said with satisfaction. "Started my seventh life figure. Seems to be going okay." Then, once more, the agonizing slide down to uncertainty and loss of conviction. "Lack of energy throughout. Wish I could learn to think, damn it. I guess one is born with an IQ. Or without one."

Then up again: "Both figures are coming along well. Went all out and bought some tools. They're expensive, but lovely." Then down: "I seem to be awfully low on energy. Don't know what is the matter. Wish I could do more, but don't feel like it." Then up: "Zorach liked my afternoon figure! He said it would take subtle handling. I know I can do it!"

Hovannes was also delighted with her morning figure, and had it photographed. Frances took the photos home, and with a certain pride, showed them to her landlady.

Mrs. Berkovitz looked at them critically. "Will you be getting your instructor to sign a certificate to say you really did these?" Then she realized she was veering away from the really important information. "When you go back to Canada, how much money will you be able to make?"

Later that afternoon, back at the school, Frances sat back and felt that it had been a fairly good day in most respects. "But I'm absolutely beat by four-thirty. Should get a shot of something to put in my coffee."

The last weekend in November was spent with Mary King in New Rochelle, a restful Thanksgiving and a welcome break before Christmas. "Beautiful day. Sawed wood, pruned bushes. Ate too much, bad night, will I ever learn?"

Back in New York she balanced her budget. "Very much in the red, but I'll clear that up with more casting for the other students." Her Toronto patron had financed her time in New York, but the grant wasn't quite sufficient for all her needs. "I did a lot of casting for my fellow students. They were all very rich, and they didn't know how to cast. Thanks to my years at the Ontario College of Art, I did, so it was to my financial advantage to do it for them, and I became a very good caster! I could finish a mould in an hour. One would think the students had never seen a proper mould! I got offers right and left. Everyone was suddenly asking my advice on casting. I cast a head for eight dollars. Eight dollars was nothing to them, but it was really welcome money for me."

To supplement her grant and extend her time in New York she decided to economize on meals. She switched to dog food. "It was only twenty-five cents a can, and I could get three meals out of it." Over the months, she would augment her meals with dog food for weeks at a time. "It was very good. Well-cooked. Good beef. Probably better than the Americans would have for themselves. Add a few vegetables and things. Very good. Quite nutritious."

"Hovannes was in this morning. He didn't think much of my figure. Started casting after lunch, had a light supper, then worked through the evening till ten. Joined some of the night class members for a coffee in their studio."

Outside on the street she still felt the pleasure of Zorach's words earlier that day. "We'll make a thrilling sculptor out of you yet," he had said. *Nice to know,* she thought. The night around her reflected her contented mood. It was fairly quiet around 11:00 p.m., crisply cold, a lovely night. She strolled east along 57th Street, crossed Seventh Avenue, passed Carnegie Hall, and continued on to Fifth Avenue, the Mecca of the upscale shopper. *More money in their pockets than I have,* she thought, but without bitterness. *More money, yes, but are they happy?* She laughed. *You bet they are!* Rather than turn south toward her room and bed, she crossed Fifth and continued east to Park Avenue. "Such a beautiful night, actually a couple of stars in the sky," and she felt the growing yuletide spirit in her heart. Then, at Park Avenue, she gazed south, and in that instant was happier than any moneyed shopper on Fifth Avenue: "Suddenly, there, spread out before me, sparkling against the buildings of lower Manhattan, were big Christmas trees all down Park Avenue!"

December's end saw Frances at New Rochelle with Mary King and her mother, Norma. Christmas day was sunny and clear, with no snow. And Santa Claus was generous. Frances's gifts were a reconditioned radio, two cartons of cigarettes, ten dollars cash from Norma, and from The Girls — the sculptors Wyle and Loring in Toronto — came a cheque. Frances could not read it through her tears. "The Girls were so kind. And all this time they were probably wondering how they were going to pay the rent. Yet, they were giving the money they didn't have to people like me."

She spent a quiet, relaxed weekend, loafing. "The birds out on the lawn were hilarious, sliding around on the frozen surface of the bird bath. Each morning after breakfast I chipped the ice off it. 'That's enough skating, fellas,' I told them. 'You'll never make it to the National Hockey League anyway, you're too small. Time for a nice sub-zero bath.'"

Then came the return to the problems at school. "Tore down the morning figure," she said, aggravated with herself. "And the next morning, after hours of work, it was still no good." Hovannes, unfortunately for her spirits, was quick to agree. "You like long slim muscles; this fat chunky figure (the model) is too much for you." His critique was prophetic. Later (and more successful) examples of her work would mirror Hovannes's words: Tall, thin female figures, slim-waisted, some might say under-nourished, though not quite as much as Giacometti's sculptures; rather Giacometti on a fuller diet. These slim figures would sometimes be found in Frances's sculpture of the late fifties and sixties.

But in these New York days, Hovanness's views were not the critical response that pleased.

She packed her bag and left for the New Year's weekend in New Rochelle.

In Manhattan, winter was moving slowly into spring. Frances's days were filled with work and study, museums and galleries, and thanks to Mrs. Berkovitz's daughter Sondra and her Broadway contacts, Frances's evenings often saw her attending plays, Broadway musicals — the premiere of *Fiddler On The Roof*, for example — and concerts, like her friend Joan Rowland's recital on the twenty-eighth of February. But mainly her days revolved around the school. The Art Students League was her world, where she felt she was growing and learning and succeeding.

Her hours at the school never seemed enough. She was doing more and more castings for her fellow students, and was producing new works of her own almost daily, which generated criticism. "Felt happy about my morning figure, but Hovanness frowned at one mean little angle. Careless; threw everything off."

March 1, 1954: "Both works much better. Tore into afternoon figure and think it much improved. Good drawing this morning." March 2: "Good figure. Hovanness? Said nothing. Must use more free expression." March 3: "Worked on my Frieda sculpture. She's one of the models. Zorach likes the figure very much."

This almost continuous activity had its effect on her diet. "I was never a good cook, and frankly, I just didn't have time for food. Could have made time, I suppose, but (shrugs) I simply wasn't that interested." And she paid the price. Most of March was spent "feeling absolutely lousy and faint … weary … feeling ill after breakfast …" Breakfast, generally, was pausing for a moment outside a restaurant and taking a deep breath. "Very nutritious. Great time-saver and you can't beat the price." These senseless eating habits contributed to an endless catalogue of various gastric illnesses. She seemed almost constantly to be getting sick, being sick, or recovering from something. Colds, stomach ailments, sore throats, flu, ulcers, muscular problems, and repeatedly bumping into, bouncing off, falling down on, tripping over, every hard object imaginable. And finally tennis elbow or carpal tunnel syndrome from sculpture, sculpture, sculpture.

"Simplify! Too complex!"

Zorach's view in three words. Other instructors would stress it just as strongly: Don't copy blindly. The subject should be a guide, to inspire your work. Exaggerate some aspects, eliminate others. Simplify. "The concept, the idea, is what is really creative," said Zorach. "The rest is work. The real act of creation is in the design." To attempt to recreate each and every detail of a subject was fatal, he said; the endless detail would hinder her impression of life, of vitality.

This was a view that Frances accepted. At this period in her training, she was prepared to follow Zorach's ideas, but tended to be open also to other methods, treatments, and new ways of looking at art, even the avant-garde, even what some might call the absurd.

She attended a lecture at the Museum of Modern Art in mid-January of 1954. The subject was abstract and cubist art. "Abstract art," said the cartoonist Al Capp, "is a product of the untalented, sold by the unprincipled to the utterly bewildered." But then Al Capp was a humorist and would be expected to say that. Frances, on the other hand, thought about it seriously. *To appreciate abstract art,* she thought, on her way back to the studio, *I have to consider that a thing can have a beauty of its own without having a resemblance to anything I know.*

Zorach, however, wasn't buying any of that avant-garde, no-talent, "no resemblance to anything" bafflegab. "The non-objective art of today is a purely visual thing," he said. "The importance it has is the importance you, yourself, give it. To read meaning into it is comparable to reading meaning into tea leaves." Zorach was not the man to leave you in any doubt. Just in case you missed that last remark on art and tea leaves, he expressed his utter amazement at how the work of some artists can be taken seriously. "Today we encourage the most infantile efforts, and admire them." He agreed that it was natural to enthuse over the daubs and splashes of a four-year-old, "but when a so-called artist does the same thing and *exhibits* it, to me it is retarded development."

In spite of Zorach's modest to favourable opinions on many of her compositions, Frances was always prone to self-criticism, little of it positive. "A good feeling," said Zorach of one of her figures. *Try not to go overboard*, thought Frances with a grim smile of acknowledgement. She worried that the gains in one area were lost in another. "I used to get a good likeness," she said, "but not a good drawing or sculpture. Now I get a good drawing and sculpture, but lose the essence of the subject."

A number of visits from Ontario friends and relatives nevertheless lightened her mood. The arrival of Keith Collver, her cousin and childhood friend, still well-loved, brought wonderful memories, and they sat over drinks till the small hours of the morning, after which he poured her into a taxi.

Her father and mother came for a two-day check on their daughter, the inexplicable sculptor. She was happy, banished the negative thoughts of their past relationship, and felt quite the cosmopolitan, almost-professional artist as she showed them the Big Town, and drew their attention to points of interest with a casual familiarity.

When she saw them off at the station the next day, she found she only had twelve cents in her pocket. Entertaining friends and relatives in New York was an expensive business.

On the nineteenth of February, she sat alone in her room. Mrs. Berkovitz was out and the house was quiet. A feeling of retrospection settled over her. A time for soul-searching. She recalled that earlier that day Zorach had said that she still hadn't "the punch of first impression," no "rhythm or emphasis," no "pulling together." *Well*, she thought grimly, *I will have it; I know I will, tomorrow, next week, next month. I will have it. I have to believe that.* Her thoughts drifted back to the time of her father's visit. Showing him the sights, telling of her days at the Art Students League, the things she learned, her enthusiasm, the compliments of the instructors; holding her treasures in her hands and offering them to her father, waiting for appreciation from the man who never gave it.

She heaved a sigh that was almost a sob. "For God's sake, I'm almost thirty years old. I have to stop substituting superficial things for the real. It's time I grew up," she said to the quiet room, the empty house. "Time to start thinking for myself."

Frances sat looking critically at the two compositions in front of her. "Hmm, fairly pleased with the afternoon figure." Notwithstanding Zorach's guarded "It is passable," she felt the morning figure was "not so hot." She had begun casting a fellow student's figure and was also busy on her own, which Hovannes had said was "a good figure." Nevertheless her constant dissatisfaction with her work, even in the face of approval, albeit grudging, continued to fester in the back of her mind: "I must buck up!"

Always the mood swings: "Both figures improving. I think. Zorach says I have a good start." Then: "I'm working so slowly! Lack ambition, not sure of my composition." Finally: "Composition blah."

Then the sudden news: "Zorach said if I wanted to return next year, I could probably get a scholarship!" And the thought of what that could do to her painfully stretched budget brought an exciting ray of sunshine into her day.

Frances felt that her current sculpture, a torso of Melba, one of the models, was shaping up very well. Zorach praised it, with the qualification that it was too static. *So much for criticism*, thought Frances. Much more satisfying, from the standpoint of appreciation of her abilities, was the invitation to assist him in casting at his home studio in Brooklyn. In early March she spent a day there, working with him. "A wonderful place. Filled with lovely New England pine furniture, and animals!"

Toward the end of March, Zorach looked at the two figures on which Frances was working. "Technically, you are okay," he said, and nodded briefly, a fleeting suggestion of approval, "but you have no imagination." *Thanks a lot, Bill,* she thought, looking bleakly at the two works. "These are studies," he said. "You have to get ideas." *All right,* she thought grimly, *enough studies; from now on I will develop ideas from the model's pose.*

And yet, she was unhappy. She felt she was still depending too much on other people's decisions. But what could she do? *Do?* She knew what she could do, and indeed had to do: Listen and learn; accept the decisions of Zorach and Hovannes; profit from their knowledge, expertise, and experience. Time enough to reject the decisions of others when you've learned, when you know what to do, and what you're capable of doing. Then, and only then, can you go your own way.

Good news followed bad, as good news often does. She was told, after X-rays and a lot of medieval poking and prodding, that she had a stomach ulcer. Then she received a letter from her Toronto patrons inviting her up for the weekend. Reports from the doctors in early April were happily positive, so her days in Toronto were carefree. "Lunch with The Girls. Oh, it was so wonderful to see them all!" She also took time to see the administrators of Tannamakoon, the summer camp in Algonquin Park, and firm up her position as counsellor for the summer months. "It felt so wonderful, spiritually, to get all my problems settled. The ulcer seems to be a thing of the past, summer camp is ahead of me, and I'll be back in New York with a scholarship, I hope."

Notwithstanding his mention of a scholarship, Zorach was not wildly enthusiastic about offers of financial assistance. "I do not believe in subsidies to artists," he said firmly. "There is only one way to subsidize art, and that is to buy it." But Frances did not subscribe to this at all. "That's all very well and good, I suppose, among established artists," she said, "but it doesn't work so well if you're a penniless student who isn't going anywhere without assistance."

This, though, was a passing response to Zorach's views; things were going too well for her to entertain negative thoughts for long. "Work is coming along better than ever, and it's nice to know that my stomach is officially all right. Now," she exulted, "now for some food!" She spent the weekend in New Rochelle "and ate too much."

She sent in her letter for the scholarship on the nineteenth of April, then banished it from her mind in the flurry of work on *Melba*, a piece that excited her immensely and gained Zorach's approval: "You have improved a lot this year!" Hovannes, too, liked her *Melba*: "It's the best yet," he said. And the final accolade: "The Art Students League," said Frances, "have taken an option on my *Melba*! That means they want to buy it! I am walking on air!"

After a celebratory supper with friends, she returned home late after perhaps a couple too many. "Woke up feeling terrible. Guess I shouldn't drink so much. But …" She brightened. "… tonight the committee will decide on my scholarship."

Later she met her friend Rowlie (Joan Rowland) for lunch, and they walked along the East River. It was a crisply cool April day and the sun sparkled on the river as they sat on a bench, watched the boats, and reminisced of their days in Ontario and at Tannamakoon summer camp. "Rowlie was a great pianist, international reputation, toured all over Europe. She studied under Mona Bates in that big old Massey mansion on Jarvis Street —519 Jarvis Street, where Barbara Howard and I lived after we graduated from the Ontario College of Art." Publicity photographs of Joan Rowland show a wide happy smile, lots of teeth. "Rowlie was kind of fat, freckles. She looked just like a little girl — until she sat down at that big grand piano. I met her at Tannamakoon. She was a good swimmer."

Rowlie laughed, recalling the days at the camp. "Remember the time I almost drowned you?" she said. "Talked you into swimming way out."

"Remember?!" said Frances. "How could I forget? I could have died!"

"Come on. I towed you in, didn't I?"

More laughter as Frances cried, "How very considerate of you!"

The end of April brought good news: Her scholarship was approved, and she could look forward to another year in New York, in circumstances substantially less strained than before. "Frieda Fraser's grant supported me at the Art Students League," said Frances, "but this was New York, and a thousand dollars didn't go very far. The scholarship made all the difference." There was, too, another source of income that benefited Frances in more ways than one. She was still doing the casting for many of the wealthier students who lacked the inclination to do it themselves. "This was fine with me. I could use the money."

May 28 was the last day of her first term at the Art Students League. "Home late. Got lost in Harlem."

Her thoughts on the train north were of Algonquin Park, the coming months at summer camp, and her friend Clancy.

Clancy was the nickname of Mary Alice Rogers, the soprano. At Tannamakoon, Rowlie would accompany her on the camp's grand piano, an instrument that had to be tuned every year because, as the old German piano tuner said, "The mice, they sheet on the keys!" And of course, it had to be tuned; Mary Alice wouldn't have accepted anything less.

"Clancy was a real prima donna," said Frances. "With Mary Alice Rogers it was always My way, or the highway! I remember once, Clancy paddled her canoe out into the lake, alone, under the moon, and sang. Her voice was so beautiful as it rose over the lake in the night." Frances laughed. "Even the loons joined in."

An artist's life is awash with disappointments, but in Frances's case, disappointments had a heyday; she seemed to invite mistakes, oversights, misdirection, and frustrating confusion of all kinds. As so many had wailed before, she would cry "But it's not my fault!" and suffer just as bitterly as if it were indeed her fault. Returning to New York from Toronto for her second year at the Art Students League, she was stopped at the border. These were the final days of the McCarthy Era in the United States. To petty border officials, every southbound train carried its sinister freight of communists. This included trains carrying Canadians, and Frances was detained for three hours while they checked with the Art Students League. "I guess they had to find out if my grandmother had been a commie spy. I was lucky; they put another girl student off the train!" Later, in dismay, she found herself in New York's Penn Station instead of Grand Central. "With my luck," she said, "it could just as easily have been Central Station in Montreal."

Frances's life in this, her second year, was marginally more comfortable than before. In addition to her Toronto patron Frieda Fraser's thousand-dollar subsidy, there was the League's scholarship. "Also, I was William Zorach's monitor that second year, which cut my fees a little bit." Her duties as monitor were minimal. "I just sort of supervised things." She also chased peeping toms out of the studios. "Crazy. I mean, they could have spent a couple of dollars and stayed the whole day, drooling over the naked models. They might even have learned how to draw."

During this second year, Frances had a small room with a Miss Corbett. Mrs. Berkovitz had rented her room when Frances left for summer camp in Ontario. Miss Corbett was on the other side of Manhattan Island, on the East River. Her apartment backed onto a courtyard, so Frances was privy to everything that went on. There were cat fights, dogs barking, and frequently a window would be raised and a voice would shout, "Shut that damned dog up!" and another window would open and a voice shout back, "You make more noise than da dog!" The usual courtyard days and nights: cat fights, people exchanging opinions. Echoes of lives.

Miss Corbett had come north from Florida, gotten a job in New York, but hadn't seen anything of the city. She worked, she came home, she watched TV, she went to bed. Frances, forever enchanted by New York, was amazed. "On top of the excitement of the school, there were concerts, plays, recitals, museums and galleries, Broadway musicals, a million-and-one sources of interest, entertainment, excitement. I, the visitor, the foreigner, ended up telling her a lot about New York she didn't know!"

Mrs. Berkovitz, her landlady of the previous year, gave her an end table for her new room with Miss Corbett. "I carried it, alternating shoulders because it was so unwieldy — carried it right across town, and not a head was turned. It just shows that in New York you can do anything!" On the way, she noticed a construction site where great piles of granite paving stones had been taken up from the street and put to one side, waiting to be carried away to the dump. The stones were large — ten-by-fifteen-by-five inches, and heavy. But Frances's sculptor's eye saw artistic possibilities, and on her way back to the school — and in the same spirit that in New York you can do anything — she hefted one of the stones and, carrying it like a religious offering, took it to the Art Students League, and began work on it.

The lowly paving stone took its place in art history under Frances's hands, becoming a stylized pelican, tightly rendered by the restrictions of the stone. "Zorach was pleased; he liked it, and suggested that in contrast to the rough surface, I should polish the beak and toes. I thought that was a great idea, and polished them up!" (Half a century later the sculpture, complete with polished beak and toes, was purchased by the author.)

The end of September 1954 saw Frances spend a couple of weekends in New Rochelle. These breaks in her school work had become islands of peace in a sea of arduous study. But the Art Students League was why she was here, and she returned from those New Rochelle weekends with renewed vigour and determination, which often was just as well, because neither Zorach nor Hovannes were ones to give credit unless credit was clearly due.

At the end of October she began a *Seated Melba*, one of a number of pieces on which she was working. Hovannes remarked favourably on a small *Carmen*, and Zorach suggested casting. This was one of those periods of euphoria, when the sculptor feels her hand, eye, and mind can do no wrong; every action is right and supremely satisfying.

Frances received a letter from Toronto on the eighteenth of November. Her friend Loring was sending the forms for admittance into the Ontario Society of Artists. Frances was of two minds about seeking membership. "I wanted to become a member, and knew I'd feel bad if for some reason I was denied."

And denied she was. The rejection arrived in mid-December. "I didn't want to think about it too much, but it was hard not to. It was … well, demeaning. They didn't have to spell it out for me. I was rejected because I was not a recognized 'artist'; I was only a student, as if that were some disgusting disease."

She continued working on her own projects and assisting other students with their casting. Even Hovannes's wonderful critique of a head she was developing failed to raise her spirits. "I knew I mustn't be bitter over the Society of Artists' rejection," she said, "but, damn it, it hurt."

Nothing worked. Even Zorach and Hovannes seemed to conspire to increase her depression. Hovannes appeared to like the figure on which she was working: "But you must simplify more!" Zorach on the other hand was indifferent: "Too simplified. Needs more oomph!" This did little for Frances's mood. "Very depressed all afternoon."

In an effort to raise her own spirits she played truant for an afternoon and took a boat cruise around Manhattan. "Couldn't afford it, but it was beautiful!" And it seemed to work; that, and a weekend in New Rochelle with Mary King and her mother, Norma. "I seem to have emerged from the depression that has gripped me for so long," she said, smiling for the first time in a week. "It may have been the cruise, and the relaxing weekend, or maybe the introspection and the realization of my limitations." She remembered Frieda's veterinarian friend, Dr. Williams, saying "Do the best you can with what you've got." Which was very smart thinking, Frances felt.

At the school, however, the "best you can do" was not always good enough. "Zorach in this afternoon," muttered Frances bleakly. "Obviously didn't think much of my queer little figure, the highly stylized one. Said something about there being some nice aspects to it, and that it was sometimes good to experiment, but …"

And with Zorach it was a big and unambiguous *but*. "Continually trying out new ways and directions leads to chaos," he said. "Innovation is not an end in itself. People think that progress is constantly going ahead, following the bandwagon of change and novelty. This is not true. Rather," he said, "the true artist expands the range of his expression, and develops greater power." He was shocked to see a mature artist change his style with the fashion, and considered him nothing but an opportunist. He sneered at the artistic insanity of rusty industrial garbage, huge hamburgers, giant cans of tomato soup; he had nothing but contempt for all the Minimalists, Conceptualists, Constructivists, and the madness of Op Art and Pop Art. To Zorach it was not art, it was anarchy. "Pop Art?" He sneered. "Pop Art is something that belongs in show business."

In later years, Frances's views on what she referred to as non-art were similar to those expressed by Zorach. "Much of the new art," she said, "is not traditional sculpture. I'm not saying they should not create what they wish; but coin a new name for it; just don't call it art, because it's not."

Christmas at New Rochelle with Mary King and her mother helped take Frances's mind off confusing art movements, as did the arrival of her Toronto friend Charlotte Sullivan, who had journeyed to New York to celebrate New Year's Eve in Times Square with Frances.

And then, on the last day of the year — and could a year end better than this? — a Mr. Jan de Ruth, a Toronto dealer, came to look at the school's work, and sent Frances to the moon when he bought her large sculpture *Barbara* for sixty dollars.

"It's going into a posh home in New York!" she cried. "I can hardly walk straight."

After the claustrophobia of the New Year's Eve crowds in Times Square, the Bronx Zoo on New Year's Day was a breath of freedom and tranquility. Frances and Charlotte arrived there shortly before noon and spent the better part of the afternoon just strolling. Charlotte was very bossy. Her first words that morning had been to complain that Frances had not called her the minute she got out of bed that morning. Her intentions were always the very best — it was, after all, for your own good — but given an inch, Charlotte always felt that to take a mile was never really enough. She seemed unaware of the liberties she tried to take with other people's personal space and private business.

Classes resumed, and almost immediately Frances received what was initially an irritating surprise. She learned that Mr. de Ruth, who had purchased Frances's sculpture for sixty dollars just ten days before, had sold it to his New York client for two hundred dollars. Frances's original irritation ebbed somewhat when she considered that a hundred dollars a week represented a good income in 1955, so someone thought enough of her work to pay two weeks salary for it.

On the seventeenth of January, Frances's mother and father came down for a two-day visit with "my daughter the sculptor," and for a brief time raised Frances from a period of despair. The negative mood had been brought on by a nasty infection in her thumb. This had adversely affected her work, "which was fine with me because my work was going nowhere." Also, someone in the night class had dropped one of her pieces, smashing it beyond repair, and simply left the mess on the floor. The thoughtlessness, the casual indifference of the act, infuriated Frances. "Okay, it was not going to end up in the Museum of Modern Art, but it was mine!"

And while the parental visit served to raise her spirits — breakfast together on their arrival, tickets for a Broadway show, shopping with her mother, a tour of the school with Frances the proud guide, and a warm and intimate supper before their departure on the train — there followed, as night follows day, the desolation generated by the all-too-brief visit, and the conflicting emotions caused by family memories both good and bad.

January 25 brought a letter from Loring in Toronto with information on Canadian government scholarships. Frances's plan was for a period of study in Paris, and to this end she spent the next week drawing up her application for Canadian government assistance. Lunch with visiting Canadian friends Jean and Cleeve Horne did little to raise her hopes. They felt the chances of a scholarship were slim.

But school work kept her spirits up. "My ceramic head is coming along so well." Then Zorach took a hand in its development, and memories of OCA and Emanuel Hahn's irritating changes to her sculpture rose in her mind. "Zorach spent half an hour working on my head!" she cried in pain. "I now own a William Zorach ceramic!" She felt sick. "What he did was good, but it is no longer my piece. All I had done was gone. I knew I shouldn't have felt that way; I learned a lot. But …"

Again there began the slide into depression, made worse by a bad cold. For someone who saw the sculptor's life as one of bliss bordering almost on ecstasy, she spent an inordinate amount of time in a depressed state. On this occasion, however, she turned to the infallible prescription: She went shopping. And went directly to that friendly emporium, Sculpture House, where, like an alcoholic with a gift certificate for the liquor store, she purchased more tools than she could carry, plus a handful of carbide-tipped chisels, and spent the rest of the afternoon carving in stone and smiling contentedly.

She spent the next weeks using her new chisels. "Slow work, but nice. Vigorous carving today; right hand is painful." *Small price to pay,* she thought, and took the afternoon off to go with Lee Bontecou, a fellow sculptor, to see Rodin's *Gate of Hell.* Bontecou, at that time an attractive twenty-three-year-old girl from Providence, Rhode Island, had been studying at the Art Students League since 1952. She, like Frances, would leave the school in 1955, and in the following decades would go on to gain international recognition as an abstract artist of striking scope and imagination.

At the school in mid-March, Frances was engaged in drawing the model who was one of her favourites: the Chinese model Chao-li-chi. He was a dancer "between engagements" who was modelling in order to keep eating.

"Chao-li-chi is coming along well; the full figure comes next in terra-cotta." That Chao-li-chi was "coming along well" might have suited Frances, but Hovannes, looking over her shoulder, said, "You know the human body, but you don't know much about sculpture," and passed on, leaving Frances to grit her teeth and mutter, "I suppose I will have to take that as a challenge. Grrr!" She had just the day before come back from a serious bout with the flu — "Finally; done nothing all week" — but surprisingly it had not left her weak and depressed; she had bounced back more determined than ever, and more and more conscious of the passage of time. "The term at the Art Students League was almost gone. Everything I wanted to do … half done." The next day she would begin Chao-li-chi in terra-cotta. "A whole new day tomorrow. God help me make the most of it." Throughout her years in New York, self-doubt was a constant companion, colouring all that was good and accenting the bad.

On a warm early April evening she had supper in Greenwich Village with her friend and fellow student Lee Bontecou. Lee came from a small family. "She was an only child," Frances remembered. "And 'child' is the right word. She was twenty-three years old, and looked like a fifteen-year-old. She was about five feet four inches tall, very slight build, dark blond hair."

Outside the restaurant windows a soft spring evening was settling over the street. Frances picked up her coffee, and frowned.

Lee said, "Weight of the world on your shoulders?"

Frances sighed. "I feel Hovannes has given me up."

Lee brushed that aside with a gesture. "All in your mind. Zorach and Hovannes think you're doing well. I saw Zorach giving you a lesson in stone. And he liked your small Chao-li-chi. Come on, don't shake your head; I distinctly heard him say it was a nice treatment."

"I think the trouble is I need more than just a nice treatment."

Frances was deeply troubled by her sense of dependence on her friends and benefactors, and the opinions of her instructors. "How am I going to get on when I'm all on my own?"

But the day after her talk with Lee Bontecou, she took to school a small sketch. Hovannes liked it. Zorach liked it. For a moment content, she thought, *I am very pleased.*

And lighthearted, too. "A week's work exploded the other day. Poor old Rose Kreb put her piece, cold, into a hot kiln. Wham! Not one shattered bit is bigger than a two-bit piece. We worked on it all day today, trying to piece it together. Talk about Humpty-Dumpty! Rose and I felt like a couple of archeologists, sifting through a bunch of Etruscan fragments."

May 7, 1955: "I have my scholarship for Paris!" With thanks to the Royal Society of Canada. "These scholarships," Frances explained, "were financed by monies owed Canada by France, and would be paid in monthly deposits, in francs, to a Paris bank."

Almost like a good-natured gesture of *au revoir,* New York gave her a TV interview with Mayor Koch. She had no idea how she had been chosen. "Maybe it was because I was a Canadian student. I guess that made me unique." Though she was thirty years old she was still in many ways a little kid, and like a child she was impudent and tactless. "The mayor didn't know much about Canada, so I brought him up to date. It was that rare time when the Canadian dollar was worth more than the American. And yet the Americans still wouldn't accept Canadian money. So I asked him about that. 'We accept yours,' I said. I guess Mayor Koch thought I was a sweet young thing, but also hoped that the earth would open and swallow me up!"

When she returned later to the Art Students League, the studio smelled like a beer hall. All the students had watched the TV show in a nearby bar.

"This was the latter part of May 1955, my last days at the League. I had phoned the cartage company about all my cartons and suitcases bound for Canada, and had been told repeatedly not to worry, they would come by tomorrow. Always tomorrow, never today. These were the sad days, too. Saying goodbye to Hovannes, forgetting the incisive criticisms that so often ruined my day; remembering instead the tremendous amount of time and effort he put into teaching me the skills I now had. The class gave me a huge goodbye party, Zorach presented me with twenty-five dollars and a beautiful pin, and the class gave me a lovely tan silk blouse. Zorach and I sang together, and my eyes were full of tears. They were all so good; how could I ever thank them for these wonderful, wonderful years! They made me feel as if I really mattered, that I was somebody special."

Later, when she returned to her apartment, she phoned the cartage company again. "They had never heard of me."

Back in Canada, with three or four months to go until her departure for Paris, she worked at odd jobs, anything to keep her alive till she arrived in France. There were the weeks in Algonquin Park as a counsellor, and some private tutoring of young would-be sculptors. Toward the end of her time in New York, she had received a letter from Florence Wyle, once more saying "Don't worry; we'll have work for you when you come back." Always there was that selfless consideration from The Girls. "They couldn't afford it," said Frances of Loring and Wyle, "but they gave me a few dollars, and in return I helped them with their castings, ran errands for them, painted their floors, washed their dishes, served drinks at their parties, and cleaned up afterward. They were just wonderful. They couldn't afford it, but they kept me working till I left for Paris. Not much pay, but that was all right. They didn't have much, but I didn't need much. I just had to hang on until I got to France. I just had to survive."

| 5 |

SOUS LES TOITS DE PARIS

FRANCES STRAINED TO LOOK BACK through the driving rain as her ship moved slowly out of the harbour. What she had hoped to see — the New York City skyline — was obliterated, a grey wall of wind and rain, nothing more. Standing in the gangway entrance, away from the rain that swept the deck clear of other tourists, she sighed, and much of the emotional high that had carried her through the last few hours evaporated and left her with just the dullness of boarding, the crowds, the noise, and the pointless running in circles.

In Toronto, before she left, dull necessity had been transformed into exciting steps in a wonderful adventure: "Train tickets for New York; check bags; go to the consulate downtown; go to the bank and get fifty dollars American for walkin'-around money." She smiled. "There was a lovely going-away party at The Girls studio, where I naturally overindulged." While she was in the downtown Toronto area, she felt it was wise to check with the immigration man about re-entry permits. Stubborn vestiges of the McCarthy era still obliged students to carry more documentation.

What a madhouse at the pier in New York! Great ships, crowds of sinister-looking men, and apparently no one to help a sweet young thing with ten thousand pieces of luggage.

Earlier that day, before boarding the ship, she had revisited the Art Students League where she had spent two wonderful years. "But I found it so terribly depressing. There was nobody there I knew." Less than six months had passed, yet in her eyes everything seemed changed. She spent a disappointing half hour there, in the rooms and hallways she had known so well. Sadly, she left. *I suppose that's the way it goes*, she thought. *Places change. People change.*

The rain continued to sweep across the deck. All around was water; grey, unfriendly, dark depths lifting and falling with the waves. She turned and went below. Her ship, the *Flandre*, was so small it barely deserved the name "ship." The cabin was tiny. "There were four of us, three French, one Canadian. I had a deck chair," she added primly, "very posh."

There were also four or five American students. "They reminded me of my years in New York," she said. "I was always embarrassed by Americans because they were so loud. They'd shout across a room to one another." *It was*, she thought with a smile, *as if they suffered the insecurity of the colonists they once were. Americans, insecure? It is to laugh*, she thought, in an attempt at the French she had yet to learn.

The five-day trip across the Atlantic was one of warm sunny days followed, in the fashion of the North Atlantic, by storms and cold winds. But her table in the dining room was happy, with lots of laughter. "Kind of sad tonight, though. Everyone is at the dance. Don't know why I didn't go. Feel very alone." That she would have felt less alone at the dance is debatable. "Everyone" would simply have been the handful of passengers and a representative number of the ship's officers, and the "dance" would probably have taken place in the dining room, on a dance floor created by the removal of one chair. To dance, you would have had to take a number.

She found, though, that one way to beat the loneliness of ocean travel, and it's a good one if you're not seasick, is food. "Never had such magnificent food, and so much of it! Duck à l'orange, and two kinds of wine!" A further pleasure occurred to her: "I didn't have to cook it, and I didn't have to wash up, either."

The exciting arrival in Le Havre, and the subsequent train journey through a romantic mist to Paris, was misleading. Most people would have realized, especially when travelling, that things simply do not go that easily. Frances learned the hard way. Getting a porter for her bags seemed almost impossible; then, inexplicably, having to find a second porter to get her a taxi was just as tough. Total cost: nine hundred francs. "Nice start," she muttered.

Before leaving Canada, she had written to the Pension Domecq, an establishment recommended by friends, to reserve a room. The pension was run by the Domecq family at 70 rue d'Assas, near the Jardin du Luxembourg and just a kilometre south of l'École des Beaux-Arts. Frances was supposed to have the room for a full week, but she had hardly arrived when she was told she'd have to leave. Her room was that of a student who was returning in forty-eight hours. Frances would have the room for only two nights. Tired and confused, and her French at this time nonexistent, she wailed (in English) "What shall I do?"

The next day she went to the Maison Canadienne and spoke to a Mr. Lemay, who promised to find her a place.

After the disappointment of the Pension Domecq, Frances was directed to the Hotel Raspail on the Boulevard Montparnasse. "The Raspail was a terrible place at that time. The only good thing about it was the statue of Balzac by Rodin that was in a small park just across the street. The hotel was poorly lit and very cold. The plumbing must have gone back to the days of Napoleon. To ask for a bath, I felt, would have provoked an international incident, with ambassadors striking each other across the face with their gloves. The hotel stank of Gauloises, those ghastly French cigarettes. In fact, I tried to stop smoking by switching to Gauloises, but I just got hooked on them instead."

Across the street from the Hotel Raspail was the Dôme, the restaurant patronized by artists and literary figures in earlier decades, the days of the English and American expatriates whose names were then virtually unknown, but who would later achieve international fame. There they wrote, sketched, and caroused, and smoked the same Gauloises cigarettes so abhorred by Frances.

The Pension Domecq was a pension for gentle ladies, all in their seventies. Though Frances was there for only a few days, she came to like the dining room, and for months she would return there for meals. "The food was good, and not too expensive. To make my finances last, I knew I had to economize." She was finally placed in the Hotel Raspail, at a daily price of eight hundred francs, but continued taking her meals at the Domecq. The Domecq, she said, was a funny little place. "Each person had their bottle of wine with their name on it. They'd drink half a glass of wine topped up with water. They were very proper elderly gentlewomen. I was a rough Canadian savage who, of course, didn't have the right kind of table manners. I would grab a pear and take a big bite. Out of the corner of my eye I could see all these ladies looking askance at the boorish colonial. You were never to touch fruit with your fingers. You picked it up with your fork, put it down, peeled and cut it, and put it in your mouth with your fork."

Unhappy with the conditions at the Hotel Raspail, Frances was still looking for accommodations, and providentially encountered Trudy Peter, a friend whose home was in Switzerland. Frances had previously met her through Barbara Howard, a fellow graduate of OCA in Toronto. Trudy was attending the Sorbonne, and living with a Madame Gérard whose children she looked after in the role of au pair. With Trudy's recommendation, Frances was offered a room in Madame Gérard´s house at number 8 rue Saint Florentin, a two-minute walk from the Tuileries and the Louvre. "It was a fifth-floor walk-up, no elevator, with light switches at each floor that you pushed. The lights were timed to go off just before you reached the next stairs." She felt the room was acceptable, but made no firm decision at the time.

Trudy, as the au pair, had a room upstairs in the "servants'" quarters. "She lived in the most incredibly primitive attic," said Frances. "She had one small skylight window that would open a little bit. She had no heat, no electricity. You had to take a candle or a flashlight to go through the dark, narrow, twisting corridors to get to her room. I just couldn't believe it; it was medieval. She showed it to me while I was there. I mean, this was the middle of the twentieth century! I didn't know of anything even remotely similar in Canada."

The arrangement made through the Canadian embassy was that Frances would study at La Grande Chaumière under Ossip Zadkine, whose work Frances admired, and whose early influence is seen in the paving-stone *Pelican* that was executed during her time in New York. La Chaumière, at 14 rue de la Grande Chaumière, was just around the corner from the Hotel Raspail, and was thus in easy walking distance from the Pension Domecq, too.

Zadkine was Russian and had arrived in Paris in 1909. During Frances's time in Paris, he was sixty-five years old and firmly set in his ways of instruction. "I went to see his class and found there were about thirty little 'Zadkines' working around him. He wouldn't allow a student to work in any style but his. Well, that wasn't for me. That wasn't what I wanted at all. So I spoke to the man at the Canadian embassy, and ultimately moved to the École des Beaux-Arts."

Frances felt the École offered her more, much more than Zadkine. Nevertheless, almost every night after supper, she would return to La Chaumière for drawing exercise. "They had very good models, and it was close to where I lived. Everything was within walking distance from where I was. It was wonderful. I was a good walker. I also had a bicycle, but that was a bit dangerous in Parisian traffic."

But nothing is free, and the evening sketching cost her a few francs, perhaps thirty cents Canadian, which was quite acceptable given the quality of the models. In summertime the models were warm enough. In winter there were pot-bellied stoves, and the models were warm on one side and cold on the other. Behind the models' stands there were always several cans of flea powder; the models all had fleas. One boy was covered by little bites. He'd run away from home and was modelling in order to live. Frances was touched. "Wherever he was staying, his room must have been full of fleas," she said sadly. "He was frightened; he'd never met them before! I felt terrible about it, but it was his decision. He was in Paris! He was part of the artist's world."

Frances found that everywhere she went in Paris there was sculpture. On every street corner, every block. "But I found the French were extremely provincial, like most Americans. If it wasn't French, it wasn't any good. Professor Louis Leygue of the École des Beaux-Arts, when he first met me, said, 'You must forget everything you have learned in America, there is no culture there.'"

Almost all the professors at the École des Beaux-Arts considered that no one outside France had done, or was doing, anything of great interest. Not even New York could produce anything much in their eyes. And this feeling of narrow nationalism prevailed among the students.

At first this caused frustration, but she put that aside and decided to benefit from the fine instruction in technique she felt she would get. Individualism was not encouraged, much like Zadkine, even though students had had fine formal training before entering the classes.

The exception to all this formal instruction was Professor Georges Saupique. "He had the carving studio: wood and stone." She sighed. "He was a wonderful man." She went drawing in the zoo, the Vincennes. "My professor, Georges Saupique, took me up to the zoo for the first time because I was planning to do a seagull, so he took me up to see the seagulls that were there, and the animals. He took me to the stone yard, and we found this scrap of Carrara marble. They gave it to us, and I carved the seagull from that. It's fun to do it that way, following the restrictions of the piece of stone instead of imposing a predetermined style on something." A year later, on her return to America, she brought the seagull back with her. Her New York cab driver bent to pick up her bag and almost fell down. "Jesus, lady, what you got in here, rocks?" She was delighted to answer, "Yes!"

It was the beginning of October at the Beaux-Arts, and Professor Leygue gazed coldly at the figure on which Frances was working. "Your figure," he said, "lacks exaltation." Frances pondered that. Exaltation; what the devil does that mean? "I'll think about it later," she muttered, banished it from her mind, and went to lunch on Boulevard St-Michel, 250 francs. Later that evening she had supper at a student restaurant for sixty-five francs. "My Paris grant, two thousand dollars, was enough money to allow an American student to live in Paris for eight months." She smiled complacently. "I lived like a *Paris* student and the money lasted me for fifteen months.

"In the student restaurants, if you had a good digestive system, you could manage. They were cheap, even compared to what you could buy for yourself. The food was good, as French food generally is. I ate and behaved like the French students, and saved money. You took what they had, of course. You sat on wooden benches at wooden tables, and you just got what they served. If you wanted wine, you brought your own. You took your bottle down to the vintners and they filled it for about thirty cents. And it was really good wine."

Frances had seen Madame Gérard's room, and at the end of October 1955, had decided to take it, starting January 1, 1956. At ten thousand francs per month, she felt it was good, and would give her the opportunity to improve her French with Madame and her two children.

Hours of study and instruction at the École des Beaux-Arts were nine to four, with a break for lunch. The French had two hours for lunch, so she would have two or three hours in the morning, then about two hours in the afternoon. "That was enough, because you can't absorb more than that, I think. And then in the evening, I'd go to La Grande Chaumière to draw. On the way, I'd pass a couple of houses of ill repute. The girls were out on the sidewalk near La Grande Chaumière. They looked quite nice." Notwithstanding the firm dedication to art, the gambling instinct was alive then as it is now. "We'd check out the girls who were there when we arrived at the Chaumière, and then make bets on who would be gone when we left later."

Evenings at La Chaumière were occasionally not as satisfying as Frances might have wished. The models were, as Frances said, generally good, but "generally" suggests that sometimes they weren't. "Drawing last night. Terrible model. Skinny, flat, and stiff as a porcupine, with a malignant stare. Last pose was on her back!"

Mid-November saw Professor Leygue laying some hard criticisms on Frances's work. "The figure is too elongated." A brusque gesture. "No excuse for it." And again the next day: "There is an unacceptable lack of planes, the flat areas." As if Frances, that untalented Canadian nonentity, wasn't aware that a plane was a flat area. Teeth clenched, Frances muttered, "I will keep trying." The following week Professor Leygue came in, glanced at the piece on which she was working, and passed on without a word. *Hey,* she thought, with just a little sarcasm, *my piece must be getting better.*

She met Trudy for lunch the next day, and after a tour of a number of galleries, ended up at the Salon d'Hiver. "Indescribably bad contemporary show," said Frances. Next they visited the Salon d'Automne. "No selectivity. Good things in with bad. Grrr." Then, having got all the beefing out of their system, they tossed the salons' pamphlets into the trash and returned to the Pension Domecq for a pleasant supper.

Happy times among the galleries? Yes and no. The galleries, being visual, were fascinating, but every day there was the ever-present problem of the language. Frances's French was still poor. She found she couldn't understand the students or the instructors at all. She began taking French lessons from a private tutor.

One day in early December she received a surprising critique from an unexpected source. One of *les anciens* (the so-called "senior" students whose irritating superior airs continually exasperated Frances) said her work was almost good enough for the Prix de Rome, an award established during the reign of Louis XIV. *Hoo-ha,* thought Frances, *wouldn't it be interesting to tell* monsieur le professeur *Louis Leygue that because of his superb instruction, I was now ready for the Prix de Rome. Great fun it would be to watch his outraged response!* She felt he had probably won the prize himself (he had, in 1931), which would increase his outrage a thousandfold.

Professor Leygue's visits to the classroom were often brief. An aloof survey of the room, one or two terse criticisms, then gone. "Not surprising, I suppose," said Frances. "It was often impossible to see much in the room. Unbelievably, they didn't have any lights! Just natural light. Imagine the conditions on a rainy overcast day. No electricity. No heat, other than a pot-bellied stove. On a rainy day my feet were always cold and wet. Who would think you'd need galoshes in a sculpture studio? In the evening sketching class there were students drawing on old wrinkled sheets of wrapping paper, much as Canada's Emily Carr had been obliged to do in earlier days, when times were lean. Makes me feel like a great fat plutocrat," Frances said, turning to a fresh page in her pad of expensive drawing paper, purchased through her two-thousand-dollar government grant.

But in early December, unsuitable studio conditions faded to irrelevance. Her thoughts turned with vast anticipation to a planned week's break at Christmas time: Across the Channel to London!

London — Big Ben, the Thames, pubs, fog. The Beatles had just emerged from their Liverpool garage, and were making a few indifferent waves in the British music scene. And Teddy Boys, in their smart Edwardian clothes, were showing the country that you could be a member of a teenage gang and still look well-dressed.

But Frances was unaware of all this. Her thoughts were only of her visit with her old alumna of Toronto art college days, Barbara Howard and her friend, the poet Richard Outram, both of whom were living and working in London.

"Christmas means gifts …" said Frances on the eve of her departure. "And I knew what would go over well, so I arrived with two suitcases — one filled with wine, the other with cheese. I think I also had a toothbrush in a pocket somewhere."

Richard's "apartment" was simply a big room that was so cold he finally put up a tent inside to help cut the icy drafts. In a letter home, he said he had taken so long to write because he'd slipped on the ice in the bathroom and hurt his elbow.

After Christmas she returned to Paris and l'École des Beaux-Arts. Despite her still-sketchy French, she made every effort to associate with the other students as much as she could. Earlier she had discovered with concern that the class initiated new students by making them pose naked and sing a song. They hadn't asked her yet, and she was keeping a low profile. "There was one American girl," she said. "She had a very hard time. She came from Chicago. She felt everybody should speak English, and she made no attempt to embrace the French way of life. For example, she had a shower every morning in the public showers — and got athlete's foot! She was so obnoxious that once they threw her in the clay bin, a large container like a gigantic bathtub, full of modelling clay. Yep, threw her in. I wasn't able to help … very much."

Art students, in Paris as elsewhere, find their amusements where they can. Frances found to her delight that students in France could get tickets to plays and concerts for the price of the tax, so she went to scores of stage productions. "You'd have to stand, but if you got there early you could often get a seat. I saw Édith Piaf in person, and a lot of violinists and string quartets. I mean, thirty cents a ticket, just the tax!"

It was the end of the year, and Madame Gérard was to have Frances's room ready for January 1, 1956, so New Year's Eve was spent in the Hotel Raspail. "I was homesick for the first time in my life," said Frances, "because all my Christmas mail had arrived. The French make much more of New Year than Christmas, so New Year's Eve was wild. I sat on my balcony. Below, there were people rushing back and forth, mostly drunk. Everyone was surprised that I would spend New Year's Eve all alone. But who would I want to spend it with except myself? All my Christmas mail … bunches of cookies … I just longed for the presence of my own people."

She had spent the afternoon of December 31 studying French and sculpture, then dined alone at the Pension Domecq. Back at the hotel, she sat in her room. On her table was a bright new candlestick. "And a red candle. I'd bought a nice candle for it." And she sighed. "All alone in Paris. Happy New Year to me."

"The first day of January 1956, damp and dismal."

She had awakened in the Hotel Raspail at seven in the morning to find the nightlife still in full swing, with fights on the sidewalk, drunks everywhere, and crowds of people coming and going in the hotel. A glance outside showed the rain sweeping across her small balcony. She shrugged, said "To hell with it," and went back to bed till nine o'clock. Then she got up and began packing for the move to Madame Gérard's room on the rue Florentin.

"I think I paid all of Madame Gérard's rent, but it was still much less than the hotel. The Raspail cost more than twice as much — eight hundred francs a day, compared to Madame Gérard's ten thousand francs a month. As a bonus, she had an eight-year-old boy named Jean-Marie who taught me most of my French. His French was just about the right level."

Frances was allowed one bath a week, and had to pay thirty francs for anything beyond that. Madame changed the bed sheets once a month. "One day, I thought, *Okay, Madame is away, so I'm going to wash my blanket.* I don't think she ever washed anything, other than the sheets. So I saved thirty francs by putting the blanket in the bath tub when I had a bath, and just walking all over it to get it clean. I discovered that what I thought was a brown blanket was actually a white one!" After that experience, Frances bought some flannel and made a sort of sleeping sack that she could use in her bed, and wash whenever Madame was away.

Madame Gérard was a small, very Gallic woman, with dark hair and dark eyes. "She was like a bird the way she flitted around. She was very quick and anxious. If I wasn't in my room, she would rush in and turn off the light because it was wasting electricity. My French wasn't good enough to tell her that it probably cost her more to turn it on and off. Her husband had been a filmmaker, and had died in a plane crash four years earlier." When Frances was living there, Madame had a little shop, selling knick-knacks and clothing, and spent the summer months in Provence where she had a small vineyard.

During the day, Madame's two children, Jean-Marie, eight, and Marie-Françoise, twelve, were in the charge of an au pair. Trudy had by this time returned to her home in Switzerland, and a young German girl had taken her place. She would take the children to school on the subway, pick them up and bring them back for lunch, then return them to school, and finally bring them home later in the afternoon. This was apparently the au pair's total responsibility; Madame took over after that, feeding them and giving them a bath. The children had first-class tickets on the subway. At that time there were two classes, First and Tourist. On the subway, Jean-Marie would say *"Quelqu'un pue!"* (somebody smells!), and the au pair would have to explain that all people couldn't have a bath every day. "They really were snobs, those kids," said Frances, "but that's the way they were brought up, to be upper middle class."

One day in mid-January, Frances had lunch with her new-found friend Paddy O'Hanlon. "Her name was given to me by a fellow student in New York. 'You must look her up,' he said. I usually try not to do that, because it rarely works out and you are stuck with someone you don't want to be stuck with. But I was lucky this time. She was a beautiful person. She was Irish. What else, with a name like that!" Paddy was moderately tall, extremely attractive, with an infectious effervescence. "She would have been nice to paint, but not to sculpt, because her bones weren't so obvious. But her colouring was lovely, so she would have made a good painting."

The two women spent happy hours touring Paris. They both had bicycles, and visited the many galleries. They sometimes had lunch on the banks of the Seine. Paddy had what many would consider the ideal working life. She appeared to have two jobs, one giving an American magazine a Paris presence, and all of France, too, undoubtedly. If the magazine wanted anything checked out or written about, Paddy was on the spot and handled it. "I think she was what was called a stringer," said Frances. "She was also the representative for McGraw-Hill, the publishers. She was perfectly bilingual. I guess that's what she was doing for McGraw-Hill, reviewing books toward possible translation for the English market."

Back at Madame Gérard's, she checked her mail. "Six letters today. Christmas cards. Merry Christmas, ho, ho, ho." And more dissatisfaction: At the Beaux-Arts she frowned at her sculpture. "I am not enthusiastic about this piece I'm working on." She looked bleakly at the young woman posing. "Model is stupid and gauche. The models are very badly treated here, but this one is just filthy, and not good."

It had snowed overnight, and under the thin morning sun the rooftops of Paris were lovely, but it was a beauty lost on Frances. Yet, as a result of the continual mood changes she underwent, the next day, in spite of a howling blizzard, Paris reached out and delighted her. "Paris looks exactly like a bride, dressed in beautiful lacy snow. The barges on the Seine are like blocks of snow, gliding down the slow green-brown water between the ragged clear areas where the thin ice has broken away. There are many barges on the river, with entire families living aboard."

It was still bitterly cold the following morning, and at the Beaux-Arts the figure on which she had been working was progressing, but only in a relative sense: more advanced than yesterday, but not terribly exciting. "*Les anciens*, the so-called senior students, push me around so much I can't see the model. They take priority of position in the studio, and they're very assertive about it. I wasn't aggressive," she added, "… in those days."

Toward the end of January, Professor Leygue offered a more comprehensive critique of Frances's piece, rather than his customary one or two words of utter rejection. Like many self-important insecure people, he seemed to feel that a compliment or implied agreement showed weakness; that only a voice raised in arrogance and harsh contempt showed that he knew what he was doing, that he was in charge, that he was number one. "He gave me a good going over. Not enough force, he said, in fact not any. Damn. I thought it was good." The next day she looked at the figure again, in agony, despair, and heart-breaking resignation. "My figure is awful. Awful."

The next day she looked for Leygue in vain. "I'm trying to do one figure, just one figure, to please him!" she cried. She sat, slumped, before the now-seen-as-utterly-appalling piece of work, and gave in to depression. "I just didn't know what to do," she said. "I was in one of those terrible paralyzing artistic lows. I had to tell myself, 'Come on, it happens. Tomorrow it will be better'. But at that time, in that hour, I knew I was lying."

One day at the end of January there was a big fuss at the Beaux-Arts. Joan, an American student Frances had met at the school — she was the Chicago girl who felt everyone should speak English — had refused to participate in the jolly initiation rites, where new students were required to strip naked and sing in front of the class. "Some did it," Frances laughed. "Joan didn't." Frances had at one time visited Joan in her room, and found her living in conditions that would not have been seen in a seventeenth century prison. "I had no idea how she got by. She had no heat, no light. Shocking, really. She was unhappy. She had a huge family, but got no help from home. But it was difficult to feel pity for her; she was a very self-centred girl. Me, me, me, all the time. Really got on your nerves. She was the one we — that is to say the students — threw in the clay bin. I didn't participate, really; I was a foreigner, too, and could easily have got the same treatment."

These happy little capers were not the general rule, and occurred only when Professor Leygue was absent, which was entirely too often so far as Frances was concerned. "I'm not a freeloader, after all. I'm paying for this. Damn. He was in this morning and gave two critiques — two critiques! — to one of the Frenchmen, his current teacher's pet.

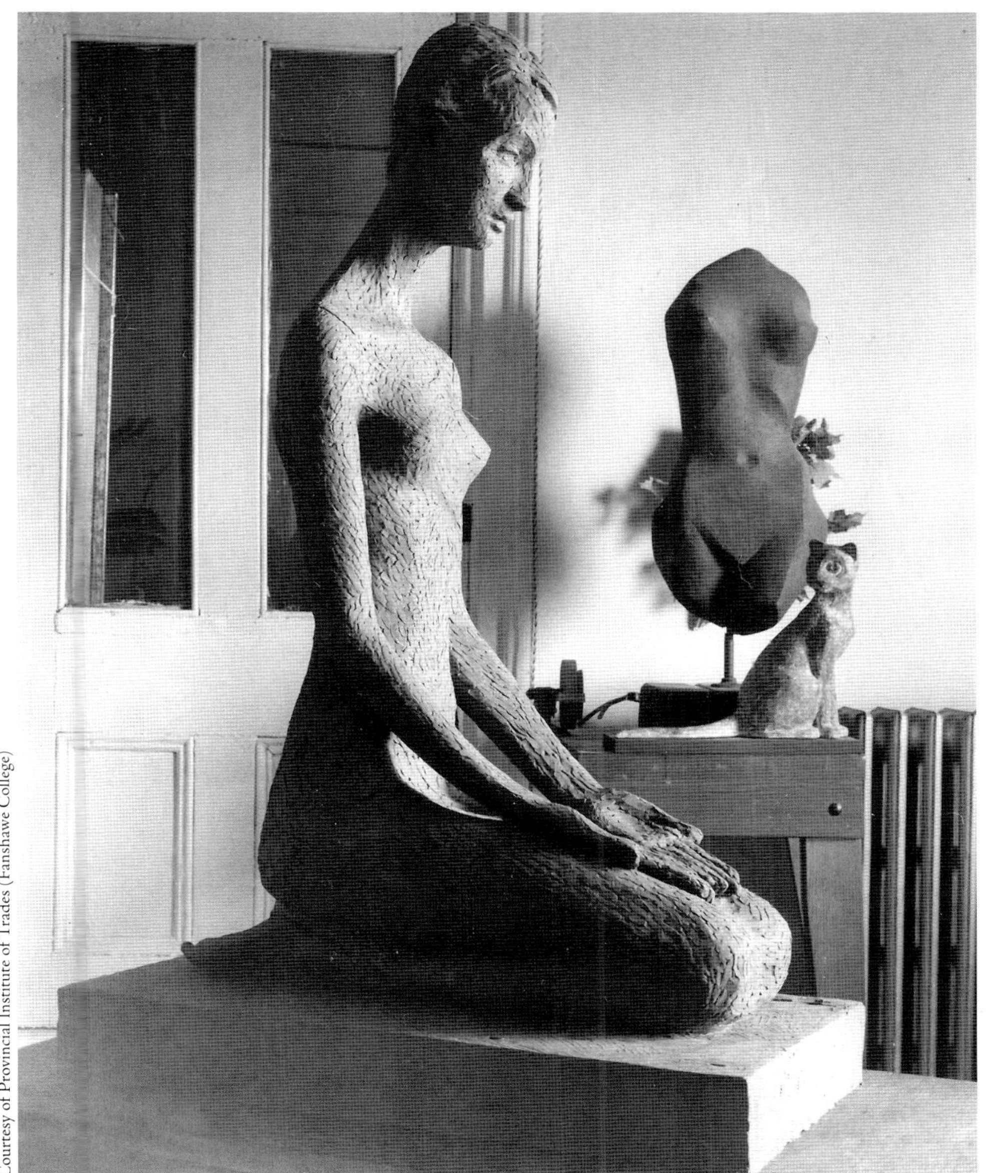

The Discovery of the Hands, 1957. The children gathered regularly to say good morning to "the statue lady."

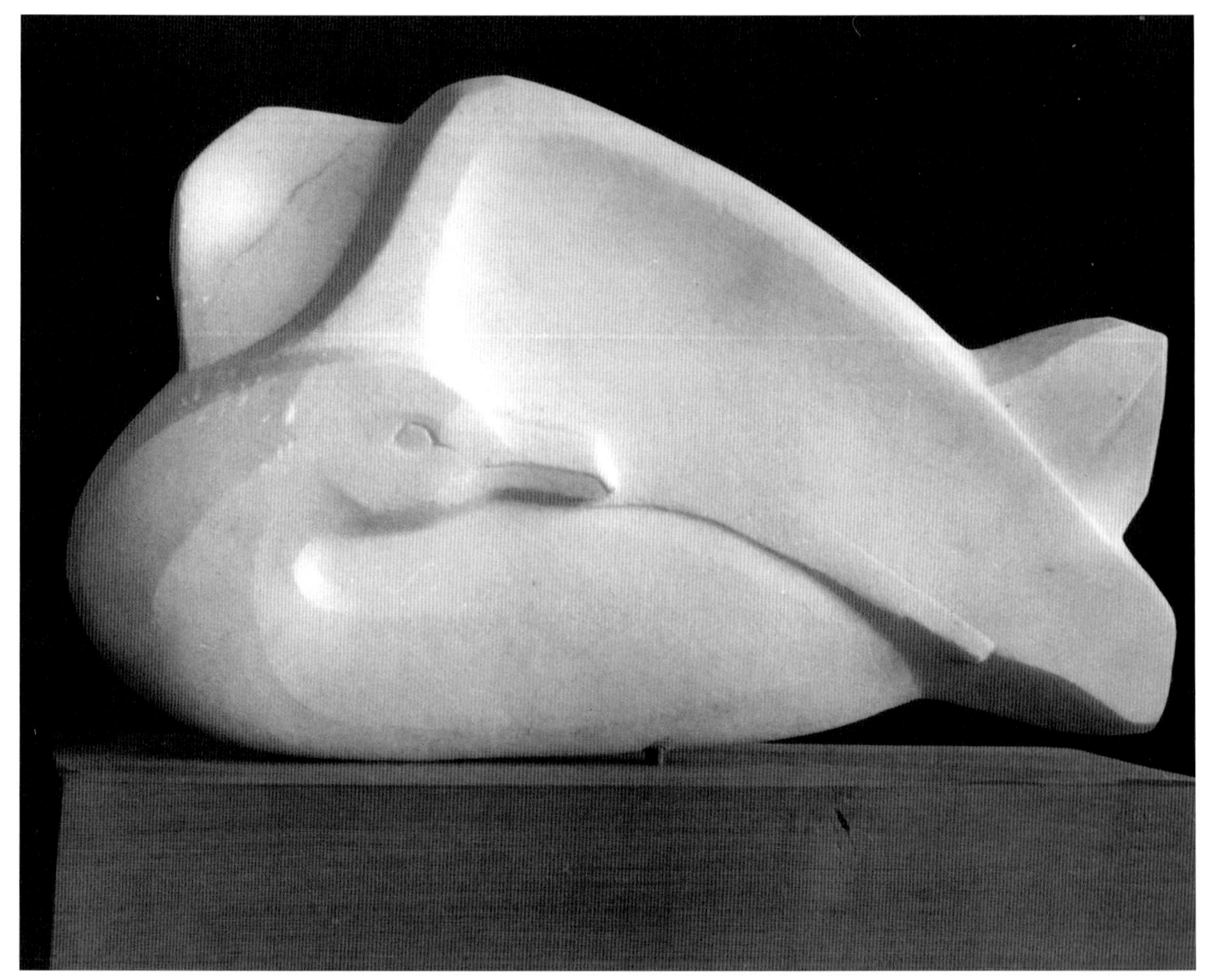

Seagull, 1958. "He took me to the Paris stone yard, and we found this scrap of Carrara marble."

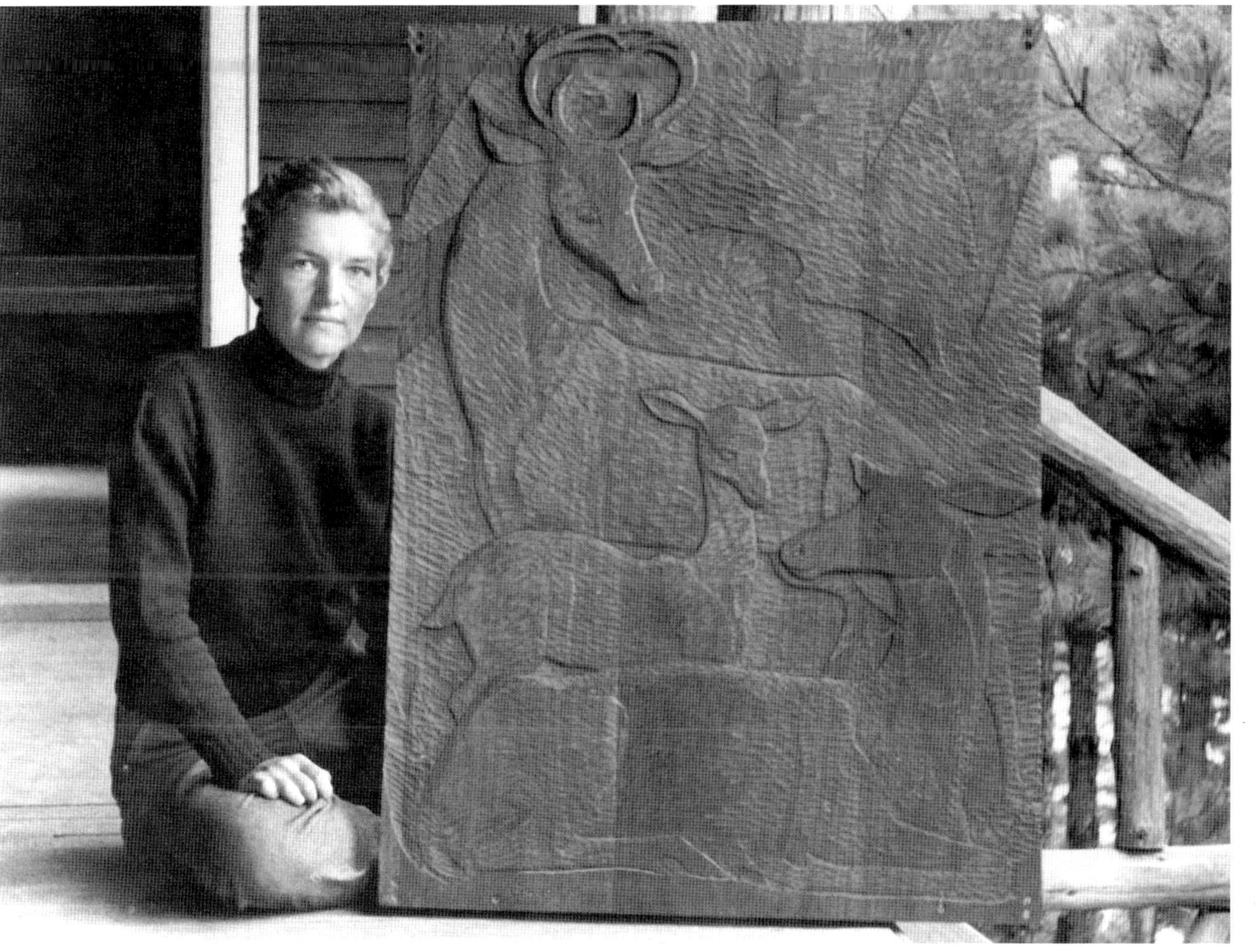

Deer Family, 1953.

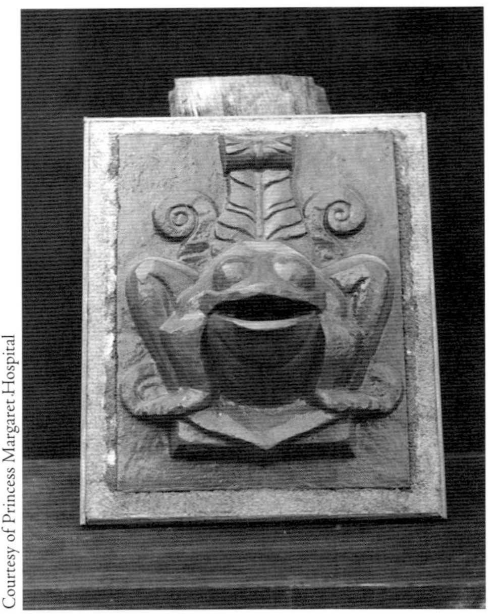

Frog Fountain, 1957.

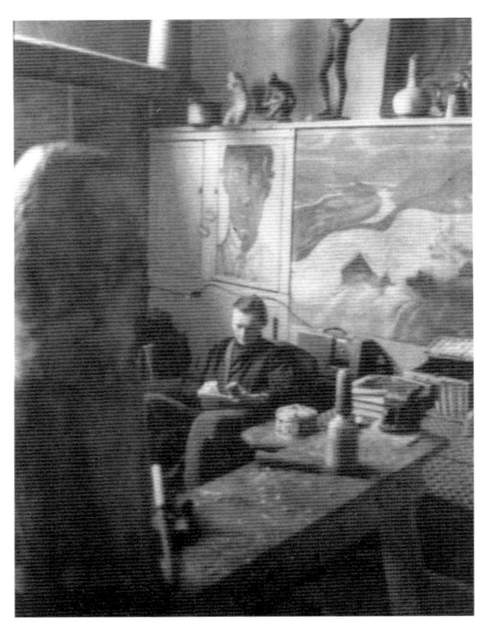

Surrounded by paintings … Frances Gage in the shack, *circa* 1958.

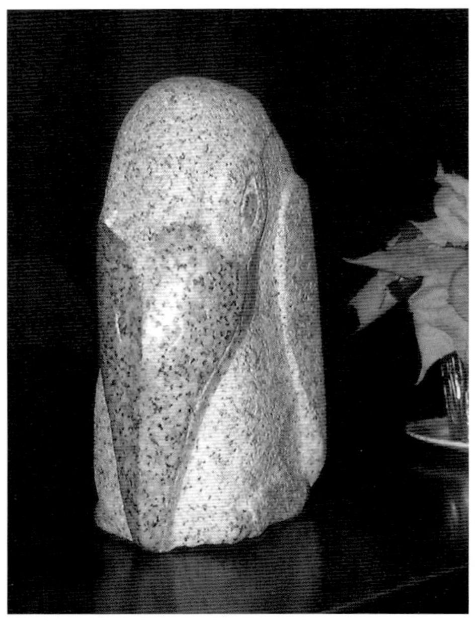

Pelican, 1954.

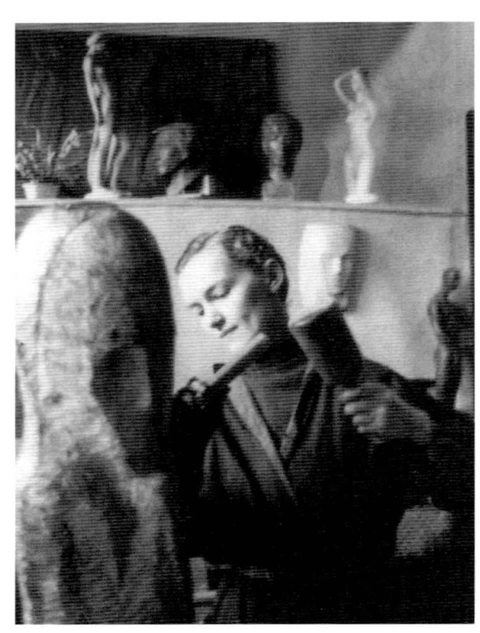

… and the spirit of Tom Thomson beside her. Frances Gage in the shack, *circa* 1958.

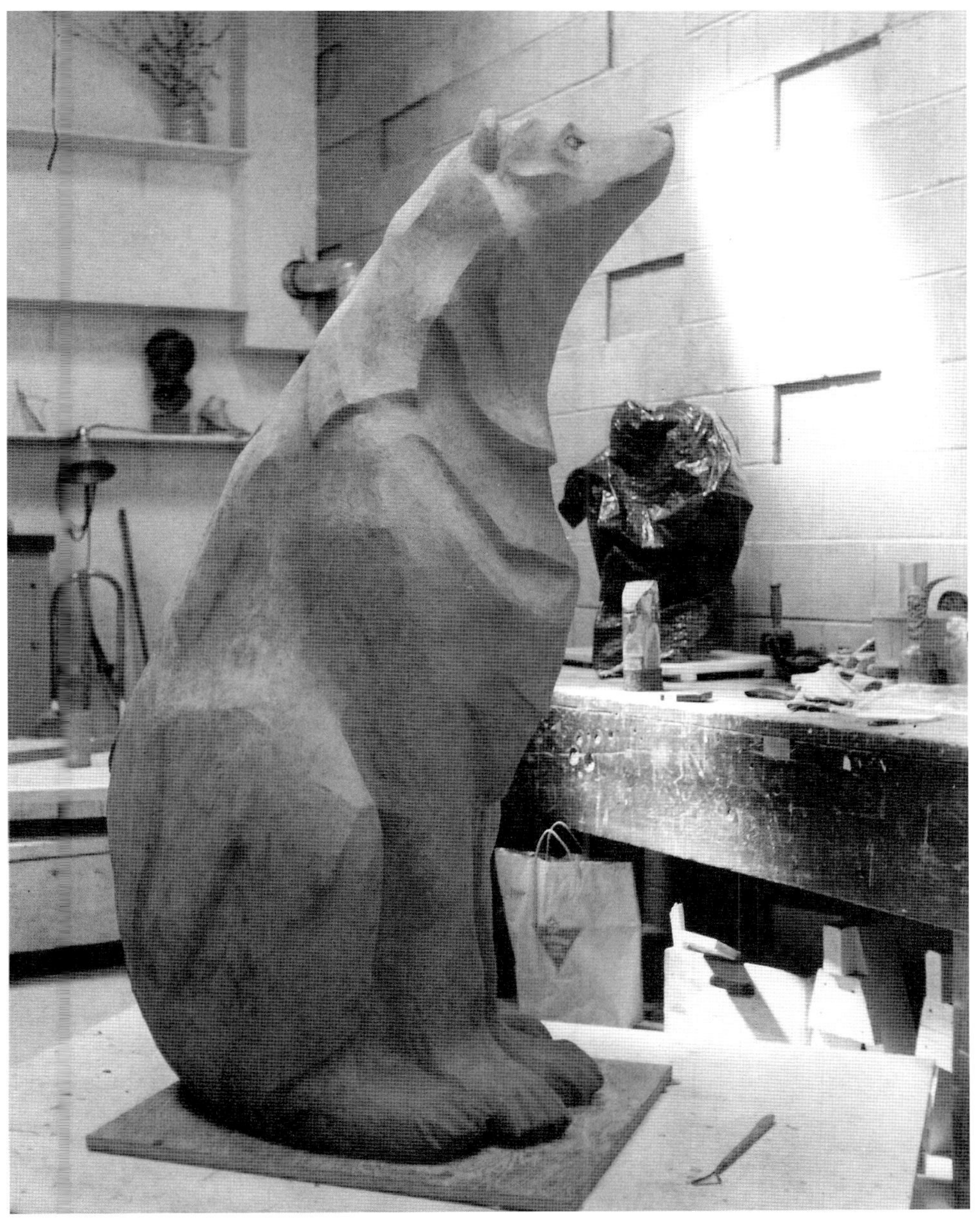

Bear, 1966. "So the Big Bear — seven feet tall and cast in concrete— was a kind of payola."

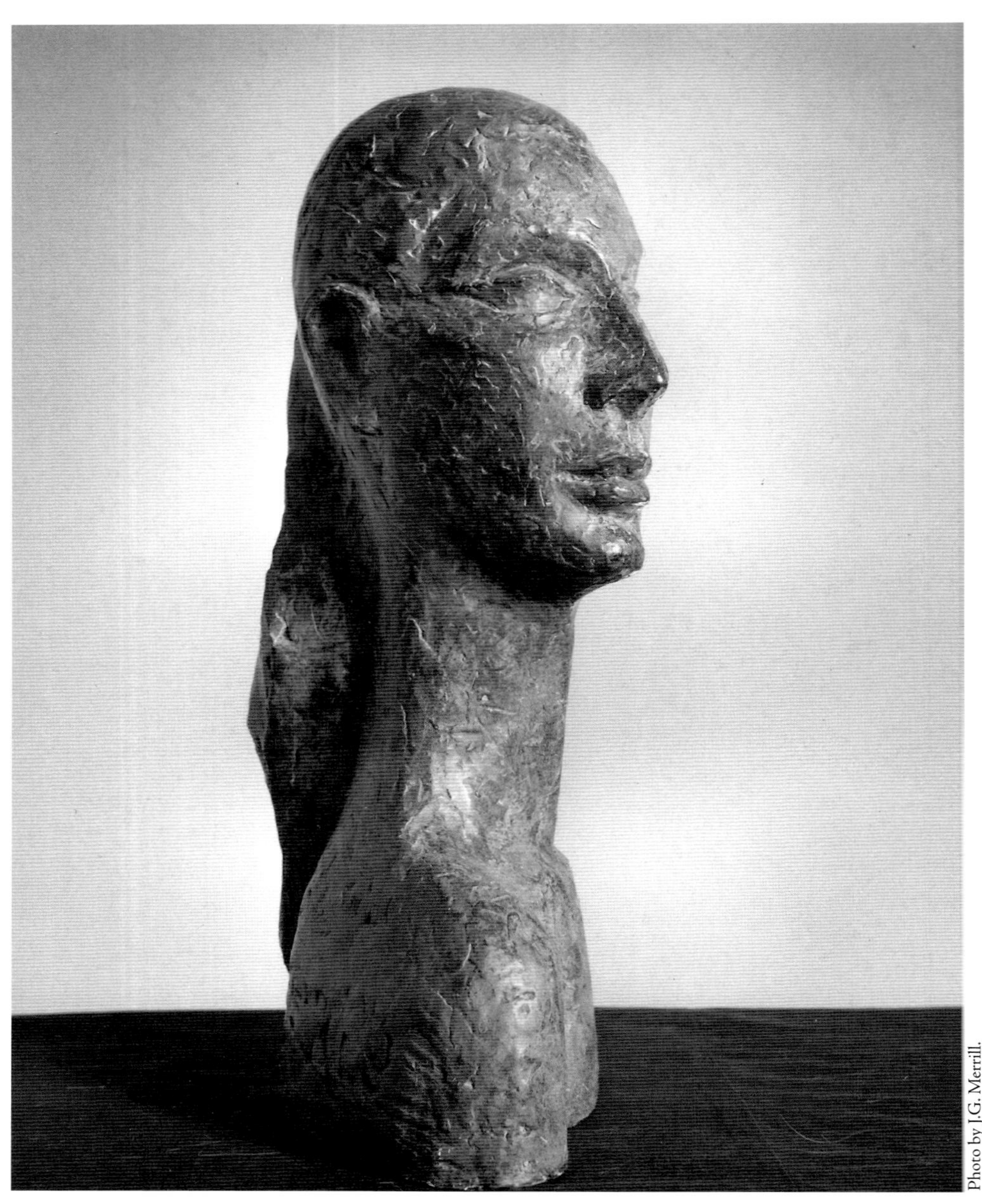

Ballerina, 1954.

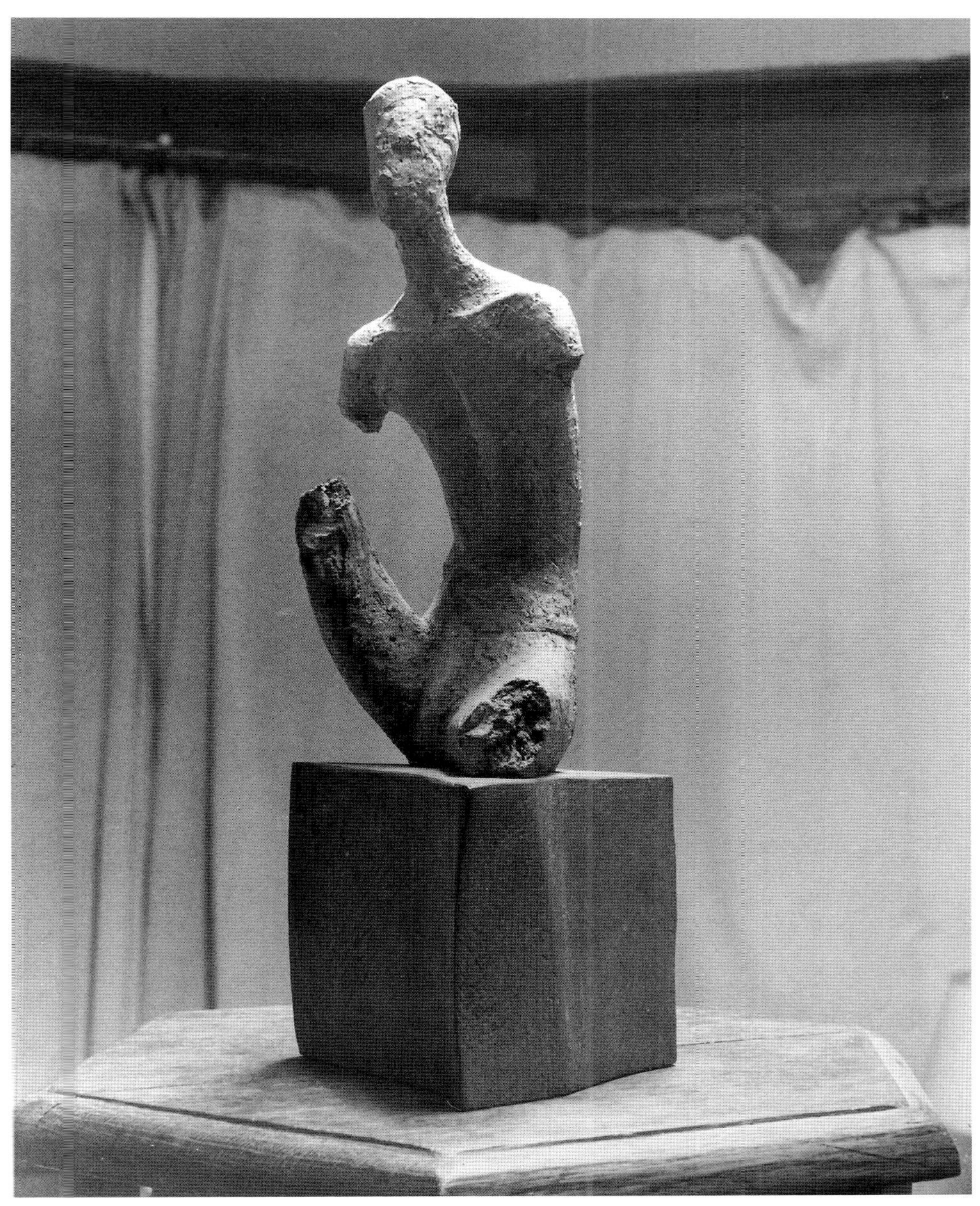

Torso of a Dancer, 1954. "The arms and legs got in my way. So I broke them off."

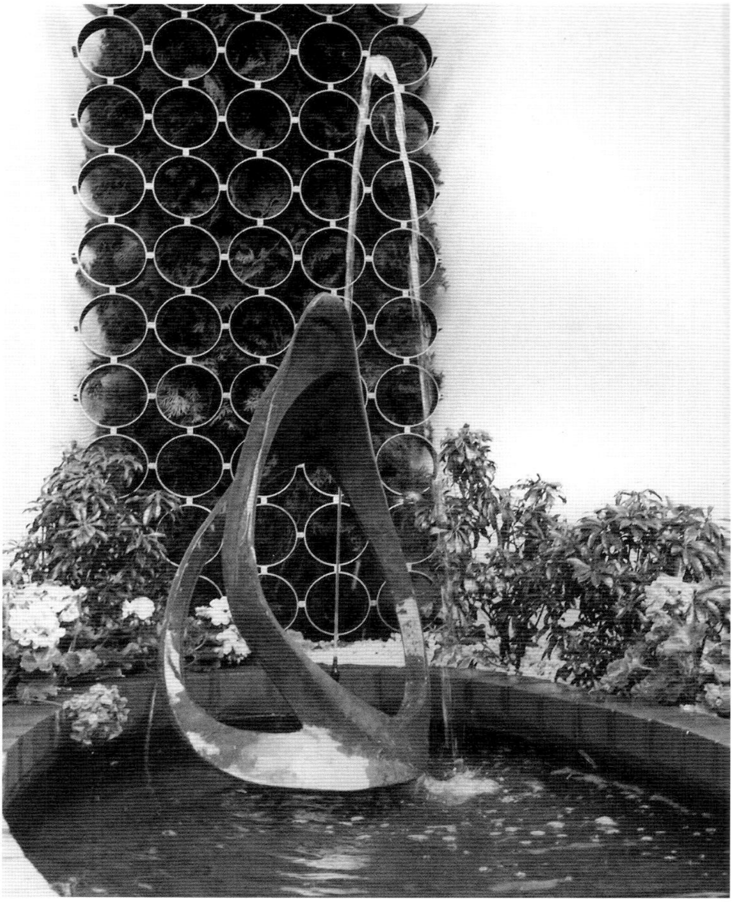

Garden Show
Winner (part),
1960.

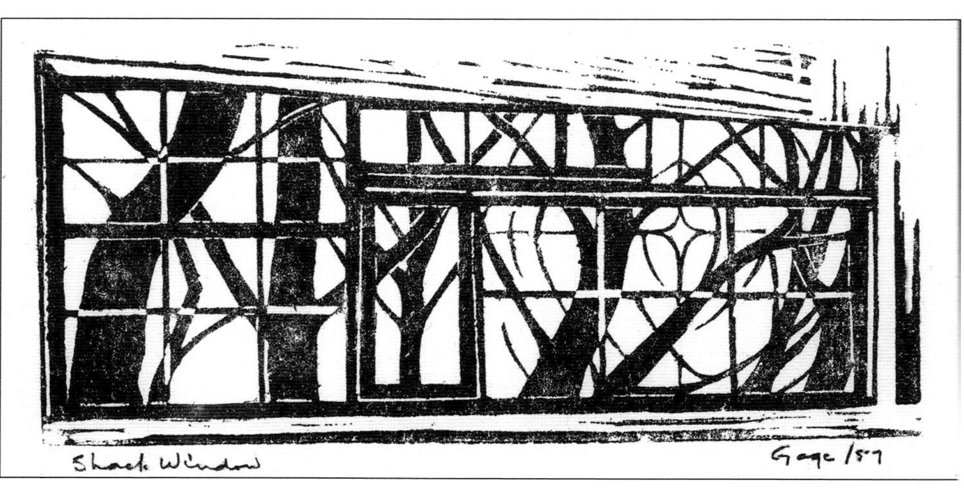

Thomson's window, 1957.

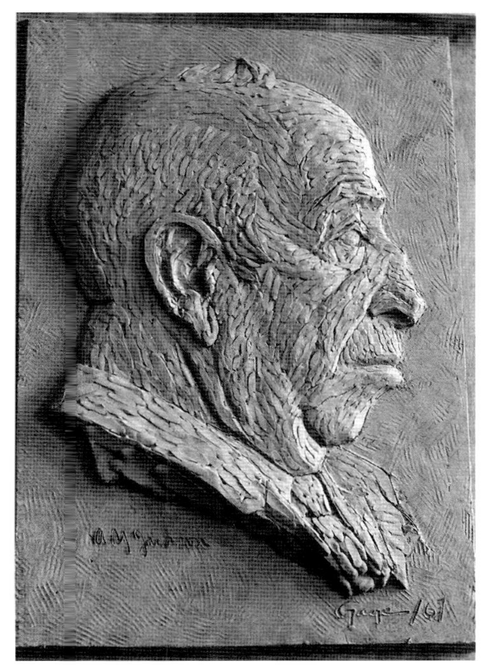

A.Y. Jackson, 1967.

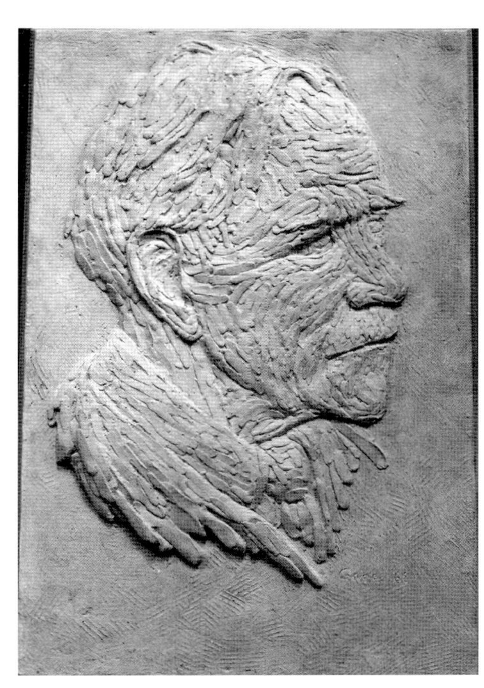

Frederick Varley, 1967.

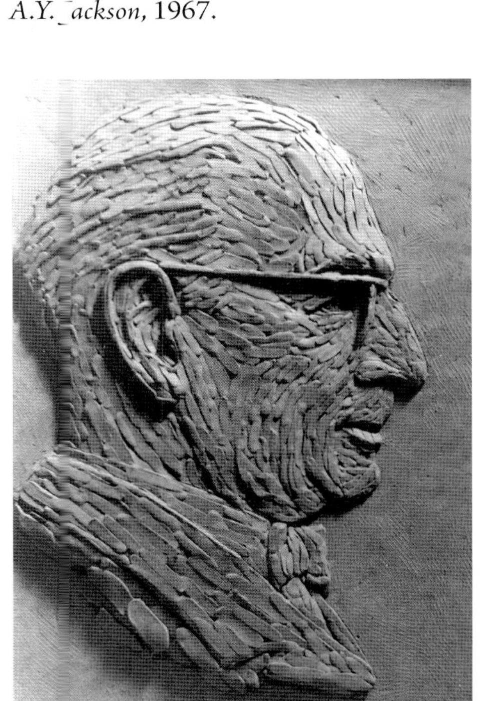

Healey Willan, 1967.

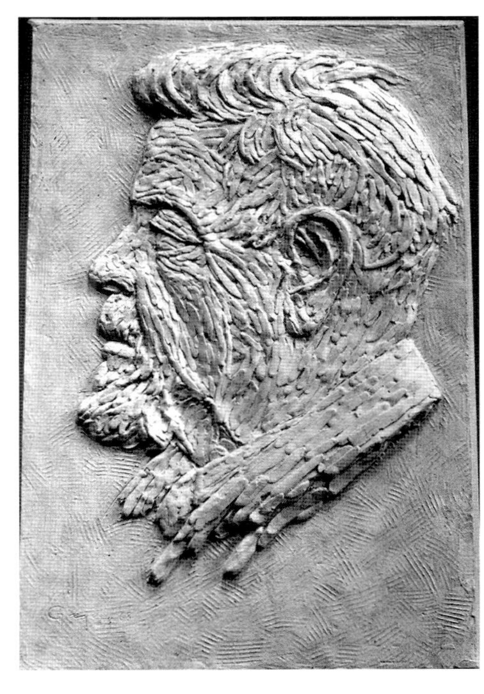

Sir Ernest McMillan, 1967.

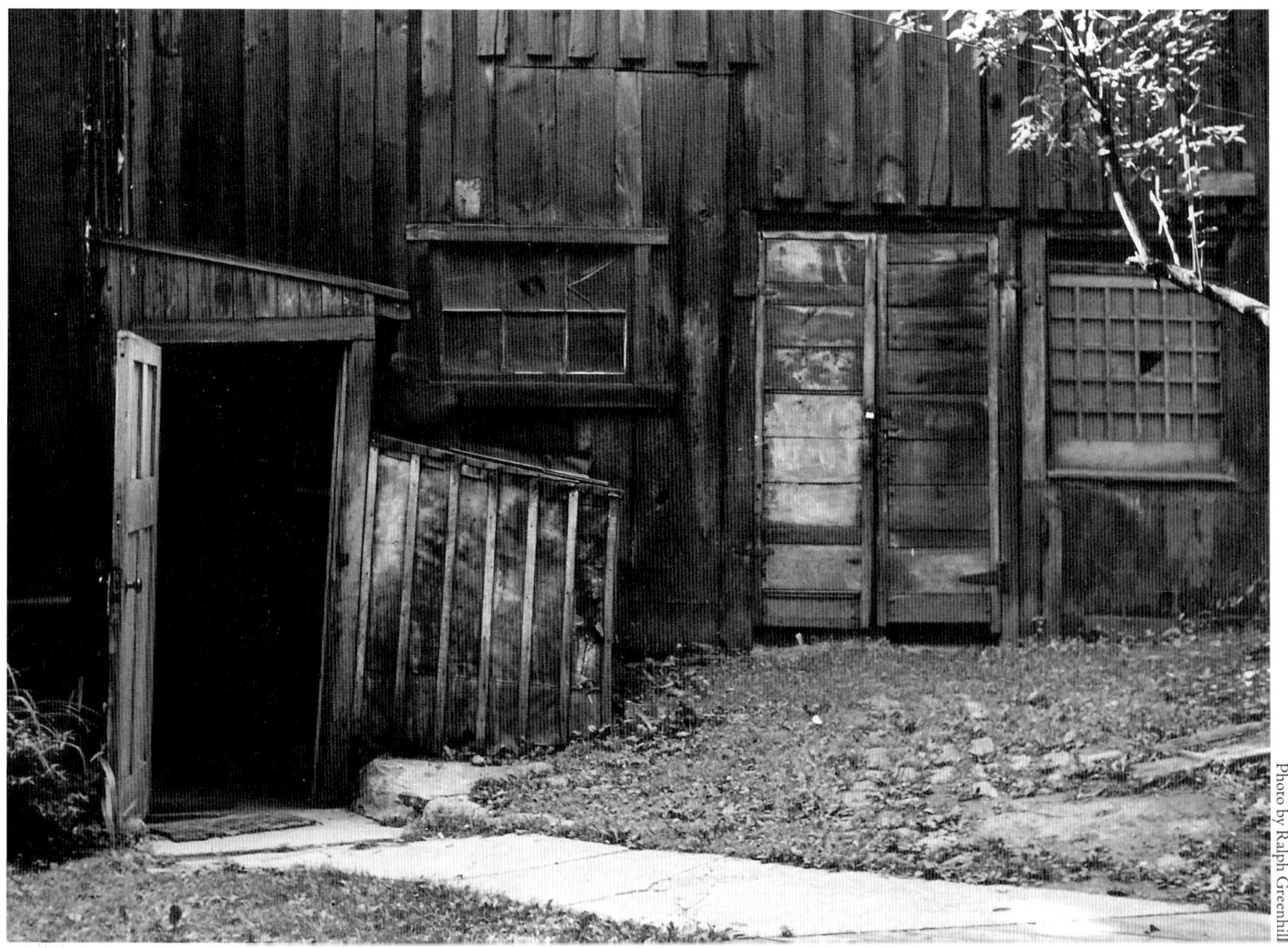

The shack, 1957. Forty years before, the shack had been the studio of Tom Thomson.

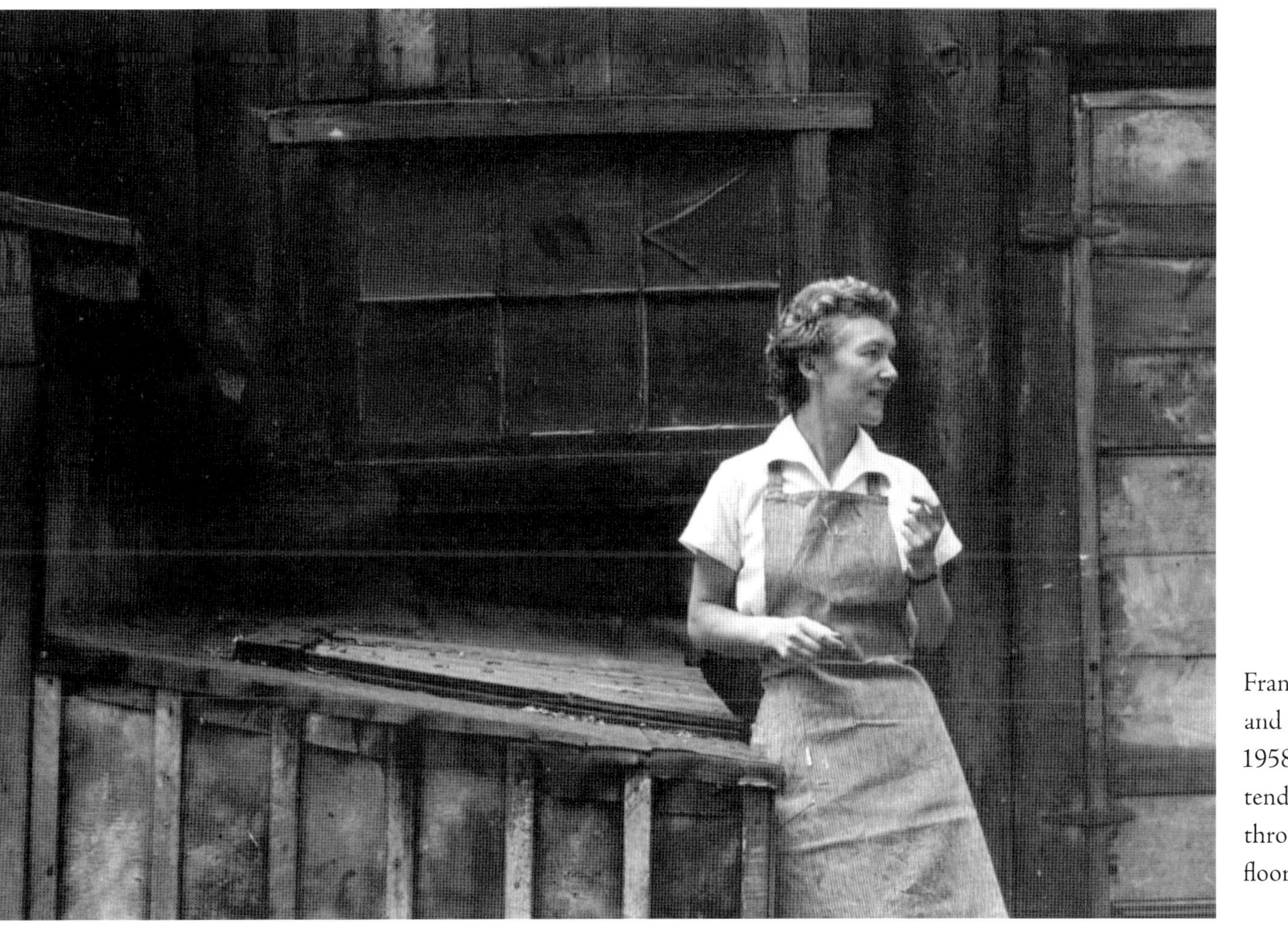

Frances Gage and the shack, 1958. "People tended to fall through the floor."

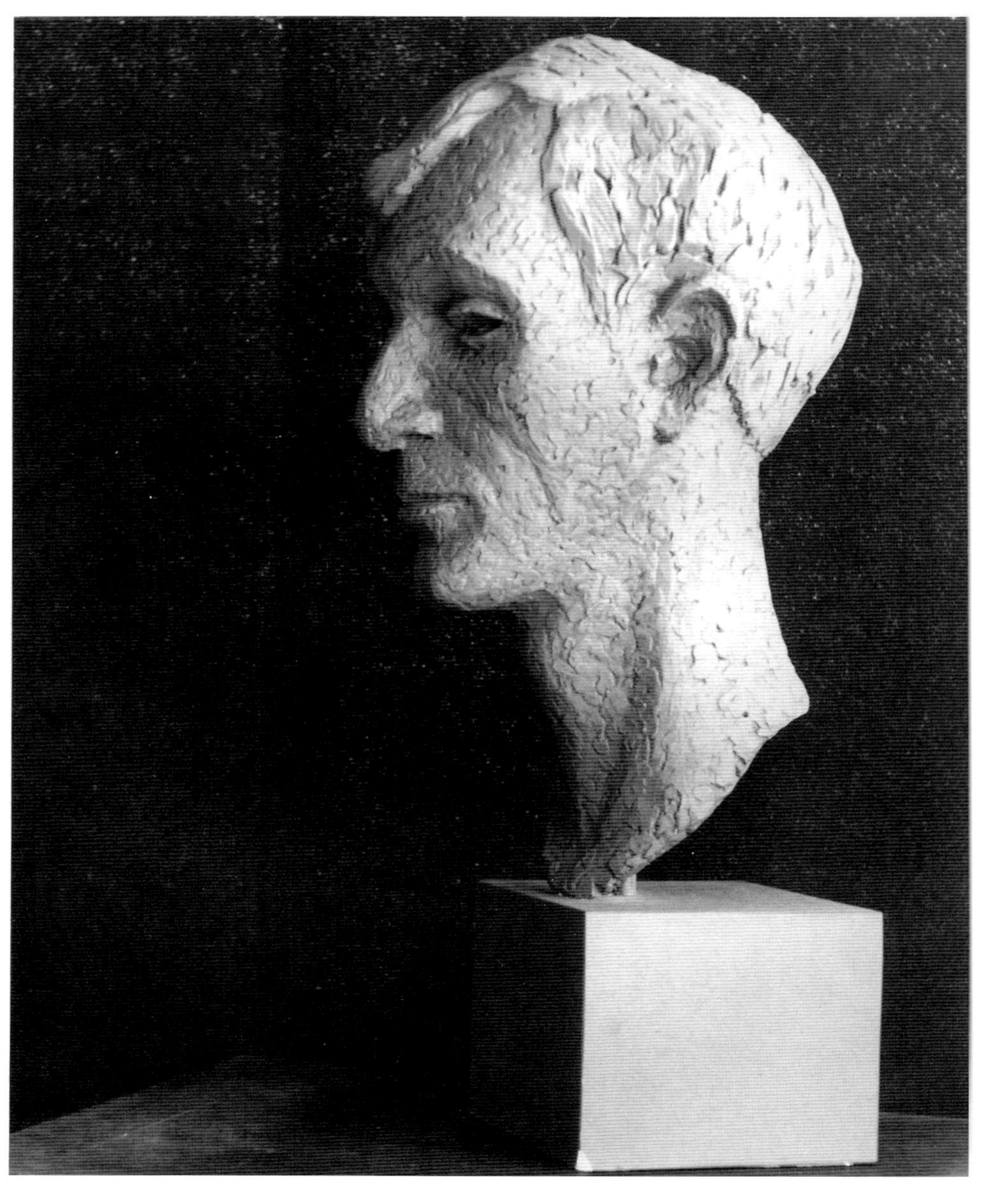

Douglas Duncan, 1957. "Some might have said Douglas Duncan was crazy ..."

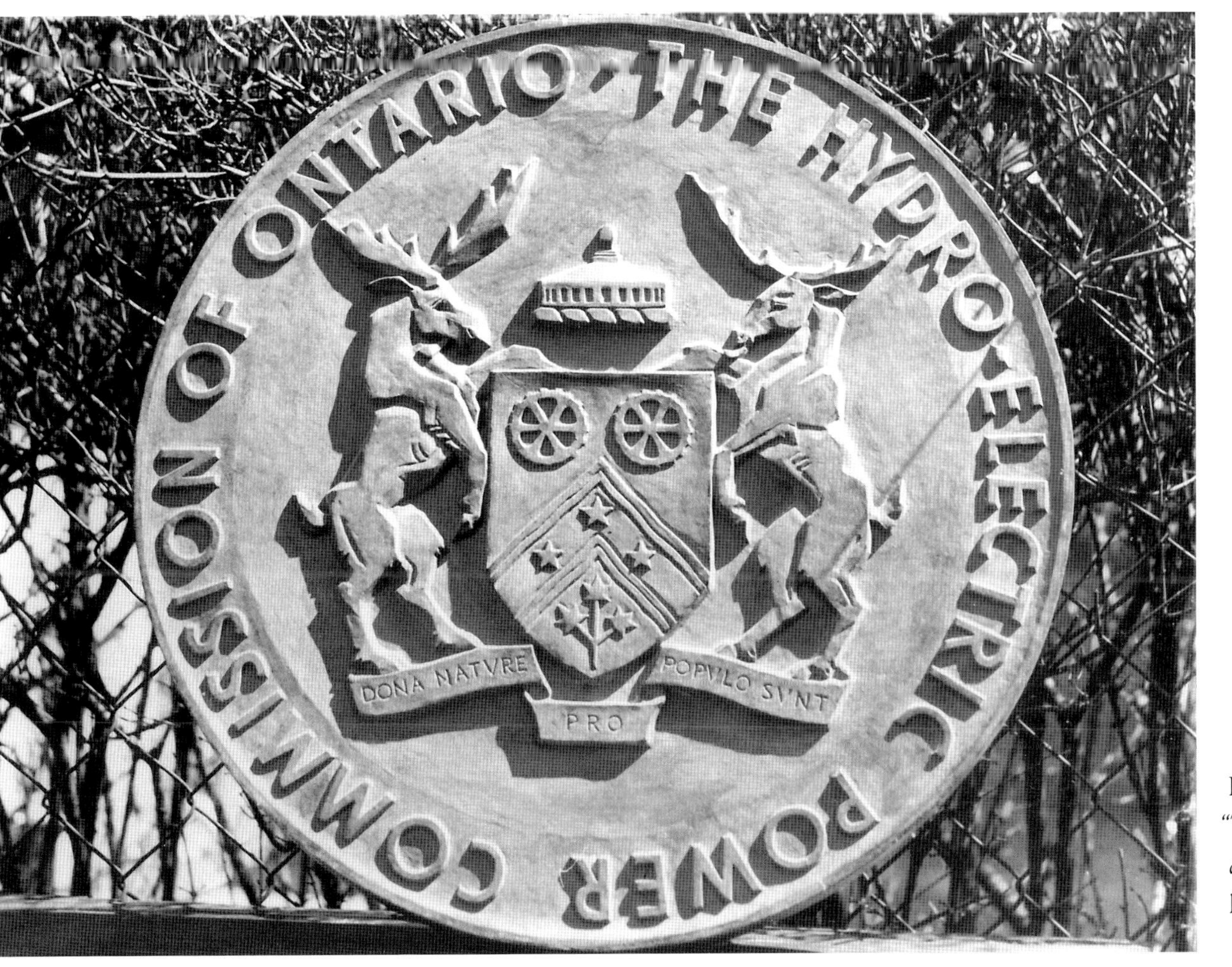

Hydro crest, 1958.
"They found that the
a in the *æ* of *Naturæ*
had been omitted."

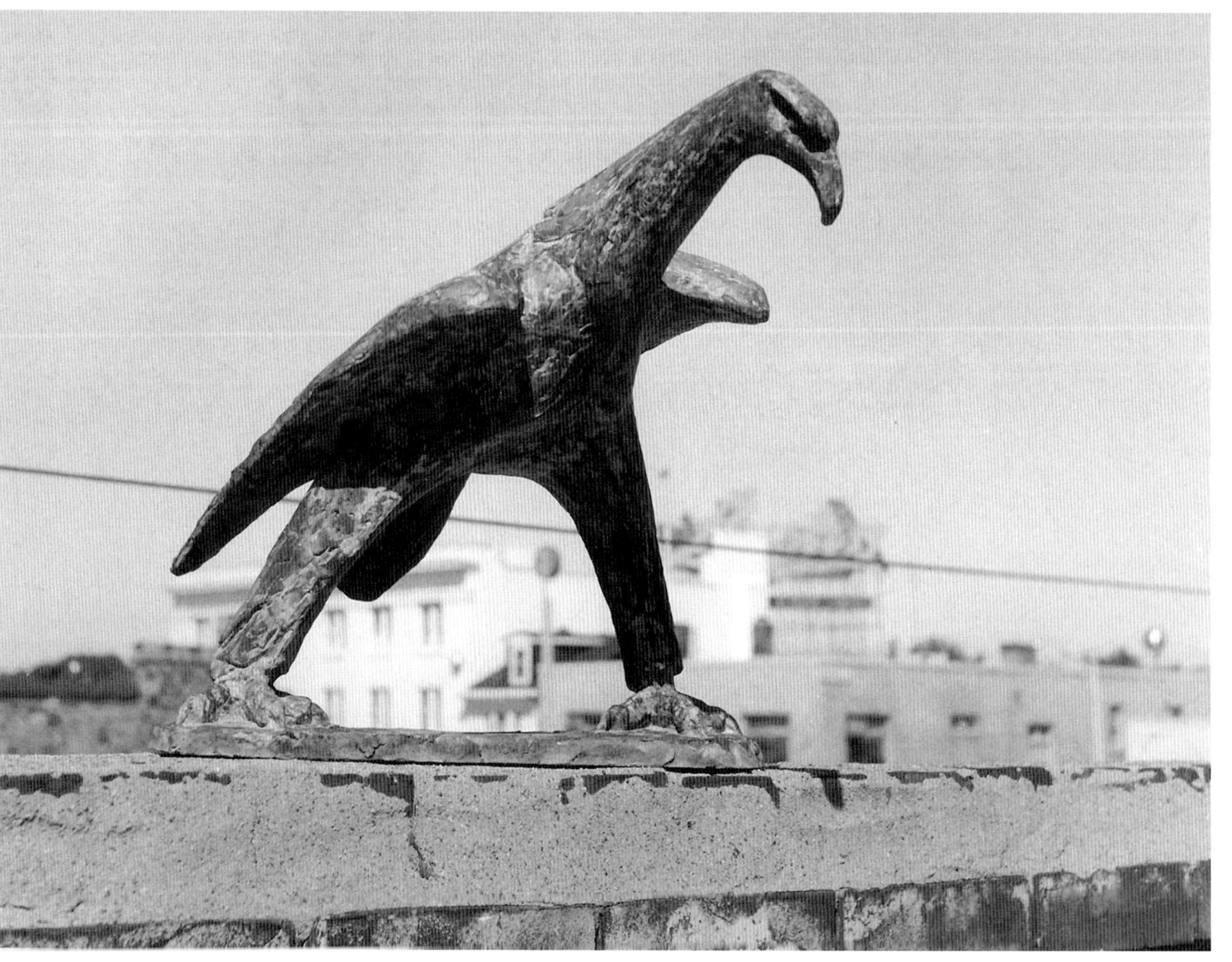

Eagle, 1959.

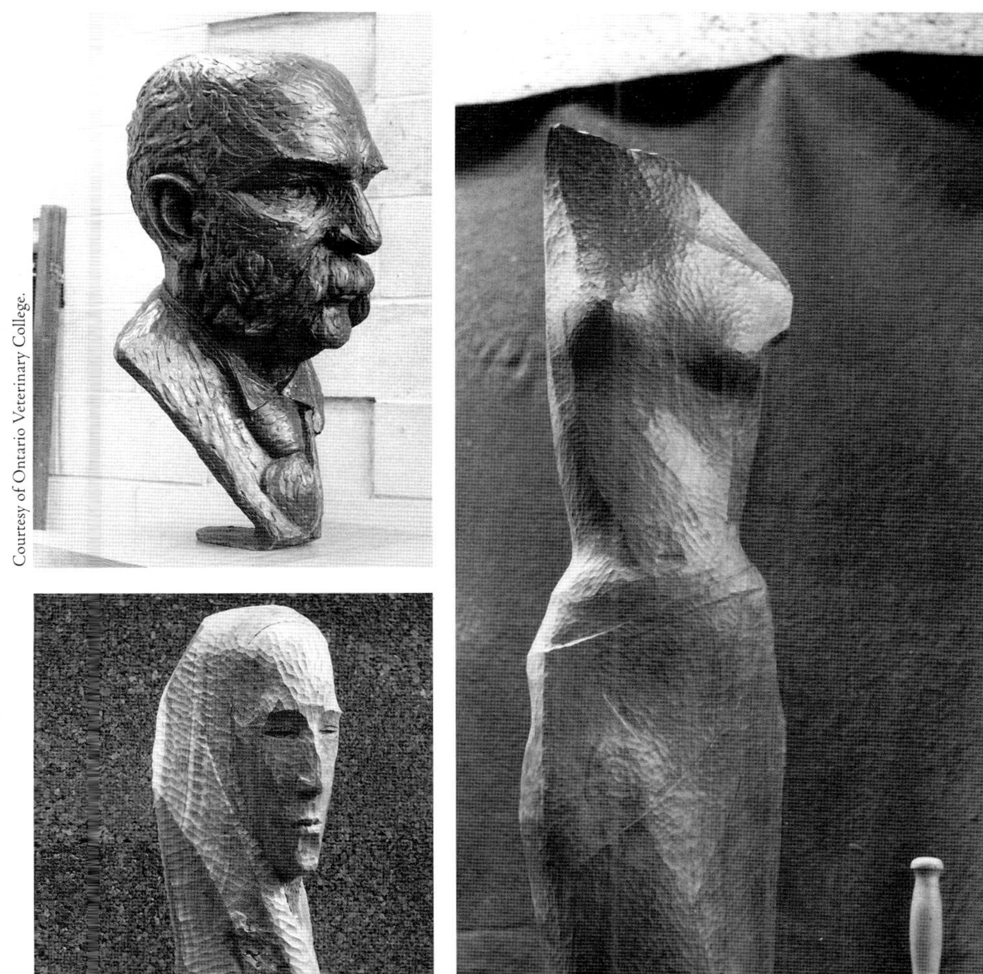

Top Left: *Dr. Andrew Smith*, 1967.

Bottom left: *Head, circa* 1967.

Right: *Torso, circa* 1967. "… in exchange for Sophia's old Volvo."

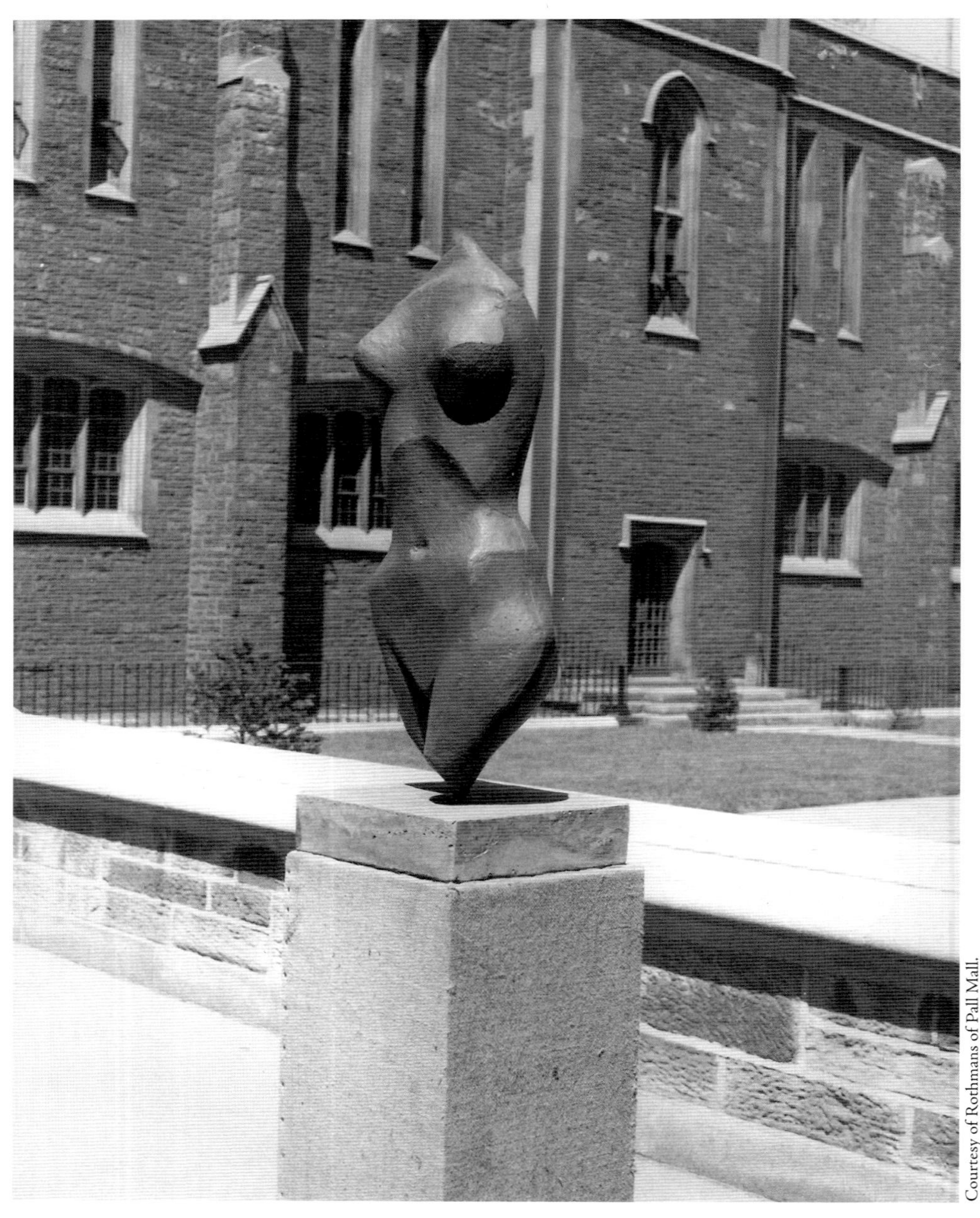

Torso, 1965. "Rothmans simply fell in love with it, and purchased it on the spot."

Leygue has given me only eight critiques in three months! But he is Monsieur Leygue, the illustrious Professor; he does as he wishes. Go complain to the management."

At the beginning of February it was the same old aggravating story: "Professor Leygue gave me hell. My figure is 'not good enough, too lax, too soft, not simple enough, not strong enough.'" She sighed. "Well, it's a critique; at least he talked to me. Or, rather, shouted at me."

The previous week she had been talking to an Israeli sculptor, who had suggested she get a studio of her own. "You're a good sculptor," he said, "and you should work alone." She was excited by the idea, but was reluctant to leave the Beaux-Arts and its professional instruction.

A few days later she went to see the Israeli in his atelier. "For the last time, let me tell you. Spent half an hour being pursued around the studio with amorous intent."

From his studio she returned to the Beaux-Arts through icy winter weather. "Minus twelve degrees Celsius with a cruel wind." Her thoughts were as cold as the weather, and not only because of the Israeli and his "artistic" plans for her. There was also Professor Leygue's apparent indifference regarding her work. "I think what he did was put on a pose, what he thought he should be from day to day, which would account for his pontifical criticisms, though God knows I don't get many!"

Leygue must have heard her plaintive voice in the wilderness. On her arrival at the Beaux-Arts he gave her a full thirty minutes of good criticism. "Wonderful!" she sighed.

Georges Saupique, the carving instructor, was, in Frances's eyes, "great," and his students "lovely, serious, friendly people," reflecting the enthusiasm and dedication of their instructor. While she struggled under the weight of Professor Leygue's burden of restraining rules and rigid procedures, Frances hoped that Saupique would allow her the freedom to express herself in her own way, and he did. The two men were, if not opposites, at least light years apart in methods and attitudes. She saw Leygue as the nineteenth-century academy professor, dogmatic, unbending, unwilling to entertain for a moment any view but his own, while Saupique, who had travelled widely, knew that art and imagination were global talents, not qualities unique to France, and — big surprise to the Parisians! — Paris was not the centre of the sculptor's world.

The one thing both instructors had in common was a cold studio. "I spent the afternoon wearing everything I had, shaking with cold. This was in Leygue's atelier. It was warmer outside in the street."

In February, Frances faced the fact that she was becoming disenchanted with her studies at the Beaux-Arts. "Yesterday Leygue went at my drawings. He doesn't like my technique, and I don't like his, but I am trying to, really. Yet, damn it, I think some of my pieces are good."

That afternoon she spent two hours walking along the Seine. It was eight degrees below zero, the air sharp and cold. *I'm disappointed,* she thought. *But what did I expect? Am I a teenager, sitting around, waiting for everything to become rosy and bright? Did I think it was all going to be so easy, so romantic — Paris, mon amour! — so exciting? Did I believe the Beaux-Arts would touch me with its magic wand, and I would be transformed overnight into a famous sculptor?* "It's so hard to do anything worthwhile at the Beaux-Arts!" she cried. Then admitted, whether she liked it or not, she had no alternative. Her grant, which was her sole source of income, was officially intended to cover her studies at the Beaux-Arts, not to set her up in a studio of her own (with or without the Israeli), or provide her with funds to do as she wished in any other way. And every day those funds ebbed. *No,* she thought, in resignation. *There's no alternative. I have to stay.*

And staying meant more bad days, more differences of opinion. "Mid-February," she said, "and not a nice start to the day: big argument with some of the students at the Beaux-Arts regarding the head I was working on. They said it was *degolas.* Couldn't find the expression in the dictionary, but what they meant was 'disgusting'. They claimed there were no such planes in the head; heads were not built like that. Hmph. *Their* work is *degolas,* all of it, everything done at the Beaux-Arts, in fact. I'm no hell, but I'm better than most of them. Time to develop some faith in myself." She dismissed them with a shrug, and prepared to cast the head, in spite of the views of *les*-bloody-*anciens*.

Looking around her at the work of many of her fellow students, and recalling, too, much of the so-called "modern" so-called "art" she had seen in the so-called "advanced" museums, she remembered Zorach in faraway New York, and felt his sensible presence. "There is a natural law in art as in life," he had said. "One school of artistic expression rises, another falls. But that which rises is not necessarily good. Continually trying out new ways and directions leads to chaos." She could still hear the exasperation in his voice. "Innovation is not an end in itself." The Dadaists, for example; an irrational art movement begun in the early twentieth century, thought to capitalize on shock, and turned to anarchy and absurdity. Zorach had nothing but contempt for sculpture from discarded junk, what some, like the Dadaists, called "found sculpture." In despair he said, "I cannot accept this. The instability of the world has penetrated into art." Frances was surprised to hear one of the Beaux-Arts students, an American, a dark and angry-looking man, and also from New York, express the same views as Zorach, but somewhat more coarsely.

"Dada?" he said. "That's not art. It's a state of mind, not a style. A pile of utter shit. Not a shred of talent. Don't listen to the bafflegab of the art critics. They are a bunch of unmitigated assholes, Dadaists and critics, both."

"Well," said Frances, weakly seeking an extenuating example, "… er, Max Ernst did some nice—"

"Ernst? Three-dimensional stuff from garbage? Crap people throw away?" He waited for her to find something nice in that.

"Uh …" she said, unequivocally.

He slammed a lump of clay on the table and thrust his cigarette butt into it. "There. 'Étude Number 27, four inches by six, mixed media, 1956'. The Dadaists would love it." He walked away.

February, and the arctic temperatures were made worse by a cold, mean wind. At the Beaux-Arts the frigid studio made life for the models and students alike a cheerless experience. The weather was reflected in Professor Leygue's equally cold attitude. "Didn't even offer us his usual curt 'Bonjour,'" said Frances. "Anyway, my head is finished. But I didn't take any chances after my little contretemps with the other students regarding my so-called 'disgusting' artistic treatment. I took the head home with me. French students had been known to destroy the work of others any time they felt like it." She shook her head, still unable to believe it. "Incredible. They did it several times to a Tunisian boy while I was there, and I think it was simply because he was Tunisian."

By the last week in February the arctic chill that had lain over much of France lifted somewhat, but the cold had been enough to seriously damage crops, and fresh fruit, vegetables, and flowers were in short supply. But Frances shrugged — "I'll find something to eat" — and toddled happily off for her first visit to the Paris Opera, and Mozart's *Die Zauberflöte*. "I was a student so I ended up standing (for thirty cents) through the whole performance, but it was wonderful!"

But attending the opera by herself only accented her French experience, her aloneness. "It's bad living by oneself," she said more than once, "with just one's own comforts and interests to think about. It still seems impossible that I'm in France. Oh, it's wonderful and all that, but I'll be glad to go home. I'm sick of being taken at every turn, sick of French hatred of foreigners, sick of the provincial narrow-mindedness that won't admit there's anything worthwhile outside of France."

Still, she liked Saupique's tendency to be closely involved with his students beyond daily sculptural requirements. He became interested in the progress Frances was making in her thesis on Roman cathedrals in France, and followed her efforts with more than just idle curiosity. The thesis was yet another expression of Frances's lifelong inquisitiveness that led her to delve into everything that caught her interest. She seemed driven by a compulsion to know, to learn more, and become knowledgeable and competent in every field that came to hand. She became a jack-of-all-trades — and pretty good at many. The thesis may also have been (if the truth were known, and let's be frank) a little something to stroke the grant-giving bureaucrats in Ottawa, something to illustrate she wasn't just taking the money and sitting on her hands.

Grants aside, it was intense interest that impelled her to probe into everything. At the beginning of March, Bob Gartshore and a couple of friends, all three of whom she had met in the fall on the boat to France, were planning a visit to Normandy. She jumped at the chance to join them.

They visited Mont St-Michel, the island off the Normandy coast, and toured its once politically powerful abbey. In a little Norman town they bought bread, cheese, and wine, and dined in a field over-looking the narrow arm of the sea that separates the tiny island of Mont St-Michel from the mainland. A few hundred metres away, the abbey towered over its small medieval town, already ancient before the Norman conquest of England.

Frances was captivated. "Mont St-Michel at sunset. So beautiful. Such an old, old rock. A weathered lump of granite rising out of the sea, almost deserted except for workers preparing for the tourists."

On the road to Paris they stopped at an ancient inn for lunch. Frances, whose kitchen skills stopped at can-opening, was delighted. Roast duck, flaming crêpes, cherry liqueur! Delicious!" Then they prepared for the cold realities of the artists' life: Biscuits in the car for supper.

Back at the Beaux-Arts, Frances received an ostensibly pleasant surprise. Professor Leygue recognized her existence on two consecu-tive days. "He praised my drawings. 'Too facile,' he said. 'Too academic.' Hmph. If this is praise, I'm glad he wasn't negative." The following day he simply glanced at her work, muttered, "You haven't understood the model at all," and passed on.

But the weather was turning warmer, and Professor Leygue's bleak critiques waned, replaced by the simple pleasure of a stroll along the banks of the Seine, and some bread and cheese in the sun with friends. Toward the end of March she sat by the river lunching with Joan. "I still liked her in spite of her American ways, and her refusal to even try to understand the French."

Frances, knowing that it might be years, if ever, before she passed this way again, wanted to learn as much as she could, wanted to see things, do things, go places, discover something — indeed anything — that was new.

With Paddy O'Hanlon she waltzed along to the Crillon Bar for cocktails — a couple of wealthy Canadian socialites, you would think, whose names don't quite spring to mind. Then Le Coq d'Or for Russian food and vodka. The following evening she went to the Olympia Music Hall to see Josephine Baker, though at that time both the Olympia and La Baker were in decline. Josephine was then fifty, but still able to mesmerize her audience. The Olympia had, two years before, been reclaimed from where it had languished as a mere movie theatre, to rise for one brief period to its former glory. But this, too, would not last. Some years later there would be plans to turn it into that universal symbol of "progress": A parking lot. Frances was witnessing the end of a glittering era.

The next day, with Joan the American student, she revisited the Louvre. "A lot of Gothic and Roman stuff. We had a bit of trouble with the guards, because Joan kept handling things." Joan left, but Frances stayed on drawing until late in the evening. When she arrived home she was suffering indigestion, and worried that her ulcer was back again.

In the morning the sore stomach was joined by a sore ankle and a sore hand. Hands were always a problem, an affliction she attributed to sculpture. "Not much I can do about that. Can't sculpt with my elbow." After an enjoyable afternoon of carving with Saupique, she once more fell victim to depression. And everything conspired to augment it: Paris, the weather, the Beaux-Arts.

On the sixth of April, she woke to snow. *Poor 'April in Paris' tourists*, she thought. She had been in agony the night before: the ulcer had returned to torment her. "Will have to go to the hospital," she decided, but like many of Frances's decisions, it was put off for the moment, elbowed aside by the thousand other things that clamoured for attention. And so the days passed, some uncomfortable, some not.

School offered little to alleviate her depression. "School this morning. No model. I left in disgust. What an institution." By the end of the second week in April, her depression was turning into self-pity. "Seems to me my life is much too dull for a life in Paris. Don't know what I can do about it. I'm all alone." And again, school didn't help. "Drawing today. Under strain caused by all the loafing *anciens*. They just hang around." In the dimness of the unlighted studio, she looked out at the grey skies, the wind that shook the trees, the ice that held the windows fast and sealed the cold within. "Weather so mean and cold this week. Atelier like an ice box." The next day was no better. Professor Leygue's studio was miserable. "So cold we all got headaches. The building simply wasn't heated. Came home with the shivers. I'm so tired of being tired, of being cold. Tired of everything."

April 19, 1956, and still depressed. "School. I'm there alone — are you ready for it? — at *ten degrees below zero Celsius*. Left at four-thirty, frozen stiff."

The weather continued relentlessly inclement. "Rainy and cold. What a country! If the sun ever comes out, I vow I'll drop everything and just sit in it like an old dog."

But Paris is Paris, and the city moved hesitantly into spring as patches of sun appeared in the streets. The temperature rose a few degrees. Frances bought a French bathing suit. She treated herself to an Italian haircut. She was smiling again.

"Professor Saupique gave me an excellent criticism," she said the next day. Her depression began to lift. She sat in the sun in the Tuileries, lunched with friends, and began to live again, in spite of the pain in her stomach. She even managed to laugh when Madame Gérard discovered Frances had a small radio, and was using electricity, *mon Dieu!* Madame promptly raised the rent by four hundred francs.

May 29, 1956, offered the French a glimpse of Canadian creativity with the opening of the "Canadian Artists in Paris" show. Frances was scheduled to exhibit some of her work, and as usual with any public display of her sculpture, she was galvanized, hyperactive, and nervous to the point of prostration. "So busy I'm going crazy with so much to do before the twenty-ninth!"

She was submitting a head and a selection of drawings, all of which Professor Saupique had liked. On the twenty-sixth, she worked all morning, then took the head home and worked until two in the morning. On the twenty-seventh it was the same story.

For Frances the show generated mixed feelings. To see her work prominently displayed was both embarrassing — "Almost like being naked in public" — and thrilling. The thrill, the pleasure, and more than just a little satisfaction, won out in the end.

And the show provided a surprising bonus. Professor Saupique had been enthusiastic about the Canadians in Paris show; he was now determined to see Frances's head in an upcoming "Judgement," a rigorous form of exhibition and examination. Frances, still somewhat down after the excitement of the Paris show — "I'm exhausted. I feel seventy years old!" — took a less-than-positive view. "What I think of the judges for the 'Judgement' I will not say," she muttered darkly, then promptly said it: "I think the judges are incompetent."

On the twenty-third of June, the day after the Judgement, she found herself in a rather uncomfortable position: "My head won second prize!" After her blunt comment on the judges' abilities, she didn't know whether to be pleased or insulted. "I mean … (weakly fighting self-esteem) I didn't think much of the other things that were exhibited." Saupique, however, was not only delighted to see the vindication of his faith in Frances's work, but amused by her struggle with vanity.

With the school winding down for the summer, Frances spent more time in social activities: entertainment, seeing friends, visiting places in and around Paris. "I did a lot of walking in Paris," Frances said. "For a brief period I even had a bicycle. Once, when I was on my bike, I got caught in l'Étoile, the roundabout at the Arc de Triomphe. A gendarme saw me wobbling by for the third time. He stopped the traffic and got me out." She laughed. "It's terrifying! You can't get out if you're in the wrong lane!"

She spent a day in the town of Beauvais, another in Amiens; she sang in the British Embassy church choir; she went strolling in the Tuileries garden — "Smells like one huge tom cat. It's full of cats, and I usually walk through it several times a day, to and from the Beaux-Arts." She attended theatres and symphonies — "Cheap enough, at the students' rate: just pennies, comparatively speaking." She had supper with a girlfriend, a fellow student from the days at the Art Students League in New York, "then a nice post-supper walk around Saint-Germain-des-Prés to the Louvre. Ladies of the evening every six metres. Then we were chased by some Frenchmen. Seems to be a standard pastime in Paris, young ladies getting chased by the natives. Just the day before, for goodness sake, two men chased me in and out of a metro station."

The next day she lunched near the Seine with two friends from the summer camp in Ontario's Algonquin Park, where she had been (and would be many times again) a counsellor for the children. It was early July, and after lunch and a brief tour of the Beaux-Arts, they walked along rue Bonaparte to the Quai Voltaire, and watched the boats on the river. Frances experienced the pleasure of playing the tour guide, gesturing casually toward the twin towers of Notre Dame on the right, and drawing attention to the Louvre just across the Seine. The river slipped slowly by, placid, casting light green tints that turned to darker greenish-blue in the shadows thrown by the bridges. Her friends were leaving that afternoon, and the "au revoirs" were heartfelt. "We'll see you when you get back to Canada!"

Later in the week she went to a matinee, and once again saw a performance by Édith Piaf — "How delightful! To enjoy La Piaf, live, in Paris!" And delightful it must have been. La Piaf, "The Little Sparrow," was then forty years old and at the height of her powers and popularity.

Frances was still suffering from her stomach ulcer. In mid-July she finally visited the hospital. "I had a bit of a fever, too. I had already made plans for a trip to Italy, and if I had to, by gosh, I was going to travel with an ulcer and a fever. One must press on, regardless."

On the twenty-ninth of August, Frances made the sad booking for her December 6 return to Canada on the boat. "I wanted to have a good cry. I realized I finally felt at home in Paris."

She was looking forward to the resumption of classes in mid-September, and while this was uppermost in her mind, thoughts of the trip to Italy kept rising and troubling her: Could she afford it? She had paid the greater part of the expense in advance — trains, hotels — but there were always a thousand little things, unanticipated items, that would erode the budget.

With the return to classes came a brief sketching interlude at the fabled Atelier Julian, the famous studio begun almost 150 years ago (1868) by Rodolphe Julian. Rodolphe was an artistic revolutionary. In those early days, the École des Beaux-Arts held firmly to the belief that it was immoral to confront the female student with a naked model (or perhaps it may have been just the arrogant condescension of the male chauvinists of the day). For whatever reason, in those days the Beaux-Arts did not accept women as students. Julian, on the other hand, did, and became famous overnight, offering instruction to female artists like Käthe Kollwitz, Marie Bashkirtseff, Elizabeth Gardner, Cécile Baudry, and a host of others. Canada's A.Y. Jackson was a student; J.W. Morrice, the Montreal artist, was there in 1890.

September 17, 1956, was Frances's first day at the Académie Julian. It was located near Boulevard Saint-Germain, a scant half-kilometre south of the École des Beaux-Arts.

"The front looked onto a dark and filthy street, rue Dragon. The rooms inside were dark, too, with low ceilings. I went up two flights of narrow creaking stairs, and found an old lady all dressed in black. She had a halo of fuzzy white hair held down by a circular grey comb, and around her shoulders she wore a black sweater with the elbows magnificently darned. Her stockings were also beautifully darned. The instructor breezed in around three. He looked like a rat, with huge pouches under tiny eyes. What a motley collection!" But she told herself that, my goodness, the Julian was a Paris legend, and they have a reputation for "originality" to maintain, so she persevered and absorbed the atmosphere.

By the twenty-fourth of September she was back attending classes at the Beaux-Arts, but her thoughts were only for Italy.

Her brief trip to Italy wasn't the happiest of holidays.

"Bad start. Arrived in Rome at two in the morning. At the hotel, I had to wake someone to let me in." The next day the hotel gave Frances a letter from her sister Marion: her mother had suffered a stroke. Frances was deeply disturbed, and the news served to increase her loneliness. Still, she played the tourist, and in standard fashion got lost somewhere between the Forum and the Coliseum. Depressed, and frightened for her mother, she sat in a nearby park among hundreds of cats. *Here she was*, she thought sadly, *the tourist and her animals, sunning themselves on the grass.*

The next day she travelled through Umbria and the dry Appian hills to Assisi, and thence to Perugia where she met Lee Bontecou, her friend from their days at the Art Students League in New York. Lee was at that time living in Rome, and would spend the next year there on a Fulbright scholarship. Artistically, both women were then unknown. Lee would later go on to create three-dimensional constructions of an avant-garde nature, as far removed from Frances's future work as it was possible to get, and both would achieve wide recognition. For the moment, though, they were two young artists enjoying a pleasant lunch in a charming Italian city.

After lunch they sat talking. "At least you had the sense to order the scaloppine," said Frances. "The restaurant wouldn't have had your favourite sandwich, anyway. Crushed dates and cheese on rye." Frances shuddered. "How can you eat that? Are you trying to be original or something?"

"Hey, cheese and dates are good," said Lee.

Frances laughed. "I bet you hate it. But people expect you, as an artist, to be kind of strange, so at least you're getting your vitamins, as well as being a bit odd. I'm surprised you're not allergic to it; you're allergic to everything else."

"Don't remind me," said Lee. "I'm allergic to my own hair!"

A late afternoon sun came through the windows of the trattoria, spreading over a corner of the room, leaving their own table in warm shade. Both girls were dark blond, hair short in the Italian manner of those days — *arruffato*: casual, ostensibly unstyled, looking as if they had just risen from their beds.

With a smile, Lee sat back comfortably in her chair. "You were saying, earlier, something about school. Problems?"

"Mmm," said Frances; an affirmative, but without enthusiasm. "Every time we meet," she said, "I seem to be complaining about something."

"Always something about sculpture, though, so your head's still in the right place."

"Yes," said Frances, "but always negative."

"Not happy at the Beaux-Arts?"

Frances slumped in her chair, and sighed. "I don't know." For a moment she was silent, pointlessly rearranging the napkin on the table. "I've been there for a year, and Leygue still treats me as if I were a two-year-old. A mentally deficient two-year-old." She tossed the napkin aside. "I'm just so … so damned disenchanted with the whole thing; Paris shouldn't be like that. I don't seem to be getting anywhere at all."

Lee leaned back in her chair. "Disenchanted? Think you're alone? How about the Impressionists — Renoir, Monet, that lot? They attended the Beaux-Arts, too. So did Degas and Manet. And they were so disenchanted they started a new art movement! Okay, they were painters, but we're not talking about painting, we're talking about disenchantment." She tapped the table decisively with her slim fingers. "You know what you have to do? You've said it before yourself, so it shouldn't come as a surprise. Remember what Zorach used to say? He said it to me, and I'm sure he must have said it to you: 'Listen, and learn, then do what's right for *you.*' Remember that." She stood up briskly. "But more important right now, remember you've got a train to catch! Have a great time in Venice!"

Frances carried on alone to Florence and La Pensione Nicoletti where she stayed for a few days, then moved on into northern Italy. She had received another letter that said her mother's condition had improved, so Frances was in much better spirits when she arrived in Venice.

And, yet again, confusion and despair. "Came to Venice in the dark. After some misdirection, I located the Continental Hotel, only to find it closed. But the desk clerk agreed to see me to the Hotel Splendide, away off in the wilderness." The clerk found a porter who took Frances's money and pushed her onto a vaporetto, one of the Venetian motor boats. Having pocketed her money and settled her on the motor boat, he waved goodbye and disappeared. "Nice, eh?" said Frances. "Bye-bye, have a nice trip, send a postcard when you arrive." She realized, with mounting concern, that she was on the Grand Canal, a broad, dark, mysterious waterway, with no idea where she was going. "I got off at the Rialto Bridge, wandered through murky streets and over bridges, asking directions on the way. I finally found the Splendide, which was anything but."

She had one day in Venice, a day of grey skies and wet streets, conditions that robbed the island city of its unique charm. Through the curtain of rain the ancient *palazzi* nevertheless still bore the signs of former magnificence, the trappings of a sumptuous and politically powerful past. But on this, the sculptor's only day there, the Queen of the Adriatic Sea hid her face from Frances, and left the lonely artist without the inspiration she might have gained; left her to stand gazing forlornly at the wavelets that lapped the very entrances of the mighty mansions. Cold and wet, Frances shared her breakfast with two cats at a sidewalk café.

"I took the train from Venice to Bologna, and then on to Florence. My companion on the train was an Irish Catholic priest, very nice. He chain-smoked cigarettes throughout the trip. The train was what they called the *rapido*. Kind of confusing; it's the slowest one, lots of stops, which must have pleased my priest. He bought a large gin at each stop. He had a flask in his pocket, as well. For the dry periods between stops."

A bleak day in Florence. "Got lost on the way to the hotel. Rained all day. Everything I own is wet."

On October 28, 1956, she left for Paris.

Within twenty-four hours of her return, she was once more, though only briefly, immersed in the satisfying routines of school, studies, and the good-bad-indifferent critiques. "Carved all day," she said in early November. "It was good to get back to work. Bird almost done." This "bird" was the seagull from the fragment of marble which was given her when she visited the stone quarry with Professor Georges Saupique. She would finish it in Toronto, and it would eventually end up in the hands of Senator Nancy Ruth.

On December 1, she said her goodbyes to Louis Leygue, and to Madame Gérard and the children. She could not bring herself to face wonderful Professor Saupique (she eventually sent him a letter).

"Funny to leave a place into which I've put so much of myself — the church, and the choir in particular — with hardly a handshake to say goodbye. No one really cares. Only me, and my ego's disturbed. Time to shake off childishness and face reality."

And so the Paris adventure came to an end. It seemed so natural, on that last night, that Paris would say goodbye, or rather *au revoir*, in the city's own special way, in the final twilight, "…with a soft fog masking everything. Paris is magic tonight!"

The uneventful boat trip across the Atlantic was anticlimactic, like the slow winding down of a clock, impressing upon her, even more than the last night in Paris, the feeling that it was the end of things. Paris seemed, already, so distant in time and space. The exciting time was over, gone, as if it were just the memory of a brief period in another person's life.

Finally there was the arrival in Toronto, and a big lunch with all her friends at The Girls' studio.

"I'm dazed," she said, almost in tears, then joined in the laughter of her friends. "Oh, it's so good to be here again," she exclaimed, and her tears were those of happiness.

The woman locked the shack and walked across the uneven ground to the narrow passageway that led to the street. The Studio Building was dark as if uninhabited; along the south wall were the shadows of trash cans. A little light filtered down from Yonge Street to the west.

She smiled to herself. It's like having a nine-to-five job, she thought. Work in the shack during the day; go home in the evening to Charlotte's apartment.

She pulled her collar closer. Cold winter wind. Be nice to get home. The shack is like an ice box.

Now, she thought with a smile, Paris is a memory, and I'm here in Toronto living with a friend at plain old Broadview and Langley Streets out east. Paris a memory? Like it was a million years ago? I'm barely back home a month. She sighed. It was so good to come back and step into the wonderful world of friends, sculptors, artists, people I'd known for years, people who had been so understanding, so supportive when I had first started out.

When I started out … She turned down Rosedale Valley Road toward Bloor Street and the streetcar that would take her home.

Started out. She felt the panic again, and thought, I'm starting out once more, but this time it's not the romantic Parisian studios and the professors teaching me new things. No, Frances my dear, it's the real world now, where no one gives a damn about your Ontario-big-deal-College of Art, or your two-year-Yankee-holiday in New York, or your oh-so-frou-frou days and nights in Paris where they don't even speak English, for Heaven's sake.

Okay, maybe not as bad as that, but not much better either. Clients are clients the world over, and they all look at artists as if they'd just found half a worm in an apple. They're businessmen, and they're going to want the best art for the least money, so that means I have to be a businesswoman as well as an artist. I guess I'll have to go back to school again. She laughed not too happily, and swung onto the Bloor streetcar.

| 6 |

THE HAPPY HEART: LIVING WITH TOM THOMSON

WITHIN A MONTH OF HER arrival back in Canada, Frances was looking for a studio. Her years at the Ontario College of Art (OCA), and the friends she had cultivated in the city, had made Toronto her artistic home, and she planned to live and work there. She had been relieved of the problem of living accommodations by Charlotte Sullivan, a professor of ichthyology at the University of Toronto, the same Charlotte who had visited Frances in New York on New Year's Eve in 1954. She was a tall, slim woman. Frances's sculptor's eye noticed particularly her long neck and lovely hands. Charlotte habitually wore her hair in braids, coiled at the back of her head. Frances met her through mutual friends, and Charlotte had offered a room in her apartment, a third floor walk-up in a building on the south corner of Broadview and Langley Avenues, overlooking Riverdale Park.

At that time there was a small zoo in the park. "They must have had some coyotes," said Frances. "At night I could hear them howling at the moon. At least I imagine they were in the zoo, though I guess they could just as easily have been in the Don Valley. There was a lot of virgin bush in that area. At first I thought it was a bunch of drunks carousing." In the distance to the west could be seen what little skyline Toronto possessed in those days.

"I met Charlotte through my friends the Coopers," said Frances. "George and June Cooper were a wonderful couple, and George was a marvellous man, helpful, considerate, and six-foot-five. I met him through June. She was a model, part Cherokee Indian, very exotic. She looked like a blue-eyed Chinese. They thought Charlotte and I would get along well, and we did. Before I left for Paris, when Charlotte asked me to come and live with her when I got back, I knew what a wonderful advantage that would be, not having to worry about where I would live when I got off the boat. It left me free to concentrate, right away, on finding a studio."

Frances stayed with Charlotte Sullivan from January to December of 1957. At first it seemed ideal. Charlotte was generous and, in her own way, considerate. She also exhibited an enthusiasm for what Frances was doing: the drawings and rough sketches for some minor sculpture on which she was working. At first Frances found this both flattering and encouraging.

But Charlotte had lived alone long enough to establish her own ways, and with time what had started as convenient habit had become inflexible routine. Shopping had to be done on Saturday; garbage was wrapped thus and so, and must not be wrapped in any other way. Everything had to be done as she was used to doing it. Frances, through the nature of her hand-to-mouth existence of those days, was not accustomed to such a rigid schedule, and found it irritating and unnecessary. Even the generosity that had at first been so heartwarming became overwhelming. "It got so I wasn't allowed to have a mind of my own. It was as if I were her tame artist that she could pet and look after, so long as the pet did as it was told. I felt she would soon start to tell me how to sculpt, point out what I was doing wrong, and show me how to correct it. She was a wonderful person, and I know she was hurt when eventually I couldn't take it anymore and moved out. But I had to be myself."

The sudden change in Frances's situation weighed heavily on her. "I found it very hard to face the reality of very little income. I had never been in that position before, at least not to such a degree. To realize toward the end of the month that I didn't have the money for next month's necessities was frightening. It wasn't that I was just a bit short of money that month; the terrifying thing was that, for all practical purposes, I didn't have any money at all! None. Nothing. And no idea where or when or from whom I could get some."

The problem of money, of some form of income, continued to oppress Frances. Through OCA graduate friends, she met Barbara Wells at the opportune moment. Barbara was planning to start an art class, which ultimately became the Artist's Workshop. Frances got a job there as an instructor. "Barbara really took a big chance with that project. She bought a coach house at Sherbourne and Bloor streets, and lined up a number of OCA grads as instructors. I remember there were Don Fraser and Gerry Scott. With them, I became one of the first instructors. All of us were OCA graduates. Barbara wasn't. Don't know where she got her training. She was a nice person, tall, slim, freckle-faced. She did some good painting and drawing. The Artist's Workshop was lovely for me, money-wise. A lot of preparation, but worth it."

Another friend, the medallist Dora de Pedery, arranged for Frances to take over her job as instructor at Northern Vocational (Norvoc), just north of Eglinton Avenue off Yonge Street. Frances had been assisting Dora, so she was the logical one to take over when Dora left. The Norvoc job paid $4.50 an hour, which paid the rent and put food on the table. "First things first," said Frances grimly. "It wasn't a particularly exciting job, but it was a job, and that put it at the very top of my list of priorities."

Fortunately, Frances was unconsciously good at meeting people and making them friends. Without being aware of it, she was a world-class networker before the word *networking* became current. Her address book would eventually become encyclopedic.

At first, finding a studio was daunting. Actually, finding one was the easy part. She looked at a number of them that would have suited her needs. The hard part was going to be finding the money with which to pay the rent they were asking.

On January 4, 1957, she saw a coach house. "Could be fixed up, and it would be perfect, but it's a hundred dollars a month; unthinkable at this stage." The next day: "Studio on Collier Street, in the Yonge and Church Street area. Nice light, two rooms, but on the third floor, and no heat or water. Must think about it." January 10: "Another studio, but way out east and not so good."

Without a car, she walked or took the streetcar to view the various studio possibilities. "Bitterly cold. No stoves in the rear of the streetcars then," she noted, bleakly, remembering the coal stoves in the trams back in the forties, when she was going to the Ontario College of Art.

In mid-January, Frances was routinely going to The Girls' old church studio for the occasional supper, and to do her laundry. Charlotte didn't have laundry facilities in her apartment, and while Frances might just as easily have toddled along to the laundromat with Charlotte, she found The Girls' cluttered studio more congenial. In return, Frances would continue as she had done years before: she'd wash The Girls' floors, do their dishes, serve drinks at their parties, and perform other minor chores.

Frances was outspoken on the subject of The Girls: "In those first six to eight weeks when I got back, before I got some teaching jobs, The Girls kept me alive. About 50 percent of the food I ate came from them. They'd also give me a few dollars for the chores I did. Where they found the money, I don't know. I wasn't the only one they helped. How did they pay their bills? Property taxes? Their own food and necessities? I just don't know. Yet Loring always seemed to have enough for a bottle of Canadian Club rye. That was another of my chores: On my way out to see them — I sometimes helped with a sculpture they were working on — Loring would tell me to pick up a bottle of whisky for her. Six dollars; the great big bottles. She liked her rye." Frances would shake her head in wonder. "And yet they'd always be there for me, with a dollar, with a meal."

The search for a studio went on.

"Teaching tonight at Northern Vocational. Same old group. News of two studios, one of them a coach house," she added without much enthusiasm.

And then, one day, Opportunity knocked softly.

"I got a call from Keith McIver. I had met him at The Girls' studio. He was a friend of theirs; he was there all the time. The Girls had a very friendly relationship with the artists of the Group of Seven — Jackson, Varley, Harris, and the rest; Keith, too, knew them all. He was their guide to the north country, up in Algonquin Park, and especially around Georgian Bay where they painted. For a long time, Keith lived in Tom Thomson's old shack that stood behind the Studio Building on Severn Street. Keith had given it up years before, and the shack was just sitting there, unoccupied." At the time of Frances's return from Paris, Keith and his wife were living in the Albion Hills north of Toronto.

"The Girls told him I was back and was looking for a studio. Though he hadn't occupied the shack for a number of years, he hadn't told anybody that he'd given it up. He had a very sentimental feeling for the shack, and was afraid the wrong kind of person might take it over. So, when he heard I was back, he called me and asked 'Would you like to have it?' Would I like to have it?!" She laughed. "I jumped at it!"

Lawren Harris (scion of one half of the Massey-Harris farm machinery people, and a noted artist himself), together with his friend, art patron Dr. James MacCallum, built the Studio Building in 1913, and its first occupant, other than Harris himself, was his Montreal friend and artist A.Y. Jackson. MacCallum philanthropically offered both Tom Thomson and A.Y. Jackson financial support for a year if they agreed to devote themselves entirely to painting. The artists accepted and shared an atelier in the Studio Building.

When Jackson left at the end of 1914 to become a war artist, Thomson was obliged for economic reasons to seek other accommodations. Harris offered him the shack at the rear of the building. The artists in the Studio Building got together and decorated the walls of the shack with their paintings. It was here, in the former tool shed, that Thomson produced some of his best paintings, including *Northern River* and *The West Wind*, which many consider his most outstanding works.

Frances knew A.Y. Jackson quite well through his frequent visits to The Girls. It was there, too, that she met Frederick Varley who was then in his mid-seventies.

"Varley had a magnetic personality. He was very close to The Girls; Florence Wyle loved him. I remember The Girls had a show at the Jack Pollock Gallery and Varley attended it. When he entered … oh, he just filled the gallery. He had a wonderful presence. He was also a womanizer, and a fairly heavy drinker. Yet, I found him very shy. When he was drinking he wasn't shy, but he was really very reclusive. I met him a few times before I did his portrait (Varley Gallery, Unionville, Ontario)."

In the autumn of 1948, the Studio Building had changed hands. Gordon MacNamara, a Toronto lawyer, allegedly purchased it for $20,000. Its assessed value in 2006 was $1.37 million. By then it had been designated a Heritage Building. In A.Y. Jackson's view the "glamour departed" when MacNamara took over. "Gordon MacNamara didn't like this and he didn't like that," said Frances, "and he forced Jackson to leave because he made too much noise crating his paintings for shipment. MacNamara took up residence in the Studio Building when he bought it."

Jackson couldn't accept the continual harping about noise. "And when I was informed that I must wear felt shoes in my studio," he said, "I gave my notice. I had (lived and worked) there for forty years."

"The shack was sort of a social club for the Group of Seven," said Frances. "Some of them had their studios in Harris's Studio Building, which was only fifty feet away. Keith McIver was there in the shack;

he knew them all, and could serve them a cup of tea, or something stronger. While Keith was living in the shack he made breakfast for A.Y. Jackson almost every morning."

The shack that Jackson and McIver knew wasn't the studio that Frances Gage inherited. Decades of neglect had changed all that.

In the years following Thomson's tragic death in 1917, the shack remained unoccupied, and with time grew dilapidated as rot weakened the floors, and the leaks in the roof let the weather in to do further damage. The back wall, built against a rise in the ground, had given way, and mud had flowed in.

This was the state of the shack when Keith McIver rented it and did what he could to make it habitable again. McIver wasn't too troubled by the prospect; he'd seen worse shacks up north. He built a new roof and put in a better floor and a concrete wall at the back. It made a good winter home for him and his dog.

McIver was a prospector who had come to Canada from Malaya, where he had been a rubber planter. In Quebec, he had worked for Frank Loring on a mining site. Loring's daughter, the noted Toronto sculptor Frances Loring, was the link that brought McIver into the artistic circles that included the future Group of Seven and Harris's Studio Building.

It was through Frances Loring that McIver came to know her friend Frances Gage, and learn of the younger woman's need for a studio.

On January 19, 1957, Frances phoned Gordon MacNamara, the owner of the Studio Building, and made an appointment to see him, and the shack.

"Saw MacNamara at eleven in the morning on January 21," said Frances. "He left me alone in the shack to think about it. I knew it would be a precarious situation. But I also knew, beyond any doubt, that I would love it!"

But it was a tool shed. It had been built, or more precisely "thrown together," more than forty years before. It had been, and still was, a utilitarian jerry-built construction of a few boards and a handful of nails in which to store a bunch of tools. It had never in those four long decades been intended for anything else.

But for one brief golden day it had been more, much more.

And it was that long-ago moment which instantly seized Frances's attention and enchanted her: Forty years before, for two short years — 1915 to 1917 — the shack had been the studio of the painter Tom Thomson.

By the time Frances moved into the shack, it had seen its finest days. McIver had lived in it for years, but by the early fifties he had built his own home in the Albion Hills northwest of Toronto, and the shack had, to be as charitable as possible, deteriorated. It was infested by rats, there was no plumbing, a single electric bulb hung from the ceiling, and the building was totally uninsulated. The floor was six inches higher in the centre than it was at the sides, which, according to Frances, made housekeeping much easier. But people tended to fall through the floor. Shortly after Frances moved in she laid down new plywood flooring and painted it orange to match the previous "décor."

Toward the end of January, Frances took physical possession of the shack. "Up to the shack this morning to measure for stove pipes and drapes for the windows. Ordered ladder, and pipes, and …"

She didn't seem to ask herself why MacNamara would rent such a hovel, would even let anyone occupy the place, let alone charge them real Canadian dollars to do so. It wasn't as if he needed the money. He was charging her ten dollars a month, which even in 1957 wouldn't have constituted an investment opportunity.

Ten dollars a month. "It was a lot of money," she said. "At least for me it was a lot." But Frances didn't really care; her mind wasn't on money. Her thoughts were only for the shack, Tom Thomson's studio. She imagined him standing where she stood, sitting where she sat; she saw him at his easel, laying the paint on as if with a shovel. (A.Y. Jackson recalled that he had "never known any painter so prodigal of paint, even when that thick, rich paint meant a thin meal.") In her mind, Frances saw Thomson mixing his palette at that very table there against the wall. Though, admittedly, this was outright fantasy; it would not have been that particular table. The solid bench, at which she visualized Thomson painting, had been made by McIver years later, during his occupation of the shack. When Frances eventually left, McIver gave it to her. "Do you want it? Take it." McIver doubtlessly felt that when Frances left, the shack would be destroyed. "Go ahead," he said, "take anything you want." She considered the table a wonderful memento — she'd worked on it for almost three years — and it followed her ever after.

For all this? Ten dollars a month was nothing.

As tool sheds go, the shack was large; the size of two or three rooms in an average home, but its condition was appalling. Only an artist would have been drawn to it, and Frances was an artist. The attraction was inevitable and powerful: there was the ghost of Thomson; there were the paintings on the walls, the magnetic memories of the Group of Seven and the world of artistic expression those memories implied. For Frances, the shack simply radiated art and artists, the whole creative process; it had a palpable aura, the very air invited you to create.

It had all this for Frances, but it didn't have much more. There was no plumbing. To obey the call of nature, she would find herself cast back in time almost to the outhouses of a previous century, and would have to stagger through sub-zero weather to the Studio Building to use the facilities there. There was a single source of electricity: a naked forty-watt light bulb hanging from the ceiling.

Frances's friend George Cooper came by to help her set up the stove pipes. "Was it cold! Lit the fire at noon, and after much nursing it gave off a feeble heat," she said, adding as she snatched at any positive straw, "The new stove pipe is beautiful!"

"A feeble heat" simply underlined how pitifully futile it was. Her heat for that first winter came from the small potbellied wood-burning stove. It fought the winter weather, and lost, taking as long as four hours to bring the shack to a "living" temperature, meaning that she only had to wear two coats and a muffler. Her feet and hands were always cold. She suffered chilblains until spring. "George helped me wash the floor, and while we were washing it the water froze, right there on the floor."

As January came to an end she was able to express her happiness. "What a full heart!" she cried. "My fire took only three hours to get going. About four o'clock I was able to remove two layers of clothing." Will Ogilvie, formerly one of her instructors at OCA, had his atelier in the Studio Building, and he dropped in for coffee and to check progress. "My first guest!" she cried with delight. "My place is all cleaned up now and I am ready to go. Spent the twilight sitting by the stove, reading about the life of Tom Thomson. I am so happy!"

On the last day of January she was sitting in the shack wondering what to do next. "I was all set for work, but … what was I going to do?" Her indecision was relieved by another visit from Will Ogilvie.

"There I was, thirty-two years old, and unmarried," said Frances. "A completely unacceptable state of affairs, so far as The Girls were concerned (neither of whom was married). They tried to play the matchmakers, attempting to set me up with Will Ogilvie. Well, he was a very attractive man. He was older than me. At that time, 1957, Will was fifty-six. He was a very lovely man — a gentleman, and a brilliant draftsman and painter. He often came down from his studio, and I made coffee or tea for us. I think he found it a nice break from his work. He had begun a little garden in the overgrown area between the Studio Building and the shack. Nothing fancy, just a few shrubs, but he liked to potter around in it."

But Will Ogilvie was not the only artist in the Studio Building. Perhaps other male occupants might have appreciated a cup of coffee with an attractive young woman, an artist like themselves … so near, so desirable … less than fifty feet away … in the shack … alone …

"Not much chance of romance with them," Frances observed, drily. "There were only about four artists in the Studio Building at that time, and most of them were gay. And for half the year the temperature in the shack would have quickly cooled any uncontrollable passions."

One day she had just poured tea for Will Ogilvie and herself, when a strange young man named Robert McMichael burst through the door unannounced. "He didn't know anyone was there, just wanted to see the shack." (Five years before, Robert and Signe McMichael had established their art gallery in Kleinburg, Ontario, and would eventually acquire the shack itself.)

The silent cold of winter was not Frances's only enemy of creativity. The sounds around her did their best to interrupt and disturb, noise generated primarily by rats and the new Toronto subway.

"The shack was full of rats. I could hear them, and at night I could see them playing in the garden. They were pretty awful. They were Norway rats crossed with domestic rats, so there were some that were multi-coloured, white and brown, with long scaly tails. They were big, too. About eight or nine inches long. Not nice."

Around this time the first of numerous cats came into Frances's life. Igor banished the rats and affectionately warmed her winter evenings. He remained with her for seventeen years, so much a part of her life that his passing was a major tragedy.

Barbara Howard, her old friend from OCA days, had phoned her. "Do you want a cat?"

Frances replied: "No."

So Barbara's future husband, Richard Outram, delivered the cat to the shack. "Barbara was not the person to accept no for an answer. Her questions were rarely questions; more 'inflected statements'. Most people would understand that 'You're going to do as I say, aren't you?' really isn't a question."

After she got Igor, the rats left. Frances felt it was the feline smell that triggered an instinctive retreat from the presence of a cat. "The cat didn't catch any, fortunately. I think it would have been very dangerous if he had tangled with them because they're pretty fierce creatures."

The rats, plus the other unhealthy aspects of the shack, made it, so far as the City was concerned, impossible for Frances to live in the place. The City's health department refused to consider it, so she continued living with Charlotte.

Though the rats left, the subway that had been completed just two years before was still there. If, in the course of her work, she forgot it existed — just on the other side of the berm behind the shack — she was reminded relentlessly. Every three or four minutes a train went by. "When I heard it coming, I had to stop what I was doing because the shack shook so much. It was impossible to do any lettering or anything precise."

There was little other traffic; the Studio Building was alone at the western end of Severn Street. To the east was Rosedale Valley Road, which was not then the busy thoroughfare it later became. Frances had a painting by Thoreau MacDonald, the son of Group of Seven member J.E.H. MacDonald. It showed Rosedale Valley Road as seen from the area in front of the Studio Building, looking south. At the time of the painting (1920) the road was little more than a dirt track. While Frances was there the road was more than a track, but not much more. To the north, Aylmer Street was paved, but by the time it reached Rosedale Valley Road it had reverted to a mere dirt path again.

Within the shack itself, however, a touch of beauty alleviated the cold and primitive conditions. In Tom Thomson's time, the artists who worked in the Studio Building got together and "decorated" Thomson's shack. Photos of Frances's period in the shack show the usual clutter of an artist's studio, and around the walls the "decorations" can be seen: paintings to brighten her days as they must have brightened Thomson's. Contemporary reports list some of the paintings: a Haworth and a Jackson occupied the back wall; there was a bird by Thoreau MacDonald, a lighthouse by George Pepper, a painting of northern Ontario by Yvonne Housser, and Lawren Harris's depiction of an island at dawn.

And then there was Florence Wyle's *Pink Nude*. Keith McIver's wife, Edith, had it painted over, not so much as an expression of Victorian rectitude, but rather out of jealousy. Frances felt that Mrs. McIver resented the time and attention Keith devoted to The Girls.

"Just before I left the shack," said Frances, "I cut all the paintings off the walls and put them under my bed at home because I thought the shack might be broken into, and, in fact, it was. But then, as soon as McMichael moved what was left of the shack to Kleinburg, I gave them back."

One of the startling structural aspects of the shack was the window Tom Thomson installed in the north wall. It was so striking that Frances made a linocut of it. "The illustration was accurate," Frances said, "but people claimed 'Oh, that's just perspective.' It wasn't; it was higher at one end than it was at the other." Thomson had scavenged several small windows from the city dump and assembled them as one window in his shack. Nothing matched. "It was three feet high at one end and about four feet high at the other. One of the windows would open, so I got a good cross-current of air in the summer. I don't know what happened to that window. It was unique, and so outrageous it was almost beautiful."

Many artists, especially those at the beginning of their careers, operate on the principle that the more people you know, the greater your chances are of making contact with (a) someone who wants your work, or (b) someone who knows someone who wants your work, or (c) all subsequent levels of "someone who knows someone who knows … " In short, get to know everyone, ab-so-lute-ly everyone, and make sure they all know who you are, how you are, where you are, who you know, and most important of all, what you do and how incredibly good you are at doing it. An enjoyable way of doing this is to socialize, and having the shack, Frances realized she possessed a unique venue in which to be sociable.

She gave suppers. This is hilarious when you remember that Frances relied on recipe books in order to boil water. But she was smart enough, and adaptable, and being an artist, creative. She also recognized the can as mankind's greatest invention.

"My suppers were always very simple," she said, and added, pedantically, "The key to a good meal is simplicity. Thank Heaven, because

I was pretty good at simple suppers. I had to cook on a hotplate, so it was usually something easy, like spaghetti with lots of spices, peppers, and a little bit of meat, or something. Just one big dish, because I couldn't cook anything too complex. I only had the two-burner hotplate. I had to cook one thing and put it aside, then make something else and put that aside. I'm not a very good cook but I usually managed to fill people up. And I had good bread, too. Bread and cheese."

The shack's role in Frances's lunches and suppers was always an iffy thing. It was unique, of course, a good conversation piece, but tended to project the "starving artist" image rather than the "successful artist" image which Frances preferred.

Still, the shack saw many meals between old friends, and was a pleasant way of keeping in touch. In mid-April she entertained three friends for lunch, Edith Williams the vet, Marjorie Jordan from Frances's navy days, and the opera singer Portia White. "Served them my gourmet specialty: Canned stew."

Portia White enjoyed somewhat less fame than she deserved, according to Frances. "I heard her on the radio when I was about sixteen, and I never heard anything so glorious." Frances met her shortly before acquiring the shack, and in the course of conversation asked "Can you teach me how to read music?" Portia responded, "I'd rather teach you how to sing." Frances wasn't going to miss a chance like that, and shortly thereafter began taking lessons from Portia. Receiving such an offer was very flattering to Frances, who recalled with nostalgia the time she had been an up-and-coming torch singer during her two years in the navy.

Portia White died of lung cancer in 1968. "Near the end," said Frances, "she telephoned me. She was gasping, and to hear just the ghost of that once-wonderful contralto almost made me cry out in pain."

The thin voice came over the line. "I'm not very well."

"Can I get you anything?" Frances asked, her own voice breaking.

"No," said Portia, "no, my brother … Bill is looking after me pretty well …"

Portia White died in poverty, her last days spent in a Toronto rooming house near Sherbourne and Bloor streets. "I don't think her agents did as much for Portia as they might have," Frances felt. "In the late forties she did a lot of tours all over North America, but she wasn't paid very much and had to cover her own expenses. Imagine today's rock stars accepting that kind of treatment. Portia was black, quite tall. Came from a large family, a dozen kids I think; her father was a Baptist minister."

Lunches and suppers in the shack maintained friendships, and also served to introduce her to new friends who in turn would invite her to supper, where she would meet others, and so the cycle went. A reasonable estimate would be that for every shack meal she served, she dined out three or four times. This is the kind of ratio that pleases the starving artist. When asked how she subsisted with so little money coming in, she would laugh and reply, "I had a lot of friends."

Lunches and suppers outside the shack continually produced, directly and indirectly, the all-important contacts. "Had dinner with Vincent. Vincent Tovell, the movie producer and director. He was related to the Masseys; in fact his middle name was Massey. He did a lot of work for the National Film Board. He eventually got the Order of Canada. Very talented man. A sculptor, too; some of the works he did were beautiful."

Around this time Frances got a chip of stone in her eye, often the price paid by sculptors who thoughtlessly overlook protective goggles. She was obliged to wear an eye patch. The evening she returned from the hospital, black eye patch in place — "Quite dramatic!" — she was scheduled to accompany Vincent Tovell to a supper and party at the Art Gallery. "He was rather mortified that I had a black patch over my eye. I think he imagined the people around us would see the patch as a cosmetic touch to hide a black eye, and would be thinking 'He must have done it'. Vincent was very fussy, everything had to be just so, and a woman simply wasn't 'just so' if she was wearing the eye patch of a pirate."

So far as the shack lunches and suppers went, her culinary efforts must have been, at the very worst, acceptable, because the shack was often crowded with people from every profession. Frequent visitors were Dr. Edith Williams (Frances's veterinary friend who looked after The Girls' cats), The Girls themselves, Dr. Frieda Fraser (the patron of Frances's New York studies), Walter Gordon (future finance minister in Pearson's government), A.Y. Jackson and most of the members of the former Group of Seven when they were in town, and a host of artists, sculptors, and painters of every variety.

The contacts Frances made through these informal suppers in the shack, and her close friendship with The Girls, produced a broad catalogue of work, including sculptures of many of the prominent people of the time: Jackson, Varley, Sir Ernest MacMillan, Samuel Bronfman, Senator Nancy Ruth, Elmer Iseler, Sam McLaughlin, and works for major corporations and various universities and colleges, hospitals, municipal buildings, parks, and memorials. The hundreds of works she produced encompassed an eclectic collection of everything from a three-inch owl to a seven-foot woman, some completed in two days, others in twelve months.

For Frances it was a life of joy, a three-dimensional expression of bliss.

But by the second week in February, Frances was experiencing severe pain in one hand. This was not something a sculptor ignores. On the eleventh she saw her doctor, and the next day the hand was in a cast. "Really affects my work. One needs two hands."

The cast on her hand came off on the nineteenth. She was now arriving at the shack as early as possible to get the stove functioning properly. "Fire hot enough at three in the afternoon for me to take off my duffel coat. Got some work done, but it's slow."

In this time of despair over the condition of her hand, Frances was pleased to read an article in the *Globe and Mail* about her days in the shack, and how she was "keeping the spirit alive." Newspaper coverage was always good public relations, and in addition to the press that pleased, Frances's sculpture, too, brought satisfaction and increased her income. "Off to the Bectels for dinner. Lovely couple. They were introduced to me by Charlotte, and they bought a couple of very nice wood carvings, two walnut reliefs twenty-four inches high."

And they were not alone:

"To the Dixons for supper. He's my eye doctor. I brought along the reliefs I did of his boys."

"To the Granite Club for dinner with Mary Hamilton and Josie Jagusak. Mary was the founder of the summer camp, Tannamakoon, where I taught. She wanted me to meet Josie, a young pianist, fifteen years old and a prodigy, one she had introduced to the camp. She brought a young musician every year. It started them off, and gave wonderful exposure to the children at the camp."

Small jobs, small contacts, but important as they meant she could look forward to her next meal, and be fairly sure it would be there. One of the smaller works in progress was the seagull begun in Paris. The bird's form was rising out of the fragment of Carrara marble she and Professor Saupique had been given at the stone yard in Paris. She had been excited by the challenge of creating the bird within the restrictions of the fragment's shape. When complete, it was scheduled to go in the upcoming Royal Academy (RCA) show.

Toward the end of February things were going well. "I was at the shack from nine in the morning till eight at night," she said, "then off to Will Ogilvie's drawing class. Got lots done. I'm happy."

She was still working well the next day. "Long dark wet afternoon. I've a leak in my roof. Must get some tar paper." In the realm of Mr. Fix-it — or rather Miss Fix-it — very little confronted Frances as an insoluble problem. She was prepared to tackle any difficulty, altering, repairing, building, changing, setting up, tearing down. No matter the problem, she could, and would, fix it.

On one of the last days in February, as she was struggling with an armload of wood while cursing the stove, she wondered if these were really the happiest years of her life. "I guess they are," she thought at the time, "in spite of aches and pains and blue skin from the cold. I could still see my breath at five o'clock this afternoon when I left. Doreen had come for lunch — in her overcoat. Still, I got some work done between fire-watching."

On February 29, Frances arrived at the shack. It was early morning and the shack was crisp and cold. She glared at the stove. The stove shuffled its feet and didn't meet her eye. "Right," she said. "I have finally got the solution to my stove problems." She kicked a chair. "What I need … is a new stove."

At some point observers must ask themselves the unavoidable question: Why?

Why did Frances embrace — and she did, with a passion — these appalling conditions in the shack? The catalogue of unrelieved negatives is endless: the bone-crushing winter cold that paralyzed her limbs, the unbelievably shabby surroundings, the unchanging bleakness, the rats, the cramped conditions, the lack of plumbing and electricity, the total inconvenience of the place! Almost nothing worked, and the odd thing that did, worked poorly.

Why did she — voluntarily, eagerly, ecstatically — choose the shack?

"First," she said, "ten dollars a month. I wouldn't have found another studio for that price anywhere in Toronto. And remember, I was young. When you're young, you don't think about 'enduring' anything; everything is an adventure. But, more than anything else, it was the aura of the shack. It was where Tom Thomson had lived and worked. It was …" She paused, far away, searching for the image. "It was being able to stand in the shack and know that I was perhaps two inches away from where, forty years ago, he lifted his brush and began painting *The West Wind*." She sighed. "It was a magic place."

Mid-March, and all the disadvantages of the shack are, for a moment, swept away. "Today there are birds, and sun! How perfectly wonderful. Wouldn't it be awful to live in a place where there was no spring. Today there are two snow drops near my door, and a glorious cardinal 'way up high."

The next day, it was still March, but "really March, stormy and dreary." She looked around for some small plus factor. "But there were crows, above, in the trees!"

"That spring I was falling in love with Ken.

"I met him that year through Barbara and Richard, at some function or other at the CBC. I was attracted to him right from the first. He was self-confident, very sure of himself. In some people this is irritating, and generates an immediate dislike. I think this is because those people have a pretty good opinion of themselves, and are not too keen about those who are also self-assured. I wonder if this means they're actually insecure? I don't know; I'll leave that to the psychoanalysts."

Frances continued to have friends over to the shack for supper. An ordinary meal, restricted as she was by the two-burner hotplate, and ordinary friends. "Frieda and Bud, sometimes The Girls, often Barbara Howard and Richard Outram, and Ken Guild. Ken pronounced his name to rhyme with *child*. I don't know why.

"I think one of the things that attracted me to Ken was his similarity to my father. Ken was fair, short, and stocky. He was about three years younger than me. He was so nice; he liked me, too. I remember once that spring we drove to Stratford to have supper and see a play. He had one of the first Volkswagen Beetles in Toronto. I teased him about it all the time. 'How can you tell if you're coming or going?' On the way back from Stratford, we drove slowly along Highway 401, snuggling closely — not hard to do in a Volkswagen Beetle — and watched the northern lights. There were no trees at that point on the highway," said Frances, "so the aurora was clearly visible."

Ken's appearance was marred somewhat by a vivid scar across his forehead, a surgical memento of a serious car accident three years before. This did not bother Frances, who was falling in love, and blind to all that might detract from the subject of her affection.

With spring, though not as a result of it, Frances's growing dissatis-faction with the Norvoc night classes — too many students, and she the sole instructor — finally came to the breaking point. "I just got so browned off. They had so many rules. You had to go up the up staircase and down the down staircase." Back in the shack she made her decision. "Work is slow, my hand is not right, I could weep. Any-way, it's Norvoc for the last time tonight — because I quit." (But not forever. She would eventually go back. Money is money, and always was in her early years.)

Quitting Norvoc was a satisfying decision. But like a lot of deci-sions that are satisfying at the moment, it would cost her money. Dra-matic independence is all very good; it gives you a nice feeling. But now she had to find another source of income.

The tentative spring was lost beneath a mantle of snow that fell on the eleventh of April. But Frances was busy, and still in love with her shack. "Dear wee shack," she cooed, almost stroking the icy walls. "Good fire. Two inches of snow this morning."

Frieda Fraser came for her initial sitting. This was Frances's first sculpture of her former patron.

While working on the Frieda portrait there were still the final touches to her seagull yet to be done. She also worked on numer-ous smaller pieces, more for herself than anything else; subjects that appealed to her: a frog, an owl, a cat. She attempted to place these in shows, galleries, and exhibitions, without much success.

"I was working in the shack most days. Still had trouble, physically, but I had to carve. Masochist, I guess, what with my freezing joints and the difficulties with my hands."

One of her projects was a sculptural portrait, slightly larger than life-size, of Douglas Duncan, who operated the Picture Loan Society. Her friend Barbara Howard had been working there, and when she left, she had recommended Frances for the job. Douglas Duncan's

Picture Loan Society offered paintings on a loan-to-purchase basis. You rented the work, and if you liked it, you bought it. "It wasn't necessarily good art," said Frances. "In fact, much of it was bad. Douglas bought and kept the best stuff for himself. Over time he acquired a wonderful collection."

When Frances first went to see Duncan, she found him to be very aristocratic. "He looked so refined. Rather distant. He was a tall man, slim, his face thin and bony. His hair was quite long and wavy. The day I went to see him he was seated in a high-backed very regal chair. He was smoking a cigarette. The ashtray beside him was sparkling crystal. It all suited him so perfectly.

Some might have said Douglas Duncan was crazy. Others, like Frances, would have called him crazy but wonderful. He had begun the Picture Loan Society in Toronto in 1936, and introduced many fine artists to the public. One of these was Will Ogilvie, Frances's friend. According to Duncan, Ogilvie was the best watercolourist in Canada. But though Duncan was instrumental in advancing the careers of a number of artists, his grasp of finance, and his "original" and exasperating treatment of his accounts — he often had to be reminded of what he owed — left him open to criticism.

Frances was still dependent on odd jobs. She was the de facto charwoman for The Girls, for example, and to augment what little money was coming in, she was also working part-time at the Picture Loan Society, situated off Charles Street in the Bloor/Yonge area.

Frances's job, primarily, was answering the phone.

"Good morning, Picture Loan. Yes sir, Mr. Duncan produces a show twice a month. There's one next week. David Milne? Yes, two of Mr. Milne's works will be shown. Fine. Mr. Duncan will look forward to seeing you."

Douglas Duncan glanced into the reception area. "Frances, I wonder if you'd frame a few of these works? Are you familiar with the framing process?"

"I have a pretty good idea of how —"

"Splendid. I'll leave it in your hands. The paintings are …" — He gestured uncertainly. — "… on the table." He hesitated, thinking. "The invitations for next week. Have you …?"

"I wrote them two weeks ago. They're in the mail."

"Ah. Good … good …" He paused for a moment, as if pondering a distant thought, murmured good once more, then wandered back to his office.

Frances spent a lot of her time fending off the people who were trying to get him to cash cheques. "Very refreshing, actually; somebody who was that rich, who didn't care about cashing cheques! Still, in most ways, he was a terrible businessman. Very vague. His detachment just drove people crazy."

On the sixth of May a representative of Morani and Morris, the architects, phoned Frances seeking advice on a piece of sculpture for a building in downtown Toronto. "I didn't get a job out of it, but I was very pleased that I was consulted." In this instance, the loss of a possible commission was secondary. To be consulted was a major step up the ladder. And the following month she did get a commission from them, a memorial water fountain for Toronto's Princess Margaret Hospital. "They brought me samples of the bricks in the existing wall so I could match the colour. Syl Apps, the hockey player, brought me the clay for that, and the bricks, too. I think he was a volunteer at the Princess Margaret. The sculpture was a frog. It squirted water into a pool."

She had a pleasant lunch with Mr. Morris on the fifth of June. There they discussed the possibility of yet another interesting commission, a large commission. After lunch they parted with mutual assurances of how nice it would be to work together, the exciting aspects of the job, and all those meaningless platitudes that spring so readily to lips that have enjoyed a satisfying lunch in comfortable surroundings. Mr. Morris picked up the tab. For Frances it was, in all ways, an excellent lunch.

Five months later the commission was awarded … to Elizabeth Wyn Wood. She knew Wyn Wood from OCA days, when Elizabeth was an instructor at Toronto's Central Technical School, and Frances was a student at the Ontario College of Art.

"They gave her the commission," Frances said through teeth clenched in angry frustration, "because I didn't have a big enough studio. It broke my heart, because I could have rented a studio." Still, even in anguished moments, Frances would give credit where it was due. "What she finally produced was nice; she was a brilliant sculptor. The Girls always said she was much better than her husband, Emanuel." Rich praise, for Emanuel Hahn was recognized as one of the most illustrious sculptors in the country.

On a sunny morning in June, Frances and Ken drove to Burlington, the city at the western end of Lake Ontario, to spend the day with Frieda Fraser and Edith Williams.

Years before, Frieda's mother had bought an old farmhouse in the area and renovated it. "It was a wonderful old home," Frances remembered, "just beautiful. The house was on part of the Niagara Escarpment, and the Bruce Trail goes along there, too. From the living room you had a view that was breathtaking. The view was south across the lake, and beautiful because the house was quite high up. The property was large, perhaps fifty acres. Ken was absolutely thrilled. He was interested in old houses, architecture, and that sort of thing. It must have been a totally wonderful day for him. Frieda was a great gardener, so the grounds were glorious. And Edith was an outstanding cook, which also delighted Ken because he had a good appetite, loved eating. Both Frieda and Edith liked Ken, probably because he buttered them up. He was quite talented when it came to flattering people." Frances, too, was exposed to the same regard when Ken would open a door for her or hold her chair when she sat; the little complimentary gestures that she found so gratifying.

While Frieda and Edith liked Ken, and could see that Frances was strongly attracted to him, they nevertheless advised Frances: "If you're thinking seriously about someone, take him on a canoe trip. A few days of rain and wet feet, and you'll find out what somebody's really like."

Frances and Ken returned home by midnight, tired, but happy after a perfect day.

Frances, however, was prey to much serious thought, and lay awake far into the night. She knew the depth of her feelings for Ken, recognized the simple truth that she loved him, but was troubled by doubt: Could she, should she, marry him? The months they had passed together … he felt the same way, she knew. Their relationship was so much more than just friends or acquaintances, more than pals, so much more than casual laughter, the superficial smile. Would he ask her?

And how would she respond? With a woman's heart, or a sculptor's head?

Frances's sister Barbara phoned on the eighth of June. Mother was ill. She had apparently been suffering little strokes over the years, and no one had paid any attention. Frances remembered her mother saying "I suppose that's my fault," an attitude that was perhaps the product of her husband's "witty" and denigrating remarks over the decades. Frances also recalled, angrily, her Aunt Agnes's remark: "Your mother is just plain lazy." That thoughtless and unsupported remark aggravated Frances beyond measure.

The next day, more negative news. "Now," said Frances, "my other hand is going." On June 10 she noted, with not a shred of enthusiasm, "Only two more physio treatments to go — for the first hand. Now the other hand is giving me trouble. I am weary and depressed. What a year this is becoming."

On the eleventh of June, Frances spent much of the day at

The Girls' studio helping Loring and Wyle cast some plaques they were producing.

She returned to the shack later that afternoon. Ken came by around four o'clock for tea, an interlude to which they both looked forward with pleasure. "He was looking awfully nice," said Frances. After a morning of working on The Girls' sculpture, she found it profoundly relaxing to sit in the shack among her own works, listen to Ken's agreeable baritone voice, laugh at his remarks, and enjoy the simple warmth of his presence.

"It was almost home-like, except for the fact that we were surrounded by the comparative disorder of the studio," said Frances. "But it was comfortably informal, just the same. With his corduroy jacket draped over the back of a chair, and dressed in jeans and a T-shirt, he was quite at home. In my home. Kind of my home, anyway."

The following evening they were once more together. "How about the Fifth Avenue again?" asked Ken. "They'll be naming the restaurant after us if we go there any more often! But the food's nice, isn't it?"

Frances never disagreed. The Fifth Avenue restaurant was on the southeast corner of Bloor and Yonge streets. Ken and Frances dined out a lot, and the Fifth Avenue was their favourite. "It wasn't cheap," said Frances, "but not really upscale. You could get anything you wanted, from hamburgers to a full-course meal. I went there by myself frequently, for over a decade. But by the late sixties I had moved farther north, and mostly ate at a place called the Rosedale Diner, off Yonge Street, near the Summerhill subway station.

"Ken and I didn't go to first-class restaurants. I don't think this was so much a conscious choice as simple indifference. We weren't restaurant oriented. When we were hungry, we ate. I often put together a meal for us in the shack. We didn't stand on ceremony. I had my two-burner hotplate, and a can opener." Frances laughed. "I'd serve one of my gourmet specials. Canned stew, or something complicated like that. In spring and summer it was pleasant enough. In the colder months, well, people just kept their coats on. And often mufflers and gloves, too!"

We know, from Frances herself, how she felt about Ken. Hers was a profound, and growing, love. By the summer of 1957, if Ken had asked her to marry him, she would have said yes. Without a moment's hesitation, without a thought for the future. An immediate and unequivocal "Yes!" But what of Ken's feelings? Why, during those happy months, did he not ask her?

"He seemed to like my sense of humour," said Frances, "and my attempts at common sense, and what he called my lack of ceremony and self-concern, which surprised me. I always felt I spent too much time thinking of me and my own difficulties. Especially in that summer, because my hands were really giving me a lot of trouble. It had become almost impossible for me to do any carving."

Ken, too, had trouble with her hands.

"He seemed indifferent to my hand problem. He would shy away from any talk of medical worries. One day during that bad summer, I was at the hospital for yet another hand examination — lots of exams, but no positive results; very depressing. Barbara and Richard were there with me, and so was Ken. I was feeling pretty low, and standing there with Ken, I took his hand. And he took his hand away. Just holding his hand was painful enough, but how much more painful it was when he took his away."

Earlier that day, in the shack, Ken had watched, frowning, while Frances fumbled painfully as she worked at a small sculpture. "Why don't you stop if it hurts so much?" He turned away, irritably. "You're too interested in your work," he said.

"That attitude kind of disappointed me," said Frances. "But I tried to take a sensible view. We all have our good days and our bad days. Nobody's perfect. What a boring world it would be if everyone was perfect. Still, it would be nice —" Ken had picked up a small carving and frowned at it "— if some people were more perfect than they are."

In the shack, Ken would sometimes be impatient if Frances was working on a sculpture and wanted him to wait five minutes until she finished before they left for supper. Again he would say: "You are too interested in your work."

The twenty-sixth of June saw the arrival of the periodic medical progress report. "It was most reassuring," said Frances, sarcastically. "The doctor said they can do nothing with this hand problem, so I might as well just carry on. Very encouraging."

The month was not one of her best.

"I seem to be in trouble today. Fingers curling. Maybe tomorrow's physio will help."

Then came the bad news. "Saw Dr. Gordon, the specialist in hand surgery. The news is most disturbing. What I have is called Dupuytren's contracture." She laughed shortly. "It's an affliction of the hands invented by Guillaume Dupuytren, a nineteenth-century French nobleman. The condition causes the fingers to contract into claws. Hope diagnosis is wrong, or something will happen to stop it."

With an early period of unusual frost came an equally cold and depressing schedule of physiotherapy at the Toronto General Hospital, in what turned out to be a futile effort to arrest the condition in Frances's hands.

Over all hung the disquieting cloud, the physical fact that her hands were becoming more painful. In addition, and much more serious so far as Frances was concerned, they were growing less capable. Work ceased. For all practical purposes, even the most basic sculpture became, if not impossible, at least arduous, and ever more painful.

She received further word from her physician. "Dr. Gardiner says fifteen more treatments. Hard to be patient. Throughout all this physio and treatments my hands were giving me pain."

Despite the difficulties with her hand, Frances grimly put the pain and reduced dexterity from her mind, continued her classes, and whenever possible, gave talks, with practical illustrations, to clubs, lunches, and women's groups. At the end of October she conducted a demonstration at the Art Gallery of Ontario. "It seemed to go well," said Frances. "I demonstrated plaster casting, and that was fun. When I was flinging the plaster around, I happened to spatter one of the ladies who was wearing a mink coat. Splat, all over her precious mink. And I said, with a merry laugh, 'Oh, that's all right, when it's dry just put it on the floor and hit it with a hammer, and it will brush right out'. The lady was not amused."

Small carvings continued to bring in a few dollars, all of which were welcome at this stage, given the mounting medical expenses. Frances took some little owls to the Owens Gallery in Toronto. "The owner wasn't terribly excited; she was sure they wouldn't sell. But they did." These small items — owls, little dogs, and other animals — all produced a significant stream of income.

At the beginning of August, Frances departed for Algonquin Park and the summer weeks as an instructor at Camp Tannamakoon.

"It was wonderful teaching the children drawing and sculpture," she said, "though when I first went there I thought: *What a bunch of spoiled brats.* They were children from wealthy families, all going to private schools. But then I discovered that the poor kids wished they could spend all their time at boarding school in the winter, and camp in the summer, which is an interesting commentary on their home lives, isn't it. I taught there for ten years and loved every minute of it."

She returned at the beginning of September. "Back from the lovely north. It's so depressing to be back in the city." Frances leaned very heavily toward Nature. Birds, animals (not too excited about fish), trees, flowers, forests, farming, growing things. She delighted in the summer camp, the children, the teaching aspects, and the natural surroundings. And every return to Toronto brought the long slide into depression. She was "back from the lovely north," back to the cold, no-nonsense realities of the city. "I cleaned up the shack. After only a few weeks in Algonquin Park, the place was mouldy and damp. I put a big fire on."

This year the depression had an even darker cast. She received word from the doctor that he would operate on her right hand on the coming Friday. "At this point," she said, "the right hand was so useless I was writing left-handed."

Just before the operation, the movie producer Brian Jupe dropped by to pick up a torso he wanted to use in a film on which he was working. "It was a little ceramic one. They planned to have it revolving slowly on a turntable, dramatic lighting, music in the background. It was one I did in New York of the wonderful Chinese model Chao-li-chi. He was a beautiful dancer, but posing is awfully hard for dancers because they have to sit still!"

By the twentieth of September, the operation on her hand was over and successful, and she found she could move her fingers slightly. "Still forty-one stitches there, but the doc is pleased."

October saw her once more struggling with the stove. She could see a repeat of the previous winter's freezing days, and their adverse effect on hand, health, and sculpture. But love laughs at icy shacks.

"Well," said Frances, "maybe not 'laughs'. That damned stove. The doctor had removed the stitches from my hand on the third of October, but the hand was still very sore, and a freezing shack didn't help."

But a few days later, Ken came by for lunch, and the hand's discomfort receded in the pleasure shared around the littered workbench that served as their dining room table.

"Lunch," said Frances. "Well, again it was probably my gourmet special: Canned stew. On bread. Something romantic like that. I was a lousy cook. But we were young, and we were hungry."

Nevertheless, the still-fractious stove was a problem that would not go away by itself.

"Right," said Frances, decisively, "enough is enough," and arranged to install a forced-air propane space heater.

On the first of October she was able to report: "Space heater is ready to be set up. I'll get the propane tanks put in outside the shack."

Mid-October: "Shack cosy and warm."

She now looked at her hand. "All stitches are out. The doc missed three; I took them out myself when I got home. I used a nail file — very delicately, let me tell you! — but I got them out. Hand is pretty darn sore." It would be almost a year before she regained full use of it.

However, with renewed abilities there came a pleasing increase in business. The Princess Margaret Hospital's frog was installed and its reception was gratifying. Also during this time, Frances produced a crest for Ontario Hydro. Cast in concrete, it was mounted about forty feet up at the main hydro station in Cornwall.

This hydro crest was not without its problems. When it was completed they discovered Frances had omitted the *a* in the ligature *æ* of the crest's Latin inscription: DONA NATURÆ PRO POPULO SUNT (The gifts of Nature are for the People). "I showed them the blueprint I had been given," said Frances. "No *a*, so I was relieved of all blame."

But her friend and fellow artist Cleeve Horne was annoyed. In the October chill of the shack he paced up and down, stamping his feet in irritation as much as to lessen the cold.

"Why did you do it, Frances?" he cried, raising his arms to Heaven. "Why? Forgetting, *forgetting*, the *a*! I recommended you for that job, Frances! Don't you know the Latin ... the, the form, the grammatical form, the singular/plural indicative or whatever? Didn't they teach you anything in college?"

"For Heaven's sake, Cleeve, it was an art college."

He turned away from her and strode to the window, hands clasped behind him, rocking fitfully back and forth, heel and toe. "You know what this makes me look like, don't you? A damned fool! I recommended you, Frances!"

"Cleeve, don't shout at me! You've seen the blueprints. There's the phone, call the architect, the designer, the draftsman. Shout at them!

They overlooked the *a*, not me!" Then she added with icy sweetness, "And let's not forget who will have to pack up her tools and go all the way out to the Hydro station in Cornwall — 250 miles, Cleeve, two, five, zero — and repair the oversight? You're going to look even worse when I send them a bill for the extra work. You know what I'm going to do? I'm going to charge them ten bucks a mile, that's what I'm going to do. Ten bucks." He stomped out the door. She shouted after him, "And ten bucks a mile coming back, too!"

Frances found his inconsiderate self-centred attitude beyond bearing. "Still," she thought later, recognizing what she felt might have been extenuating circumstances, "his wife had the money, he didn't, and it may have rankled. Ego, and all that. Couldn't stand being wrong; everything had to be his way." Despite her own feelings, however, she had to add: "And yet he was a superb artist. He did a portrait of Jeanne Sauvé — she was at that time the governor general. It was in the National Gallery in Ottawa. I can imagine his feelings after the installation of the painting, when he stood looking up the broad expanse of the grand stairway, and there at the top, dominating the entire wall, was his portrait of Madame Sauvé for all the world to see. It must have been his moment of glory."

Ken's concern over his relationship with Frances must have been growing over these weeks, through October to the beginning of November. Growing, and becoming ever darker and more troubling.

For Frances it was love, plain and simple, and her days were bright with it. For Ken, too, it must have been love, but a love stained by the knowledge that he would always hold second place in Frances's life, whether or not she consciously intended it.

On November 7, Ken came to the shack. The studio was as cold as his intentions. He knew what he must say, and knew he would hate the answer, whatever it might be. How to begin? "You are too involved with your work." Or should he be blunt and unequivocal? "I will never play second fiddle to a statue." Or should he risk the selfish image? "I must come first."

What answer could he expect? What answer would be acceptable? To either Frances or himself? What could Frances possibly say to his words? "Yes, you will always hold second place in my heart"? Or "You will always be first, and I will agree to banish art and sculpture forever from that same heart"?

He stood for a moment outside the shack. He was already cold, and half-paralyzed by indecision. *I shouldn't have come*, he thought, *but what would have been gained?* He uttered a ragged sigh, and went in to Frances.

Ken stood near the window, staring bleakly out at nothing. Having taken the blunt route, and stated his case, he must then have felt like the stern unforgiving father rejecting a wayward daughter at the second act curtain of a Victorian melodrama. But Frances, shocked and confused, saw no humour or satire, and struggled to find words of her own.

"You first? I must look after you?" she said. "You know I would. But give up sculpture?" Her voice broke. "How can you ask that? How can you not understand? Ken, you're in the creative world, too — CBC, radio, TV, the actors, the writers, the costume designers. You must know what art means."

Ken turned and smiled for an instant, but only an instant. "Yes, I know actors, and artists. And if you were as shallow as some of them — artists because they like the name and can swan around the arty bars, and talk about art; beats working for a living — if you were like them, there wouldn't be a problem, you could drop sculpture overnight." He sat across from her at the table. "But you're not like them, are you? I'd never see you. Every hour you'd be in your studio, chopping away at ..."

"Chopping?!"

He brushed it aside, impatiently. "You know what I mean, Frankie. We'd be together, but a million miles apart."

"Would we? I can't believe we would." She was silent for a moment. "Ken, I spent four years at OCA, studying to be an artist, a sculptor. I spent two years in New York, studying sculpture. I was in Paris for a year and a half, studying sculpture. I *am* a sculptor. I know how it's done, and I'm good at it. I have the imagination, and yes, damn it, I have the talent."

She reached suddenly across the table and took his hand — to keep him from turning aside, to stop him from moving away from her. "You can't ask me to throw it all away. I wouldn't ask you to do that. How can you ask me?"

Ken did not answer, and they sat, still and mute, the chasm widening between them. After awhile, Ken stood. Frances remained at the table, lost and unaware, as Ken left.

> Unlike what poets often claim,
> a love won't swiftly change its name,
> nor does it on the instant die,
> but lingers, asking sadly: Why?[1]

December's grey unfriendly skies were mirrored in Frances's heart. To say goodbye because he believed he would not be first? In the days following Ken's devastating announcement, she could not understand. Her mind seemed unable to grasp the truth. Could all those happy summer days be so easily erased? Were they just a silly dream from which she had now been abruptly awakened?

But as the days passed, her common sense reasserted itself. "It was hell accepting it, but, you know what? He was right, and it didn't take me long to realize it. You can't marry if you're going to devote your life to

---

1 Anonymous.

your work. Some people do, but they don't do it very well. I would have loved to have children. I had all my nieces and nephews, but I would have loved to have children of my own. But being an artist is demanding, and so is being a mother. I don't think I could have done both. Something would have suffered. So, I made my choice, and that was that."

She smiled wryly. "I guess you could say that both Ken and I made our choices, and in the end, we were both right."

Many have turned to art in retirement as a satisfying hobby. Frances couldn't accept that.

"Sculpture, as a hobby?" Frances cried. "All those years of study … all to end as training for a retirement hobby?" Her fist came down on the table. "Never!"

Ken was no less the realist, and saw this as his future: As sure as the morning sun would rise in the east, he would hold second place in their lives, forever subservient to art.

And he, too, said "Never."

These early winter days at the end of her first year in the shack were undeniably among the most traumatic of Frances's life, and were further marred by her deteriorating relations with Charlotte. Frances felt she was suffocating under Charlotte's overpowering consideration and generosity. The kindest heart becomes difficult to bear when it's everywhere and always. The nature of Frances's work was solitary, not committee-oriented. Charlotte's constant presence, commentary, and often advice, grew impossible to support. "It's just too much," Frances realized. "I'll have to leave soon."

She sought the opinion of Dr. Edith Williams, her veterinary friend, and invited her to visit at the shack. Dr. Williams came with one of her elderly acquaintances, a Mrs. McIntyre. "Mrs. M. was celebrating her eightieth birthday," Frances recalled. "As a present I had bought her an axe. That's what she wanted, for trimming trees. Shortly after that, she fell out of a tree and broke her arm."

On the subject of Charlotte, Dr. Williams agreed with Frances. "Get away from her," she said. "Just get away and have nothing more to do with her."

Frances even explained the situation to Charlotte's family. "They understood," she said. "She had a history of taking people over. I told them I was sorry, and the sister-in-law said 'Did you think we wouldn't understand?' It's a pity; I think this happened with every friend she had, she just became so needy that they drew away. Her problem was that she was brought up with five brothers, and the brothers got everything. They all got a bicycle when they were sixteen, but that was only for the boys."

Frances found it easy to imagine the conversation Charlotte must have had with her father:

"Dad, why can't I have a bicycle, too?"

Father looks at her as if she had just arrived from Mars. "Bicycle?" he says. "What do you want a bicycle for? Girls don't need bicycles. All you'd do is ride around on it. We'll get you a nice dress instead," he says, and continues reading the newspaper.

Frances smiled thinly. "It was a fairly standard attitude toward a girl in Charlotte's younger days, so when she grew older she had to prove she could do anything a man could do, and better, and she was quite aggressive."

Frances said goodbye to Charlotte's apartment at the beginning of December, and moved into rooms with her friend Rose Fujita, a young Japanese woman who lived in a semi-detached house on Glen Road in the Bloor/Sherbourne area. She had been one of Frances's students at the Artist's Workshop, and they had become friends. Rose worked in the music department of the Canadian Broadcasting Corporation (CBC).

The move to Glen Road and Rose Fujita could be seen as a turning point in Frances's fortunes. She was soon awarded a commission by the Ontario Provincial Institute of Trades (Fanshawe College) in London, Ontario. It was her largest work to date and one of the largest she ever produced. Entitled *The Discovery of the Hands*, it was eventually situated in a pool in the Institute's courtyard.

Frances had by that time learned an important lesson from the bitter loss of the Marani and Morris job to Wyn Wood, because "her studio was too small." Never again would she lose a commission because of studio size. In early 1962 she would take an atelier on Pears Avenue at Dupont and Davenport streets.

"From the start," said Frances, "I saw this commission, *Discovery of the Hands,* as the down payment on my own house and studio, wherever and whenever I found them. But I had to complete the job first, and the studio on Pears Ave would be ideal, I knew. It was a coach house, a wonderful atelier called the Now and Then Studio, appropriately named because the owner, Debora Johnston, was a part-time painter. She was the heiress to the Coulson Industries, quite wealthy. I hadn't done the commission yet, and I was still conscious of money," said Frances. "So I arranged to give Deb lessons in sculpture in lieu of rent. Worked out fine."

During this penultimate summer in the shack — Frances would leave in September 1959 — she was busy with more and more money-making projects and activities. Earlier, she had taken a studio at 1 Yorkville Avenue in Toronto's downtown core. In that location she produced the initial work on her first major sculpture, major in both the financial sense and that of prestige, the 1,500-pound *Discovery of the Hands,* which she completed in the studio on Pears Avenue in 1963–64. These multiple studios — the shack, Yorkville, and eventually Pears Avenue — gave her the opportunity to work at a number of projects at the same time, which made for busy days, but productive ones, and not incidentally remunerative.

Busy indeed; she was also conducting workshops, giving demonstrations, and instructing at evening classes. At the same time, she was still working part-time at Douglas Duncan's Picture Loan Society, and looked forward to her summer instructing the children at Tannamakoon.

Busy days, all in all, and mostly happy and productive. Occasionally, or perhaps rarely might be a better term, in the early days, Frances would accept an invitation to participate in a charitable exhibition. "It was generally the same old story," said Frances. "The artist would be asked to donate a piece of sculpture. A purchaser then bought the piece for an attractive price, the charity got the dollars, all of them, and the artist got nothing, other than perhaps a thank you. I very quickly got tired of that sort of thing."

Rose Fujita, Frances's friend, planned to spend the early sixties in Japan. Frances was thus obliged to seek other accommodations. She would have been prepared to move to her Yorkville studio, but was prevented by the Department of Health from living there. "I had the Yorkville studio for about three years," said Frances. "I stayed there sometimes, when I had to, but it was illegal. Like the shack, it had been condemned by the City." Providentially, Dr. Williams and Frieda Fraser offered her accommodations in their home on Burlington Crescent.

When Frances gave up the shack, she was afraid that it would be torn down the moment she left it. Impulsively, she paid a year's rent in advance to prevent that happening. Why? Instead of being torn down when she left, it would have been torn down a year later. And yet, she paid out $120 she could ill afford. What was gained?

"It was such a wonderful place," she said. "I guess I just didn't want to think of it being destroyed. There was so much atmosphere, so much of Thomson and the Group of Seven, you felt you could almost talk to them, reach out and touch them. The shack? It was nothing, it was appalling. And yet ... the very air I breathed was so heavy with memories, of art, of artists, of a still-real creativity ... still there, still alive, in the walls themselves. I knew I would never again know the joy, the pure bliss, of working in a studio like that."

| 7 |

THE BRIGHTENING
FLAME FLICKERS

IT WAS 1960, AND FRANCES'S first major commission was still three years in the future. In the meantime she was comfortably settled in the Williams/Fraser household at 28 Burlington Crescent just west of Toronto's very up-market district of Forest Hill.

While not for a moment turning her back on a seventy-five-dollar project, she was getting more of the $250 variety. Not many more, just more; her accountant was not getting rich handling her financial affairs.

One of her works was on show in the Eaton's department store in Toronto. Ah, one might think, another sale? "I was exhibiting," said Frances. "The Eaton's never bought anything. That's how the rich stay rich."

It was at this time, in early 1960, that The Crucifix Affair occurred.

Some days nothing goes right, and Frances endured an aggravating series of such days after she accepted the project offered her by Canon Fielding, a clergyman who required a copy of an old crucifix, which Frances undertook to produce with the assistance of a jeweller. In the course of production, the jeweller, whose only function was to produce the copy of the halo, lost the original halo. The canon was not pleased. "The jeweller made a replacement, of course, at no charge," said Frances, "but the item was very old, and in the canon's eyes, a very valuable crucifix had been damaged beyond recall." The canon's loving hands caressed the crucifix, then withdrew in revulsion as they touched the new halo, the undeniably foreign replacement.

"I made some pretty heavy apologies, which accomplished nothing toward mollifying the canon. It was just a disaster from start to finish."

The entire first half of the year seemed to be characterized by disaster. Hardly had Canon Fielding left, muttering, than Frances was admitted, hemorrhaging, into Women's College Hospital at the end of March. This was the second time; she was there in February, and would be back in again in July. Same diagnosis: Ovarian cysts.

During the summer of 1960 Frances was looking for a suitable house. Three years would pass before she found one.

July 18, 1960: "Fourteen acres, Albion Hills, northwest of Toronto." Sigh. "Fourteen thousand dollars." She did not have the money. "I just had the desire. I loved the Albion Hills. Caledon. Up there around Bolton. Keith McIver had his place there. So lovely, that area."

One day that summer, Frances's mother and father came to visit. "Fortunately, I was no longer in the shack," said Frances. "I don't think they could have handled that! It was startling enough when I took them to meet The Girls."

For her parents it was another world.

"My father was always very embarrassed by sculpture. By naked people. I remember him looking at a book on Rodin's work. He was leafing through it, and his face grew red, and he said, 'Now this, to me, is just plain stupid'. It was an education for him. And remember, The Girls' studio was full of sculpture. The visit was a shocking experience for him."

At the annual Home and Garden Show that year, Frances had contributed a small free-form piece, "with water pouring over it," which was part of a water garden, another gardener's larger project. "The water garden actually won top prize." she said.

Hmm. "Actually won top prize" suggests she was surprised. "Well," she said, casually buffing her fingernails on her lapel, "I probably wasn't surprised. My contribution was a nice piece. The Heintzmans bought it; just my free-form piece. The Heintzmans were related to the piano company."

The following year, 1961, was not a year that would shine in Frances's memory. It started with minor problems, and subsequent months didn't see much change.

In the early months of the year she had submitted the necessary forms along with a sculpture to the Ontario Sculpture Association for exhibition in their April 15 show. "Should have known better as regards the OSA. I got a call from them and had to go to the Gallery — this was not the Art Gallery of Ontario; it was the Art Gallery of Toronto at that time — to pick up the sculpture I had submitted for the show. It had been smashed. They told me the piece was too fragile. Like, it was my fault, you know? Very bad feelings all 'round."

This was frustrating, and was not helped by conditions at Burlington Crescent. "I'm having trouble with Dr. Edith Williams. Won't leave me alone. She's behaving much like Charlotte." And again in June: "Not one moment's peace in this house, day or night. I'm not allowed to work."

For better or worse, and Frances would have been hard pressed to tell you which it was, October saw her back teaching at Northern Vocational, a dubious move, but money was still money, then as before, and also in the foreseeable future. "On the very first night, there were twenty-two students, and one instructor: Me. And in addition," she said, amazed, "there was actually a waiting list for that class." She shook her head in disbelief. "You know, I wouldn't have put my own name on that list. Even with me as instructor."

A welcome break came in May with a three-day holiday in New York City. She renewed acquaintance with her old friend Lee Bontecou. A non-artist would marvel at the friendship between two artists of such wildly divergent styles. Bontecou's hallucinating constructions radiated a strange, incomprehensible, almost threatening vitality, while Frances's work exhibited a delicate, imaginative, yet instantly recognizable beauty. Masculine aggression on the one hand, and feminine grace and accessibility on the other, and yet the two women were the best of friends.

While in New York she also had lunch with Zorach, and was transported back almost ten years, to the days at the Art Students League. The old problems disappeared and they talked only of the good times. She would have undoubtedly shown him photographs of her work, and though there is no record of his comments, he would have been pleased to see the justification of his prophetic remarks of a decade past: "Frances Gage, a young lady who is going places!"

Back in Toronto she suffered shoulder problems, which banished the pleasures of New York and reminded her of the real world and the difficulties of the sculptor's life: physical distress, caused by the nature of sculpting, and not made any better when the sculptor continues to sculpt in spite of it.

On the last day of April 1962, Frances officially decided to take the Pears Avenue studio. Not too much serious thought was involved; she had the commission from the Ontario Provincial Institute of Trades (Fanshawe College) for *The Discovery of the Hands* sculpture, and she would need the space the Pears Avenue location offered her. And you couldn't beat the price: sculpture lessons for the studio owner, Debora Johnston, in lieu of rent.

At this time the CBC produced a program on portrait sculpture. Frances was the sculptor, the actor Paul Soles was the model. "In the show," said Frances, "I pointed out the difficulties in doing a portrait. More than anything else, it's the large number of views you get of your work. What is right from one viewpoint is out of kilter from another, so you must keep changing it. You must pay as much attention to the back of the head as the front."

Paul Soles, the actor and model, liked the result so much he bought it.

"I was naturally pleased that he liked the head, so I sold it to him for peanuts — four hundred dollars." Frances frowned at the memory.

His cheque bounced. So she went to his house and handed him his rubber cheque.

"Your cheque bounced," she said.

"Yes, I know," said Paul Soles.

"You know?" she cried. Then, coldly determined: "Gimme my head," she said, and took it away.

"A few days later," she said, "he came back for it, and gave me the four hundred dollars — cash."

The memory of the Paul Soles incident remained in her mind, irritating her for months afterward, illustrating a sad naïveté that appeared so often in Frances's dealings with others: her storybook expectation that people will do what they say they will do; will act with fairness and consideration; will not go out of their way to make things difficult. In some ways Paul Soles was one such instance; there were many others. It was a surprising character trait, because Frances was, to a substantial degree, a successful businesswoman, an artist in business for herself. It is hard to believe that naïveté can be a winning quality in the successful entrepreneur. It makes you a nicer person, perhaps, but … what is it they say about nice guys and their position at the finish line? The answer to that happened more than once to Frances in later years.

Still, these months were not a wholly monotonous series of irritations. In October 1963, there was the pleasure Frances gained from the interest in her work shown by the neighbourhood children. She had taken the Pears Avenue studio the year before and produced the initial sketches and small models of what would, be *The Discovery of the Hands*. While working on the final sculpture, she would often put in a fourteen-hour day, dressed in her stained and dusty overalls under which she wore long johns to cut the draft that came in under the large shipping doors.

From start to finish, the sculpture took eight months to complete. But word passed quickly, and soon the neighbourhood children gathered regularly to say good morning to "the statue lady," an ingenuous way of checking out the developing sculpture. The children came to call it simply "the lady." Frances took it as a form of coffee break, and let the children in to see what she was doing, and talked to them about the how/what/why of the work-in-progress.

When the finished statue left in the summer of 1964, the children, as well as Frances, watched with proprietary concern as the 1,500-pound sculpture was loaded onto a truck. As the truck drove away, the young sidewalk superintendents waved and yelled, "Goodbye, lady!"

With delivery of "Hands" and the welcome infusion of cash — this was no seventy-five-dollar job; in the end she netted three thousand dollars — she now began seriously to look for a house of her own, and could do so with a price range in mind she could support.

But first, a welcome break: Christmas 1964 in the lovely Albion Hills. Her old friend Rosemary Kilbourn had her home there, a former schoolhouse she had named "The Dingle."

With a sigh of contentment Frances turned away from business, money, home-hunting, sculpture, and the whole hurly-burly and uncertainty of her life, and just relaxed with Rosemary. She was delighted to see deer tracks in the snow, and the deer themselves near the pond at midnight under a full moon. "Oh, the magic of the place!" she cried. The air, the quality of the light, made a deep and enduring impression on her. Was it the hypnotic charm of Rosemary's home and surroundings that sowed the seeds of desire for a similar place for herself? Rural isolation? A home made-to-measure? With its own studio? Dreams? Perhaps. But still some distance away; you can only do so much with three thousand dollars. But maybe, just over that hill there, to the west?

Maybe. So many maybes.

"I kept looking in the newspaper," said Frances, "and the first time I went up to see number 60 Birch Avenue, I just got off the subway and walked around, checking it out."

To the south were the railway tracks with freight cars on a siding. Noisy neighbours were in the process of being noisy while Frances stood in the street. On the south side, just east of the house, was a row of shacks. On the north side was another row of shacks, and number 60 was at the western end. Across the street was a park, a characterless expanse, merely a flat green playing field, but it lent an openness, a vista of sorts, seen from the windows of Number 60.

"The house was like a New York railway flat," said Frances. "It was about a dozen feet wide and it went way, way back." She looked around, horrified, at the street, the houses — no, huts; hovels in which you wouldn't even consider parking your car. *God,* she thought in dismay, *I can't live here!*

Then, involuntarily, her eye recorded the north-facing rear of the house — there would be good north light — where already her mind was building her studio, her own studio. She frowned. With only three thousand dollars as a down payment it would be heavy to carry the purchase price of 14,500 dollars (Twenty years later, in the madness of the Toronto real estate market, she would sell the house for half a million dollars).

"Dr. Williams and Frieda said you must never buy anything unless you can buy it outright." Frances smiled grimly. "They were rich. They could afford to say that."

She made her decision. It was a commercial area, which she needed; it had good light for a sculptor's studio. "And above all," she said, "I could afford it." She later learned that the present owner had bought the house three months before for nine thousand dollars, giving him a profit of five thousand dollars in ninety days.

So, in early 1965, Frances had a house of her own, an uncomfortable eleven-thousand-dollar mortgage, and already plans for a studio addition which would eventually cost twenty thousand dollars. She shrugged fatalistically. "I felt that if I lost everything, then I ... well, I lost everything, that's all."

But she still had friends.

"I had most of the studio built in exchange for sculpture," she said. "Tadek Wisniewski, the builder, who, with his wife Rosamond, were great friends, arranged with a wonderful young German, Gunther

Ivans, to build the studio. In exchange I did the *Big Bear* for Tadek. An architect friend of Tadek drew up the plans for the building. I paid the builder, but the architect had drawn the plans for nothing, so the *Big Bear* — seven feet tall, cast in concrete — was a kind of payola."

Still, no matter how many friends you have, there is always some supplier who refuses sculpture and insists on cash (the "I already have pink flamingos in my front yard" type of supplier). Frances's father came through with the remaining cash required to complete the project. "He gave me the money — at 7 percent."

Frances recognized this as very real help; there would not have been too many lenders prepared to take a chance on an unknown, penniless artist. But — she sighed — that 7 percent. There was nothing fundamentally wrong with him charging interest; if someone provides a much-needed financial service, a service unavailable elsewhere, well, to be compensated for that service is not out of line. Frances had to admit it was perfectly acceptable business procedure.

"But my father. I mean …" She shook her head. "Funny man — funny strange, not funny ha-ha. He couldn't just lend me the money. Couldn't just say 'Pay it back in two years,' or five years, or whatever. No. That's the way he was. Seven percent."

But she paid him off. This was a good period for Frances, providentially one of the best from a money standpoint. Within the next four years she would produce two of her biggest works, and the money from them would more than cover the costs of the studio.

And Frances, being Frances, was not without her own resources. "I finished the studio myself," she said. "I put on the siding, installed the ceiling, and did all the insulation in the walls. Hey, I was more than just a pretty face. Okay, I had a few friends to help me; good strong men, guys who could lift and move things."

One sweltering summer day during the studio's construction, Gunther Ivans saw his men doing the brickwork on Frances's studio, and his heart went out to them as they sweated under the summer sun. So he bought them a case of beer.

That same evening, when Frances looked at the new studio, she noticed that some of the bricks were slightly out of line; some were grossly out of line. "I called the builder, and he was furious. He made the men take all the bricks out and put them back in properly. The builder had made a terrible mistake giving beer to the hot workers because, inspired by his case of beer, they had bought themselves a second case. They thought they were doing such a fine job."

Frances the sculptor was one of three or four small businesses on Birch Avenue. The street itself is not long, perhaps four hundred metres, bordered on the south side by the park and Cottingham School at its western end, and farther south by the railway tracks. Its eastern end begins at Yonge Street, a short block south of the Summerhill subway station.

Among the other small businesses on the street was Neil Sneyd's Animal Art Gallery, and next to him the Shaw-Rimington Gallery. And, of course, on the north side of the street, struggling along with her new studio at the rear of her house at number 60, was Frances.

But the street was not completely art-oriented. Next door was an extended family of gypsies, the Dury family. "Their name was originally Dura," said Frances. "I've no idea why they changed it. Maybe they didn't want people to know they were gypsies. Me being a sculptor didn't seem to matter to them one way or another. We got along well.

"Mr. Dury was a junk collector. He had a rattletrap old truck, and he used to collect all sorts of stuff and take it to the dump. Some of the stuff he collected I collected afterward. A studio chair, and things like that. Once he brought home ten old lithographer's stones. Beautiful Bavarian limestone. Don't know where he got them. I laid them down as a path leading to the studio. Just gorgeous stones; a dollar apiece from Mr. Dury."

The Dury's two grandchildren, John and David, were three or four years old, and were into everything, usually where they shouldn't have been. One day John came to Frances's door and held out a small bouquet of tulips. "'These are for you,' he said. I was so deeply moved," said

Frances, "I almost cried. Until I realized they were *my* tulips, torn up from my garden."

Early in January 1966, Frances learned that both The Girls were in hospital. By April, Florence Wyle was very low.

During that month, Frances was torn two ways: on the one hand she was concerned for The Girls, and on the other she had her involvement in an upcoming show of her work. On April 13, she was preparing her entry in the first outdoor sculpture exhibition at the Stratford Shakespearean Festival. The exhibition was co-sponsored by Rothmans of Pall Mall, the tobacco company. As they were preparing exhibits for the show, the company's representatives quite plainly and simply fell in love with Frances's entry, a life-size female torso, and purchased it on the spot for five hundred dollars. After the outdoor exhibition, the sculpture moved to the company's new head office.

In June, Frances went into hospital for a knee operation. "Torn ligament, lateral meniscus," she said, tossing off the medical terms like a seasoned pro. "I was in a cast from hip to ankle. When the cast came off I went in for physio. When I came out I found I couldn't walk. Ended up in downtown Toronto on Wellesley Street, hanging onto a telephone pole until I could flag a cab. Must have looked like a drunk."

Good times, bad times. To help with the mortgage, Frances took in a series of roomers. "The money was certainly welcome," she admitted, "but I had the devil's own luck with them. It was rarely a comfortable relationship. One had trouble with a possessive father, another was having an affair with her professor. Never-ending problems. One was an acquaintance named Richard Gross. He was brilliant, but strange. He created beautiful line drawings, then just departed, leaving a box full of these gorgeous illustrations. I kept them under my chair for years. He never returned."

Never one to pass up combining business with pleasure, on July 3, Frances enjoyed an excellent supper at the Heintzman's home, and discussed the progress of the garden sculpture she was doing for them, a commission given earlier in the year. "It was a large piece, a five-foot free-form. After the death of his wife, Mr. Heintzman moved into an apartment. The sculpture was too big, so he gave it to the Mount Pleasant Cemetery for their sculpture garden."

In the fall of 1966, Richard Outram's new book of poetry, *Exultate Jubilate*, was published, and Frances held a launching in her studio. Forty people came, and the party lasted till 3:00 a.m. "People brought liquor, but Barbara Howard took it home so I wouldn't drink it."

Frances had never been a teetotaler; the frequency of social exposure to liquor made it almost impossible to refuse an occasional drink, but occasional was what it was. Until now. By the end of 1966, the occasions were becoming more frequent, the glasses slightly larger, and closer together.

There are a hundred reasons why people, who until a certain point in their lives are the most moderate of drinkers, slowly but inexorably change. Some of us, fortunately, have the help of friends. At Richard Outram's poetry book launching, Barbara Howard, his wife and Frances's long-time friend, wisely removed temptation from her path.

"I was always an early riser," said Frances. "I loved the sunrise. But to get up early means going to bed early. This cuts into most people's drinking time. I didn't have time for serious drinking." She laughed. "Just recreational drinking."

Frances believed the turning point came later with the death of her mother toward the end of 1967. "It hurt me so deeply. I felt she had never lived, never had the chance to live her own life. Never doing what she might have wanted to do, always living someone else's life, suffering my father's put-downs and sarcastic remarks, never seeming to have a value that was recognized and appreciated. She must have been happy sometimes, I guess. I have no idea when that might have been.

"After she died, I found, since we had never been allowed to cry as children, that alcohol allowed me to cry, encouraged me to cry. At Birch Avenue I'd drink until I fell off my stool in front of the fire. Then

I went to bed. I found that crying was a wonderful relief; I felt, rightly or wrongly, more able to express my feelings when I was heavily under the influence, and I felt better for it.

"I found release this way. I didn't, at the time, consider what it would cost me in the end." She thought about this for a moment. "Funny," she added, "so many alcoholics are like that: the only way they can express their feelings is when they're drinking. I found this is common, and I've talked to a lot of them."

Mr. Lempiki, the Toronto builder, had completed the apartment complex at 50 Prince Arthur Avenue. Tadek Wisniewski was his nephew. Wisniewski and Frances were friends; she was producing a bear for Tadek and his wife, Rosamond, the tacit payoff for Tadek's assistance in the construction of her studio. It was thus natural that when they decided to place a sculpture in front of the new apartment building, Lempiki would turn to Frances.

On May 5, 1967, Frances began the preliminary sketches for what would be a reclining figure called *Rosamond*, after Tadek's wife.

This was a gratifying time of intense activity for Frances. She was working on the bear for Tadek's wife, and in July her sketches for *Rosamond* were accepted and the real work began.

She also started a series of four reliefs for Spencer Clark of the Guild Inn.

"Spencer had this place called the Guild Inn, 'The Guild of all Arts,' in Scarborough. He and his wife, Rosa Breithaupt, ran the place and that's where we did the work on the four reliefs: the two from the Group of Seven, A.Y. Jackson and Frederick Varley; and Sir Ernest MacMillan and Healey Willan, both very big in the Canadian music world. Spencer Clark put us up in the Guild Inn for a few days where we worked in this little studio, kind of a log cabin. That was the Guild of all Arts. Spencer collected the remains of sculpture and things like that from buildings that were being torn down, and he had them all there at the Guild. There's a train station there now called Guildwood. When I went out there it was a little old dirt road with a tiny train stop."

At this time, June–July 1967, in addition to the Varley relief for Spencer Clark, Frances had been asked by Varley's companion Kathleen McKay to do a portrait of the eighty-six-year-old artist.

Charles Band, a financier and a great friend of both Varley and McKay, had a magnificent collection of Varley's paintings. Band, who was also a close friend of Frances, recommended her when McKay wanted a portrait of Varley.

Frances spent three days in Varley's Unionville home, working on his sculpture. "It was a devastating experience," she said, "doing his portrait — or trying to. I stayed there, in the Unionville house, which is now the Varley Gallery, but Kathleen McKay would never leave us alone. Even Varley got a bit ticked off about that. She must have thought I was going to rape him." Frances laughed. "I might have, too, if I'd known how." Talking to Kathleen McKay one time, Frances recalled Kathleen saying that between herself and Frederick there was never any sex. "So says Kathleen," said Frances. "Ho, ho, ho, and another cow flew by."

In the end, Frances found conditions in Unionville simply impossible. "I knew I couldn't work on Varley's sculpture in that house, so I destroyed the piece, and did a 'study from memory' back in my own studio. I think that's what perhaps makes the sculpture stronger, because it was my feeling of Varley."

Still another project in this productive period was the commission to do a head of Dr. Andrew Smith, who founded the Ontario Veterinary College in 1862, the oldest such college in North America. The work was commissioned by Dr. W.G. Ballard of Vancouver, an alumnus of the OVC. "So," Frances smiled, "I was, in a sense, finally 'admitted' into the vet college, twenty years after I first applied, following my years in the navy."

Closer to home, Brian McFarlane, the sportscaster, dropped by and asked after Frances Loring's sculpture of a hockey player, a goalkeeper.

According to Frances Gage he wanted to buy it, but he said the pads would have to be altered in keeping with current design.

Frances hooted with glee. "Change the already-cast-in-bronze sculpture, Brian?" (And not incidentally put pads designed in the latter half of the twentieth century on a sculpture created in the first half of the twentieth century.)

Another visitor was Richard Outram. Frances mentioned to him that she would be acting as "security officer" the next day at The Girls' church studio. The CBC was doing a show there. "I was to protect the place against the destructive behaviour of the TV people. What surprised me at the time was that the 'destructive behaviour' was expected. Kind of flattering, I guess, that the organizers thought I would be able to control them." She laughed. "If I ever have to look for another job, I can add 'bouncer' to my résumé." When Richard, who worked at the CBC, heard about her security duties at The Girls' church, he was aghast. "Don't let them in there!" he cried. "They'll dance on the piano!" Apparently radio and TV people — creative types in general — have a reputation for all manner of irresponsibility. "It was quite an experience," said Frances. "Seven a.m. to 6:00 p.m. Incredible mess of equipment."

In early autumn Frances attended a gallery preview of ten of her sculptures. It was the Sonneck Gallery in Kitchener, an area very familiar to Frances; her brother Robert was professor of physics at the University of Guelph. It was also in Guelph that she taught sculpture and woodcarving. By now she had been teaching for almost ten years and had a number of classes in Toronto. "An artist," she maintained, "needs contact with people. I find my students very stimulating. You can get much too introverted working alone all the time." One of the pieces in the gallery preview was the seagull in Carrara marble she had begun while a student in Paris and had ultimately completed in Toronto.

Three days later her mother suffered a stroke and was hospitalized in London, Ontario. A week afterward her father was struck by a coronary (but survived); within five days her mother was dead.

A desperate end to the year. Three months passed, then, hardly two weeks into January 1968, Florence Wyle died; The Girls were then, for a heartbeat, only one. Three weeks later, Frances Loring, Florence's friend for so many decades, passed away in a Newmarket hospital, and the era of The Girls was over.

"We had a wake for The Girls," said Frances. "It was at their church studio and a lot of people came. Walter Gordon, the former finance minister, had been very friendly with The Girls. He was there, and brought a whole case of rye whisky. Walker's Canadian Club it was, in memory of Frances Loring's taste in whisky."

By mid-February Frances felt she just couldn't support all the deaths. She had sunk into a terrible depression. Not a day passed without a heart-wrenching reminder of what was, and was no more. She seemed surrounded by mementos: a Loring figurine, a Wyle sketch, a mother's letter. She had to get away from everything. Her own sculpture offered her an answer.

Her friend Tadek saw her sorrow, and asked, "How is *Rosamond* coming along?"

"You've seen it; it's complete," said Frances. "It'll soon be off to Norway for casting."

He noted the lacklustre eyes, and thought he saw an answer. "Why don't you go to Norway with the sculpture? It might be better, for everyone."

She thought about it for a day, then made her decision: She would cross the Atlantic with the sculpture.

In early April 1968, Frances made shipping arrangements for *Rosamond*. She had chosen Norway because of the remarkable difference in cost. A New York firm had quoted her 8,500 dollars. The foundry in Oslo, Norway, was asking three thousand.

At the same time, Frances produced a memorial for Mount Allison University in New Brunswick. It was commissioned by the husband of Cecil Record Johns. Ms. Johns was a former faculty member in the university's department of music (1927–1932). The commemorative piece was a free-form sculpture entitled *Song in the Wind*, cast in bronze and mounted on a piece of the local New Brunswick red sandstone. Frances's price was one thousand dollars. She took the sculpture to Norway for casting along with *Rosamond* and a number of other small items. *Song in the Wind* would be installed at Mount Allison in the spring of the following year.

Frances also produced a piece, cast in concrete, called *Ship of Earth*, a rugged, stylized vision of a ship atop a rock. This made a huge impression on Mr. Johns's daughters, and pleased as he was with Frances's work on his wife's memorial, he bought the piece for his girls.

On May 1, 1968, Frances travelled to Montreal to board the *Byklefjell* for Norway. *Rosamond* was scheduled for another vessel, the *Sagahölm*.

Earlier she had been in discussions with Women's College Hospital (WCH) regarding a sculpture for their foyer. As the Norwegian ship stopped for an hour at Sept-Îles at the mouth of the St. Lawrence River, Frances jumped ashore and mailed her preparatory sketches to the hospital in Toronto, then continued on her way to Oslo.

During the trip to Norway there was sometimes a gathering in the ship's common room. "A bunch of us got drunk together, and I thought I could draw like an angel! But when I looked in my sketch books in the morning, I thought, *What turkey's been wandering around in my sketch book?*" She laughed. "But at the time I remember thinking it was so good." At these common room gatherings there was always a lot of singing, too. "I could always sing all right; when I was drunk, I could sing even better." She frowned. "At least, I think so."

Two days out, the birds which had been with the vessel from shore returned to the mainland. "All except a white-throated sparrow," said Frances. "He stayed and took up residence in our cabin. He slept in a light sconce, and became the ship's mascot."

The following morning, she found the little bird had gone, flown out an open porthole.

But the next day he was back. "We discovered he had managed to re-enter through another porthole. He was pretty frazzled and missing a few feathers. He was with us for almost the entire trip, occasionally perched on a chair, singing. A day out from land he left us for the coast of Norway." She wondered at the time how a new kind of bird might have been received by the local Norwegian birds, how he would have fared in a strange new habitat, surrounded by different birds, and how he might have adapted to new food, and, indeed, new dangers.

In most things Frances seemed the very embodiment of Murphy's Law: If anything can go wrong, it will. When they arrived off the west coast of Norway, en route to Oslo in the southeast, Frances's captain dropped her unceremoniously at Sognafjorden, a coastal town 290 kilometres west of Oslo. The captain, according to Frances, decided to bring his wife aboard and needed the cabin occupied by Frances and her roommates. Frances was left standing in Sognafjorden. *Beautiful day*, she thought, seeking some shred of optimism in the situation. There was neither train nor bus, and 290 kilometres is a long walk, so she hired a car. "Forty dollars. The road had just been opened; snow banks were twenty feet high."

She was in Oslo for a week before *Rosamond* arrived, and during that time she produced a number of small pieces, courtesy of the foundry. "Mr. Erno, the manager at the foundry — lovely man; very considerate — gave me a studio I could use while I was there, so I was able to do a few small items for my own benefit. I think I did about fifteen sculptures."

When *Rosamond* arrived she was cut up — head, arms, down the middle. The maximum size of a one-piece casting naturally depends on the size of the foundry's kiln.

On the first of June she exclaimed "Beautiful day again!" then "but a disappointing lunch. Salt herring. That was an experience like eating cod head. First time I had cod head was on the ship, the *Byklefjell*, coming over. You slice the head longitudinally to get two halves of the face. You eat the cheeks and the eye. I couldn't —" She shivered. "— just *couldn't* eat the eye."

By mid-June she was finished. *Rosamond* would be shipped, and Frances was free to enjoy a brief holiday. She flew to Copenhagen, to Zurich, then by bus to Wiesendangen, and spent a quiet few days in the Swiss mountains with her old friend Trudy, the former au pair for madame Gérard in Paris.

On her return to Toronto she began the preparatory models for what would be *Woman*, one of her career's major works.

"It was a real job of love," she recalled. "They liked it, and I liked it, and I liked them. They liked my first sketch, too. And it was carved for that particular location in the hospital's foyer."

She carried on, working, developing, even though she had yet to receive the official okay to proceed. Everything felt so right.

At the same time, she completed a piece for Seagram's, the distillers. It was a stylized sheaf of wheat that went on display in the Toronto-Dominion Centre. Concurrently she worked on a portrait/bust of Dr. J.B. Collip who had been head of the department of medical research at the University of Western Ontario. Collip had laboured beside Banting and Best on their insulin project. Frances's sculpture would be positioned in the rotunda of the Medical Sciences Building.

In mid-October, Frances was negotiating with representatives of Roy Thomson Hall in downtown Toronto to do a head of Elmer Iseler, the outstanding choir conductor. It was planned for the hall's foyer. This was at the discussion stage; actual production was still in the future.

On October 28, *Rosamond* returned from Norway. Frances met the truck at the warehouse, and arrived with the sculpture at 50 Prince Arthur Avenue. "Started at ten, through by eleven-thirty," said Frances. "Lots of press, but I was exhausted. We were on TV, *Metro News* at six-thirty." This was the official installation of *Rosamond*.

But annoying things were happening at Frances's Pears Avenue studio. Again for financial reasons, Frances was conducting sculpture classes at Debora Johnston's Now and Then Studio there. On

October 28, Frances was depressed. "The model didn't show up, which was bad enough. But there was also Katherine, one of my students and one of Debora's old drinking buddies. She was Katherine Christie, the very spoiled heiress of Christie Biscuits, and a real pain." Frances claimed that Katherine's grandmother used to sit on the steps of the factory smoking a clay pipe. "Right off the boat, man!" Frances laughed heartily. "Katherine's pampered ego wouldn't have accepted any of that, of course. She would have gone up the wall if you had dared remind her of that."

One of the contentious issues between Katherine and Frances was Katherine's belief that she had been responsible for getting Frances the Birch Avenue property, and later had recommended Frances for Debora Johnston's Now and Then Studio, and Frances simply wasn't showing enough appreciation. There was some shouting and abrasive words, and lots of melodramatic waving of arms. "She was very disruptive," said Frances. "So much so that Debora threw her out."

And if these contretemps were not enough, there were more problems with Frances's roomers. Recently one roomer had decided to have a baby (maybe even get married, too). "Not in *my* house," said Frances, and the roomer was invited to leave. She was followed by a young student who had a million friends, all of whom visited at the same time and never left, it seemed to Frances. This roomer, too, was soon history. The next one had a nervous breakdown; by this time Frances was ready to have one, too. These roomers brought in money, admittedly, but you have to wonder why Frances didn't seek another less nerve-wracking source of extra income.

Still, despite the difficulties at home, in her studio at the rear of the house her work was progressing on the sculpture for Women's College Hospital. Mr. Luigi Temporale, the Italian carver, was the man who would prepare the marble for Frances's sculpture, *Woman*. On November 11, he arrived with a sample of the marble that would come from Italy, so she could be sure she was getting the right material. "You can't trust those Italians," he said. Frances gave Mr. Luigi Temporale a cool stare, and murmured, "But I have to, don't I?" Trust seemed to be much in vogue those days: she still had not received the official approval to go ahead with the sculpture.

During these weeks, Frances had been suffering a numbness in one hand. Her physician, Dr. Davis, diagnosed it as carpal tunnel syndrome; sculpture has its price. Frances's response was, in effect, "Thanks very much. I'll get back to you on that." Convinced as she was that Women's College Hospital would endorse her commission for *Woman*, she was not prepared to entertain for a single moment anything that might interfere with its execution. She did not appear to consider that by ignoring Dr. Davis's opinion, she could be creating a much more serious obstacle to the work, and her own future abilities.

Christmas came. "Miserable Christmas Eve," said Frances. "My own fault, I guess. I got moderately bombed while opening Christmas presents, then continued drinking."

But the coming year promised better things.

On February 21, 1969, Frances finally received the official okay to proceed on *Woman*.

For the rest of the year the WCH sculpture was her major occupation. The marble had arrived in Toronto's port in June. It was nothing more than a one-and-a-half-ton block of stone when it came off the boat. From there it went to nearby Port Credit and the Italian carver Luigi Temporale, who then roughed out the statue according to the sketches Frances supplied. Now she began to give form to the stone, working on it in her Birch Avenue studio until the beginning of 1970, when it was removed to the hospital's foyer.

On an icy morning in February 1970, one year after WCH gave the go-ahead, the statue, reduced to a mere two thousand pounds by this time, was taken in hand by Robert Flaherty, the monument setter, moved from Frances's Birch Avenue studio, across the city to its final position in the foyer of Women's College Hospital. Three men and three hours were needed to set the half-formed statue in its location beneath a skylight. It was enclosed by a glassed-in area at the entrance to the hospital's large foyer. It would ultimately rest in a pool, the pure white marble shimmering in the water.

To create an attractive bed for the pool, Frances went to Grand Bend on Lake Huron and scoured the shore for stones. She was familiar with that part of the lake, and knew she would find a wealth of beautiful coloured pebbles.

"I had a five-quart basket, and I was moseying along the beach, picking up a stone here and one there, and a young man went by, stopped, watched me for a minute, then said 'Look, lady, if you're going to clean up this beach, you're gonna to have to work faster than that!'

"In the foyer there was also a cement bowl near the pool," Frances said, "where people could throw their money to avoid having them throw it all over the place. In the pool, for example. Imagine the job you'd have getting the small coins out from between the pebbles, one by one. But somebody tried to steal the bowl, even though it was cemented down. It damaged the sculpture a bit, so later they drained the pool. Shortly after, they moved the sculpture back to where it was before. For all this moving they insured it for 100 thousand dollars. The statue had cost them eight thousand."

In the last months of the project Frances worked at the hospital, starting late in the evening and continuing on until the small hours. "When employees began arriving for work, I'd pack up my stuff and go home. I felt I had to work under consistent light conditions; the day's sunlight was not reliable, and not uniform when it was there. Also, the sunlight on the white marble was blinding. The artificial light at night was consistent. I must have looked like someone from Mars; the dust of the marble was like talcum powder, so I wore a mask to keep it out of my lungs, goggles to keep it out of my eyes, and put on my old navy hat cover from my days as a Wren."

There was a contest to name the statue. The local postman, Bruce Hunter, won. "There's only one name for that," he said. "Woman. I've had four daughters born in this hospital, and they're all beautiful." He pointed at the sculpture. "And she's beautiful, too."

In April 1969, one era ended and another began: The McMichaels moved Tom Thomson's shack from the obscurity of the Studio Building to a position of relative importance at their art gallery in Kleinburg, Ontario. And Frances returned the paintings that had decorated the walls of the shack, the ones she had taken down and stored under her bed for safekeeping.

The same month saw the installation ceremonies at Mount Allison University of Frances's *Song in the Wind*, the tribute to Cecil Record Johns.

In mid-June, Frances noted that between five and seven thousand dollars was left in the estate of The Girls. "This money," said Frances, "went, at The Girls' request, into a trust fund to buy the works of young artists. 'If you want to help artists, you have to buy their work,' Florence Wyle had said. I remembered that William Zorach, years before when I was in New York, had said the same thing: 'It does no good to subsidize an artist, you must buy his or her work!'"

On October 13, Frances left once more for Oslo, Norway, and her luggage was filled with work. Douglas Duncan, founder of the Picture Loan Society, had died the year before, in June 1968, but was fondly remembered by his former part-time employee Frances Gage. She had done a bust of him, and took it to Oslo for casting in an edition of three. One went to Spencer Clark of the Guild Inn, another to R.L. Pepall, a friend of Duncan, and the last was placed in Toronto's Gallerie Dresdnere. While in Oslo, Frances produced four A.Y. Jacksons, three *Young Girls* by Florence Wyle, and saw her own *Boy with Dog* made ready for the kiln. "A very satisfying and productive trip," said Frances.

The spring and summer months of 1970 were a quiet, rewarding period. The lull before the storm, as it turned out, because in mid-summer occurred "The Moore-Ede Affair."

It was a small matter, really, what many might consider just a minor business reverse. Unless you were the sculptor Frances Gage. For Frances it was to have a terrible effect initially, completely beyond the admittedly irritating facts of the matter, and it would remain a painful memory for the rest of her life.

Still, in the pleasant months beforehand, she was continuing her classes at the University of Toronto. There was an essay for her English course, plus work in the other courses she was taking — anthropology, anatomy, history, and geology. (Why was she engaged in all this studying? "I was interested," she said.) Beyond these activities, she was exhibiting some of her work at the O'Keefe Centre on the third of March; attending the installation of her *Boy with Dog* at 50 Elderwood Drive in the very posh Forest Hill area of Toronto; and dropping off her *Torso of a Dancer* to be placed in the Forest Hill Learning Resources Centre.

She was also checking a growing list of realty "opportunities," some more opportune than others. While not rolling in money, she was now in a position to at least consider her "Dream Home."

Frances was that rare contradiction: the gregarious loner. She made friends easily, and she had hundreds of them. Yet, she longed for a studio lost in rural solitude. A place of her own, built the way she wanted it built, away from everything. She loved animals, and longed to be near them. She once came within a split second of cuddling a porcupine. She was on a first name basis with hundreds of different birds, and thought crows and peacocks equally beautiful. Plants of all kinds fascinated her, and her knowledge of them grew daily, even in solidly urban surroundings like Birch Avenue.

So, during the period before The Moore-Ede Affair, she spent many summer days driving through the southern Ontario countryside, checking land packages big and small — "seventy-five acres, forty thousand dollars." She laughed, with overtones of hysteria. Or "Lovely little handyman's delight; seven hundred square feet; ten-foot frontage," at a price that was halfway to the moon.

Opportunities. Some to die for, others simply ridiculous.

And then, in the middle of all this, came the commission from Amy Moore-Ede.

"In the summer of 1970," said Frances, "Amy Moore-Ede, an ex-student of sculpture, a good amateur painter, and not incidentally a friend, asked me to do a piece for their pool. I did several maquettes and they chose a bear, which I christened *Narcissus*. He was to be situated in their pool, looking at his reflection in the water."

The bear was specially reinforced so that their grandson could ride on him. Frances's price was 750 dollars, which was surprisingly low, given the time (1970) and the custom nature of the commission. All were pleased when he was installed in the pool, just before their daughter's wedding.

Three months later, on the twenty-third of September, Dr. Moore-Ede phoned — it was late at night — to say that they did not like the piece anymore.

"I was devastated," Frances cried. "But agreed to take it back and refund their money."

"Devastated" is an indication of Frances's feelings for the sculpture, and you would not need to be a knowledgeable critic of things artistic to find a sweet beauty in the piece: the small bear, perched on his little rock, gazing at his reflection in the water — the birth of vanity. It is ineffably charming.

So far as *refunding* the 750 dollars is concerned …! Another earthier artist might have suggested to Dr. Moore-Ede what he could do with his request for a refund. But Frances, confused by the late hour — it was her habit to retire early, and she had been asleep when the call came — she had simply acquiesced, hung up the phone, and sat stunned, and devastated.

A few days later, Frances and John Murphy, her trucker, went to the Moore-Ede home early in the morning. A thin mist hung over the pool, half-hiding the doctor's house. The sculptor and trucker stood in the shallow water in their rubber boots. Between them the bear studied his image on the water's surface.

"Technically speaking," murmured John, "we're trespassing."

"We are retrieving my property," said Frances, firmly. "Right, sweetheart?" She patted the bear on the nose.

"Why don't you just go up to the door?" said the trucker. "Tell them you're going to …"

"Nothing would be gained by making a scene, John. And if I spoke a single word to them, face to face, there would be a scene." She turned to the silent sculpture. Her voice broke. "Please … help me with my bear, John," she said, her arm around the animal, as she began to cry. John paused, waited for the moment to pass, then lifted the front of the sculpture.

They loaded the bear onto John's truck and took it to Kitchener, as a gift for Frances's friend Fran Bean. "We put it in her pool, where someone would love it," said Frances.

"The whole incident left me with a terrible feeling of betrayal," Frances said. "Dr. Moore-Ede was, I believe, chief of staff at a Toronto Hospital; he and his wife were very wealthy." Frances added, in unrelenting bitterness, "I cannot forgive them."

The sculpture was later moved to the west coast. It may still be there, bringing a quiet pleasure into someone's life. Nothing more has been heard of it. Its present location is unknown.

The first three months of 1971 were taken up mainly with the development and production of a commemorative medal of Samuel Bronfman, founder in 1924 of Distillers Corporation, which later (1928) merged with the Canadian firm of Seagram's to become the largest distillery in the world. The Bronfman family gained a fortune through export liquor sales to the United States during the American Prohibition period (1920–1933), and devoted much of their wealth to philanthropic activities.

Frances's commission for this medal may have resulted from the simple sheaf of wheat she did for Seagram's two years previously. In any event, the twenty-eighth of January found her travelling from Toronto to Montreal to discuss the project with the Bronfmans, "despite a train fire," said Frances, "on that disaster-on-wheels, the Turbo, the railway company's answer to the tricycle. Did it ever work? I don't remember it ever working." But her ideas for the Bronfman project were accepted, and by mid-February she was carving the medal. On the seventh of March she was again in Montreal for the medal's presentation. "Gorgeous celebratory banquet, in spite of a blizzard." Sadly, Samuel Bronfman died four months later.

Two other projects were completed in the first half of the year: the four reliefs — Jackson, Varley, McMillan, and Willan — were delivered to Spencer Clark at the Guild Inn, and on May 19, 1971, Frances noted with vast satisfaction: "Finished stone at 4:00 a.m. at Women's College Hospital. *Woman* is complete."

There was a further note: a photo-op at the Women's College Hospital. Frances smiled with unavoidable pride. "Prime Minister Trudeau officially unveiled the hospital's new wing — and *Woman*, my sculpture."

Throughout the year, when time and circumstances permitted, Frances continued doggedly to search for her dream house, her dream property.

"Eleven acres, near Rockwood, about twenty-five miles west of Toronto. Forty-five thousand dollars. A steal."

"Property ten miles from Guelph. Sounds like another steal at eighty-six thousand. And it was," she said, "but too much for me."

Together with her old friend Fran Bean she actually bought what seemed a suitable property near Guelph. The ink was hardly dry on the deed when the Grand Valley Conservation Authority stepped in and flooded the area. "No great loss, financially," said Frances, "to either Fran or me, but we both felt we'd been hard done by."

Frances, almost in desperation you might say, even considered buying a wonderful old hotel (the Washington Hotel) which was on the highway between London and Kitchener. What she would have done, as a sculptor, with a hotel is unknown.

In the late fall of 1971, Frances was in Kitchener, visiting the Kitchener Art Mart. "I had a few pieces on exhibit there, hoping for sales — vainly as it turned out, but you have to keep trying. I was showing a bear for seven hundred dollars. Rather large dollars for that area, but as I say, you have to keep trying. There was also a small head, and a couple of birds."

While in the Kitchener/Waterloo area, Frances carried on fifteen kilometres west to visit her friend Fran Bean. Fran and her husband David had a farm near the tiny community of Crosshill.

Fran had told Frances of a seventy-five-acre parcel of land that abutted their property, about a kilometre and a half from Crosshill itself.

Frances arrived, looked at the property, and her heart beat strongly. This was on November 10, 1971. By the thirteenth she had taken notes, considered the extent of the property, pondered price, discussed the possibility of taking twenty-five acres while Fran and David took the remaining fifty acres, looked coldly and realistically at her own financial situation — "I could not afford to be foolish." But she was hooked.

November 13: "All alone this morning at Crosshill, wandering around, looking at the property. Magnificent black cherry trees, almost three feet in diameter!" The place wasn't hers yet, no papers signed. But she was committed, irrevocably.

A month later she was back at Crosshill, happily pruning "her" apple trees in the wind and cold of a bright December day.

Frances had encountered many problems, artistic and otherwise, in the past years; she had met trouble, and survived. In her new-found paradise, she was to find that she had never known the real meaning of the word *trouble*.

She would learn that every paradise has its inferno.

| 8 |

PARADISE AND INFERNO

Halfway along the road of Life, I came upon a dark wood, and lost my way.

— Dante

"I WAS FORTY-SEVEN YEARS OLD," said Frances, "gazing out across twenty-five acres of … well, dense woods for the most part.

"I knew the Beans before my move to Crosshill. Fran was a sculpture student in my Guelph group. Then this seventy-five acres came up for sale; it was adjacent to their farm." Frances would ultimately buy one third, twenty-five acres, for seventy-five dollars an acre. The remaining fifty acres would be purchased by the Beans.

The beginning of February — this is a Canadian February, with all the weather conditions that implies — on the hill of what would eventually be her rural property, open to the wind, with not a living soul or habitation in sight, wouldn't seem at first glance the wisest place to be, dressed only in a city topcoat and no hat. But then you would not be Frances Gage, internationally famous sculptor and owner of a vast rural estate … er, okay, after the Crosshill purchase, impoverished sculptor, who owns a lot of virgin bush. But it made not a bit of difference to Frances. On February 5, 1972, she smiled broadly: "Off to Kitchener and Crosshill. Minus twenty-five degrees Celsius, cold, cruel, and gorgeous. Checking property." Checking property indeed; already the "Mistress of the Manor."

Frances's obvious enchantment with her new property, which henceforth she would refer to as "Crosshill," after the crossroads a mile away, was marred somewhat by the usual round of irritating, but apparently unavoidable contretemps.

As an experienced Ms. Fix-it, she needed a tool shed for her Crosshill property, so she ordered a prefab item from Simpson's, and invited friends over for a house-raising, or rather shed-raising. The shipping carton arrived, and was found to contain two floors but no ceiling. She complained to Simpson's, and a long and frustrating story began.

Factotums in large companies refuse to admit a mistake, through self-preservation or simply innate arrogance. At Simpson's, the factotum she contacted claimed the problem was that the address Frances had given them was an "undeliverable address." Frances looked at the phone in her hand as if it were a strange animal. "Undeliverable?" she asked. "Then how did I get the two floors and no ceiling?"

Two months passed, and finally Frances, remembering the old axiom "If you want something done, you don't talk to the office boy," contacted the president who, with apologies, sent another unit, and Frances had her friends in again for a proper shed-raising. "The tin shed is now a reality," she said. "I was so teed off, I almost sued Simpson's."

The next day she was back at Crosshill again. This was one of the first of a million 120-kilometre trips to and from the farm and her Birch Avenue house. "Off to Crosshill. Snowshoeing. Home to Birch by 9:00 p.m. for a late supper." And again, a few days later: "Went out to the farm early. Glorious, lots of tracks. Had supper with the Beans, then home late to Birch Ave."

During her frequent walks through the woods, Frances found that in the eyes of many of the wilder residents of the Crosshill forest, she was not welcome. "Toward the end of March, I was out walking among the trees, and a red-tailed hawk dive-bombed me. Yes, 'bombed,' with talons out front. You ended up with your arms over your head, staggering around, looking for somewhere to hide. They would follow you all the way through the woods until you were out of range of their nest, then they'd go away. Oh, they were fierce."

In May 1972, there was the theft of a piece of sculpture from Frances's Crosshill property. "I was living in a tent," she said. "My house hadn't even been started yet, and I had left the sculpture out on a rock." The local newspaper, the Kitchener/Waterloo *Record*, interviewed her about the theft, and the story was a nice bit of public relations for Frances.

But the item that catches the ear was Frances's remark "I was living in a tent ..." Living in a tent is, in itself, not particularly noteworthy; everyone has spent a night in a tent at least once in their lives.

But Frances lived in that tent — large, it slept six — for five years, 1972 to 1976, while her house was being built. And this, too, poses yet another interesting question: Five years? To build a house?

Regarding the construction of her house, Frances was faced with a financial problem: A builder could erect a house in no more than six months, but at the end of that time he would expect to be paid. In full. Frances was not financially able to do that, thus no builder would even consider her. So far as loans were concerned, the bank's attitude was cool and uncooperative.

But Frances, as always, had friends, and one of those friends was Menno Martin, a local Mennonite builder, who agreed to build as much of her house as she could afford, when she could afford it.

Sitting beneath the marquee of her tent, Frances would gaze across the open ground and see visions of her house rising before her. An imaginary rooftop here, perhaps a window there, through which she could almost see her soon-to-be studio.

Then she got a call from Dick Hungerford, her lawyer.

"Looks bad," he said. "The township will not give you a permit to build."

No permit?

Frances was staggered. *Wait a minute!* she thought in panic. "No permit?" she cried. "Where am I going to live?" She realized her voice was becoming a shriek; only dogs would have heard the last few words.

"I talked with them yesterday," said Hungerford. "They weren't happy about you building a …"

"Dick," said Frances, desperately, "what do they want me to do? Build a nest in a tree someplace? I couldn't do that. The red-tailed hawks would go crazy, they'd tear me to pieces!" She stopped, then said, with poisonous sweetness, "Dick, isn't it just a little bit on the late side for the township, and you, my lawyer, to be telling me this? For Heaven's sake, I'll have to live in a tent! Forever!" In anguish she paced up and down in front of her tent, her future home. 'I'll have to get another tent for my studio!" She wept when she thought how much it meant to her. "To come so close, and then be refused …!"

They went to the township and stated her case. The township's fear was that the town would be faced with unforeseen and onerous road maintenance, and (panic-stricken gestures and cries of dismay) extra costs! Money going out, not coming in! Frances had heard it all before; bureaucrats were bureaucrats the world over, and all of them considered *cost* a four-letter word. And *maintenance* was an eleven-letter word, almost three times worse.

"Finally, they said that if I agreed to maintain the road from the highway to my building site — a distance of perhaps eight hundred metres — and not ask them for any help whatsoever, well, they *might* reconsider the building permit."

For the first half of July 1972, she gardened, both at Crosshill and Birch Avenue. Gardened blindly, like an animal acting instinctively, anything to avoid thinking of the township's final decision. "At Crosshill I was alone, digging, planting, with only my neighbour's cows for company, and even they were indifferent."

Then, on the first day of November, she attended once more the township council meeting. Permission to build was granted, but on the clear understanding, in writing, regarding Frances's responsibility for road maintenance. Frances collapsed into a chair with a big smile, and before she was out of the building, she was planning, planning …

There were somewhat the same problems on Birch Avenue, too. Frances, like most of us, was never happy with people who thought themselves better than others. So, when the residents of Birch Avenue decided to improve their image by getting rid of the street's businesses — art galleries, hardware store, and the lone sculptor — by having the street rezoned Residential Only, they discovered the small businesses had found a relentless champion in Frances.

"There was a big meeting at City Hall," Frances remembered. "I went, of course. I was on the opposing side, naturally. I needed a commercial area. Even though I was no longer physically the official resident of the house, I still conducted sculpture classes there, and without a studio at that time in Crosshill, I had to use my Birch Avenue studio for all my own work." For this reason, Frances did not sell the Birch house; she rented it to her friend Rebecca Sisler, a fellow artist, for 250 dollars a month, and Rebecca, too, benefited from Frances's studio. This was the situation that remained in effect over all the years Frances was at Crosshill, thus this meant that commercial zoning was of prime importance to her, as it was for the other businesses. "They were all quiet enterprises, art galleries, that sort of thing, no heavy industry. So I went to the City Hall, and in my plea I said, 'They moved in, and now they say the natives can stay — if they're nice.' That kind of remark didn't make me very popular with the 'Residential Only' faction. Years later we finally got 'Single Non-Conforming Use.' But, you know, it wasn't right that they should move in and say, 'Okay, we're here now, so everything has to be the way we want it.' It just wasn't right."

Incredibly, the battle raged for years, with bitter skirmishes a monthly occurrence. The business people finally won — fifteen years later.

Frances had ordered an aerial photo of her Crosshill property, and in mid-May it arrived. Its original purpose had been simply for reference, the manse-at-a-glance. But when she gazed at the cold no-nonsense photograph, she felt her heart swell with pride. Her twenty-five acres seemed to stretch to the horizon, *and it's all mine!* she thought with delight.

The photo showed a vast sea of trees, some clear parts, and in the middle of one of those clear parts was a large tent. The aerial photo didn't show Frances, but she was there. "Morning on my hill (already it's 'my hill'). Planted ten red pine and ten white pine." Twenty trees, the first of the thousands to come. "Mosquitoes a torture." The first of the billions to come. "Orchard, garden, and bugs. I spent two days planting. Fantastic northern lights!"

When asked about her house, she might have replied that progress was immeasurable, in the literal sense that it could not be measured; there was none. "Fourteen months since I signed for Crosshill. No water yet, not even any foundations."

Her relationship with her tent was a good one; she was happy in it. This was just as well, as she had little alternative. The summer months, even late spring and early fall, posed no problem. If sculpturing responsibilities permitted, she could drive to Crosshill, live in the tent, and sleep there. The winter was another matter. She stayed at the Beans' farm, bedding down on a cot in their living room. David Bean was a physician, and his practice was in Kitchener. In the winter, both he and his wife Fran would come up to the farm on weekends and holidays; Fran would be there almost daily to attend to the cattle. In late fall, Frances would take her tent down in preparation for winter.

Over the years Frances came to know many of her neighbours, among them Aaron and Emma Gerber, a Mennonite family — "They were wonderful people" — and a neighbour she referred to only as "Attila." Attila seemed to harbour a dislike of Frances that bordered on insanity. To a casual observer, Frances's descriptions of the numerous incredible acts committed by him would lead that observer to see Frances as a paranoid old woman with an active, but twisted, imagination. But Frances was not old (not yet fifty). And she was not paranoid; she was scared to death.

"I think he was crazy," Frances claimed. "I feel he persecuted me because I was a woman daring to live alone, and self-sufficient, and it offended his sense of masculine superiority."

Sometimes the actions of Attila were simply annoying, aimed at causing inconvenience. Once Frances went down to get her car, which was often parked in the town. At the bottom of her lane, about eight hundred metres from her house, she found her gate had been wired shut. "By Attila. Who else? I think he knew I'd get down to the gate, then have to go all the way back and get the wire cutters, because it was heavy wire he used."

Her calls to the Ontario Provincial Police were frequent enough that a cruiser became a common sight. "I arrived at Crosshill around three o'clock this afternoon. A police car drove out as I drove in." She smiled wryly. "My guardians."

But the guardians, though they were 100 percent effective while they were there, could not be there all the time.

"One day I had some friends visiting," said Frances, "and we were walking out to my car to go to lunch with David Bean. Attila began to shoot over our heads. That's right, shoot; bullets! We could hear the bullets going by, and hear them hit the trees. I have never again experienced that sense of unreality, like being in a terrible dream and unable to wake up. Then, with the sun shining quietly on my fields and trees around us, to know, horrified, that it was real, the bullets were real, hitting the trees behind us, and the blind panic was real, too — 'The house! Run, get inside!' — as we crouched running, one of my friends stumbling but scrabbling to her feet and running on, toward the house that never before seemed so far away. We hurried inside and called the police. The constables questioned him, but what could they do? He didn't do it, he said, with injured innocence; he had been inside all day. The police could do nothing about him."

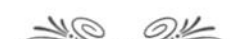

After the deaths of The Girls, Frances Gage was one of their executors. She was also on the board of the trust formed by the Royal Academy from the monies that came from the Loring/Wyle estate, "and later the Jacobean Jones estate, and a couple of architects," said Frances. "We gave scholarships every year, perhaps two, sometimes three. Scholarships, or we bought works of art; gave money to the galleries to buy works of art. About three thousand dollars a year. We'd give the money to the gallery, and they would choose someone, and send us a photo of the recipient(s). We tried to choose galleries all over the country."

The year 1972 saw Frances inducted into the Royal Canadian Academy of Arts (RCA), considered by many as the ultimate recognition of her work. It was also the year Frances began one of her major sculptures.

In August 1971, at a Wren reunion in Victoria, British Columbia, the idea of a unique project had been born: To erect a statue to honour the thousands of young women who joined the Women's Royal Canadian Naval Service (WRCNS, or Wrens) in the Second World War. The choice of Frances as the sculptor was a logical one. "I was known as an artist, and I'd been a Wren myself."

The location for the statue was, at first, just as logical. The city of Galt, Ontario, was the natural choice. It was where the "land ship" HMCS *Conestoga* had been established as a training centre for the Wrens back in the early forties.

But from the beginning, the selection of the artist and the choice of locale were the only two decisions that were made smoothly. Galt as the location was accepted, but immediately a bitter debate arose between the mayor, the members of council, and the parks and recreation committee: Galt okay, but where in Galt? Some favoured the site of the Gore centennial fountain, others were irrevocably opposed. On the periphery of this squabble, Frances shrugged. "It was to have been designed for the Gore fountain spot," she said. "But if they don't want it there, it can always go somewhere else." But the wrangling went on and on.

It got to the point where the ex-Wrens were prepared to wash their hands of the entire affair, and select another city for their ten-thousand-dollar statue. Finally — cooler heads and all that — the mayor and the Wren committee settled on the Central Branch of the Cambridge Public Library (Galt merged with Cambridge in 1973), on the south side facing Queen's Square.

With the location established, the field of conflict, with its loudly expressed differences of opinion, moved on to Phase Two: the statue itself. What at the outset had been internal bickering between the mayor and his committees, now involved the sculptor, Frances, and the committees. The "discussion" — if such a word can be seen as synonymous with "rigid" and "unbending" — the discussion turned on the statue and its appearance. What image would it, should it, project to the viewer?

Frances was approached. "The sculpture committee came to me saying they wanted somebody (the statue) rigidly at attention, stiff, sober. I didn't agree," said Frances the ex-Wren. So she decided unilaterally to do it her way.

She had, at the very start, christened the project *Jenny*, and from then on that was the sculpture's name. "I felt *Jenny* should be seen as an ex-Wren would remember her: Young, light-hearted; the way we were. I tried to loosen it up a bit. I saw her as slim, confident, alive. I even put a wren on her shoulder, but the committee wouldn't have any of that."

There was a lot of discussion over details, like insignia and buttons. The committee was reluctant to move from a strict, almost photographic representation of a Wren, while Frances leaned away from rigid realism toward an impressionistic treatment. "I tried, but they were firmly committed to realism. It meant more to them. 'We have to please a lot of people' they kept saying."

But all the petty disputes were swept away like smoke on the wind when, on October 8, 1972, Jenny the Wren was unveiled to reveal the bronze figure of a five-foot young woman in her Second World War naval uniform, standing on a three-foot stone pedestal. Over four hundred former Wrens attended. So did Frances's father. "It was the first time I saw Father cry."

Frances was understandably pleased by the *Jenny* project and its reception by the City of Galt, but even more so by the response shown by the Wrens. They saw this memorial as the concrete, official recognition of the important part they played in the war, and the statue's quiet pride affected them all.

For Frances, however, gratification was shortly to be clouded by sorrow. Sadly, it was also the year her cat Igor died. A small thing, compared to the Wren memorial? Not for Frances. He had been her close companion since the earliest days in Tom Thomson's shack in 1957, and carried with him all the memories of those years, the ups and downs of their first steps together in the art world.

The painful gap caused by Igor's passing was filled, indirectly, by Frances's friends the Chapmans. Chris Chapman was a filmmaker, and he and his wife Penny lived on Rosedale Valley Road, near the Studio Building. Frances had known them since her years in the shack. A wild cat had got into the habit of eating with their own cat, so they packed the wild one off to the Humane Society. But Frances interceded and claimed the animal. She brought him home on the subway and let him loose in the studio.

"The first day he ate a whole can of dog food while he was alone," said Frances. "Each time I went into the studio, he ran across the floor at me, growling. It occurred to me that he might never become tame, and I'd have to put him down. Then one day I sat next to him while he ate, and dared to touch his shoulder, and he leaned into my hand. Everything went fine after that. I called him Kaspar, which is a good cat name."

While doing her planting she cut some poplars. "For Chapman's beaver. Chris Chapman had acquired a young beaver," said Frances. "He planned to do a film involving the animal, but something happened, the film didn't come off, so his wife Penny got the beaver. She took the beaver around the schools. What a wonderful idea! But the

Chapmans didn't have any poplar trees, so I cut poplar saplings to take in to them. The beavers eat the bark."

The rest of that first year was devoted to sculpture, culminating in her first one-woman show at the Dresdnere Gallery in Toronto. "When I saw all those people, all of them coming in to look at my work, I felt as if I were standing there naked." Still, as a pleasant end to the year, she sold an eagle. "Twelve hundred dollars," Frances said happily. "Less Simon Dresdnere's four-hundred-dollar commission." A pleasant year end indeed. Even after Dresdnere's commission, eight hundred in 1972 dollars represented a month's salary for most people.

In mid-summer of 1973, on her Crosshill farm, Frances became aware that instead of admiring her sunflowers, she was noticing their absence. Groundhogs were eating them. They were also dispatching her poppies. "Why do I put the accent on sunflowers and poppies?" she asked herself in dismay. "The only things the groundhogs don't eat are the steers and the stones in the field. If it was a vegetable, they ate it."

Before the end of summer, her garden, in which she had taken such pride, was reduced to nothing.

"It was an excavation!" she cried. "My garden was wiped out. It became a groundhog burrow. I'd laid out the garden on an old barn foundation, maybe nine by twelve metres. I thought I had it fenced. Hah! Groundhogs, I was horrified to discover, can get through anything. They weren't coming from somewhere else to raid my garden; these guys weren't commuters, they were living right there in my garden. They'd found the Promised Land, and were waiting for me to plant something else."

One morning she saw a baby groundhog in the garden. "The next generation," said Frances, noting that there were fewer lettuce and parsnips than before.

Notwithstanding the groundhogs, to a great degree Frances was achieving her aim of becoming self-sufficient so far as vegetables were concerned. But it was hard work. In such a vegetable paradise, with Frances doing all the heavy lifting, the groundhogs were multiplying, and were unbelievably voracious.

The groundhog war extended beyond the vegetable garden. The groundhogs, joined by rabbits, attacked the very trees themselves. They liked the bark, at the trees' expense.

"The rabbits were so cute," Frances the animal lover said, though remembering, despite their cuteness, how they decimated her vegetable garden. "Still, they weren't all bad; they were competition for the groundhogs."

Competition? It's a bit difficult to follow the logic in that.

She couldn't bring herself to shoot them, but that was resolved later with the advent of her dog, Mindemoya (meaning "old woman"). Mindy's mother was a malamute, her father a German shepherd/wolf cross. Shortly after her arrival, Mindy mounted a relentless crusade against the groundhogs. But Mindy did not appear until the summer of 1975; Frances fought bravely on, alone, for two years. Then Mindy took over.

In the spring of 1973, Frances was still involved in a low key, but nonetheless bitter struggle with the township over the status of her lane. This roadway ran a distance of perhaps eight hundred metres from her tent to her gate on the road which led to the village of Crosshill. Frances wanted the lane to be private, but the township was afraid they would still be obliged to maintain it. Incredibly, but in standard bureaucratic fashion, this had seemed to have been resolved when Frances got permission to build. But politicians, like Hamlet, "know not 'seems,' madam," and are strangers to any agreement that seems, or even is, simple. Months of backing and filling, of committees, forms, amendments, and endless consultations appear obligatory — even to break for coffee.

"The document that was finally drawn up by my lawyer stated that it was my road, no one else could use it." She sighed. "But people did — and I had to maintain it. I had to clear it myself in the winter, until I got rich enough to pay someone to do it for me. Snow drifts were sometimes over two metres high."

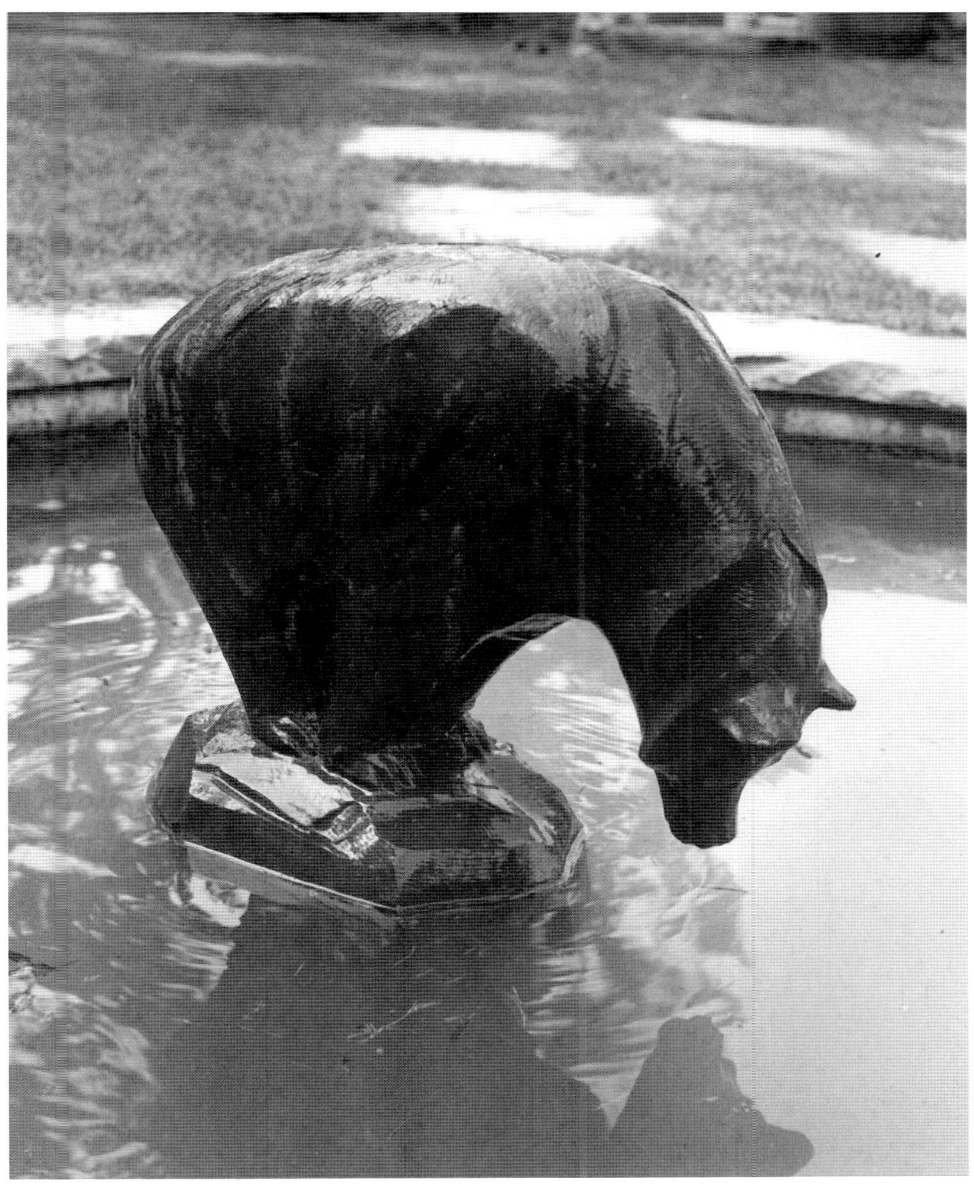

Narcissus, 1970. They gave it to Frances's friend. "We put it in her pool, where we knew someone would love it."

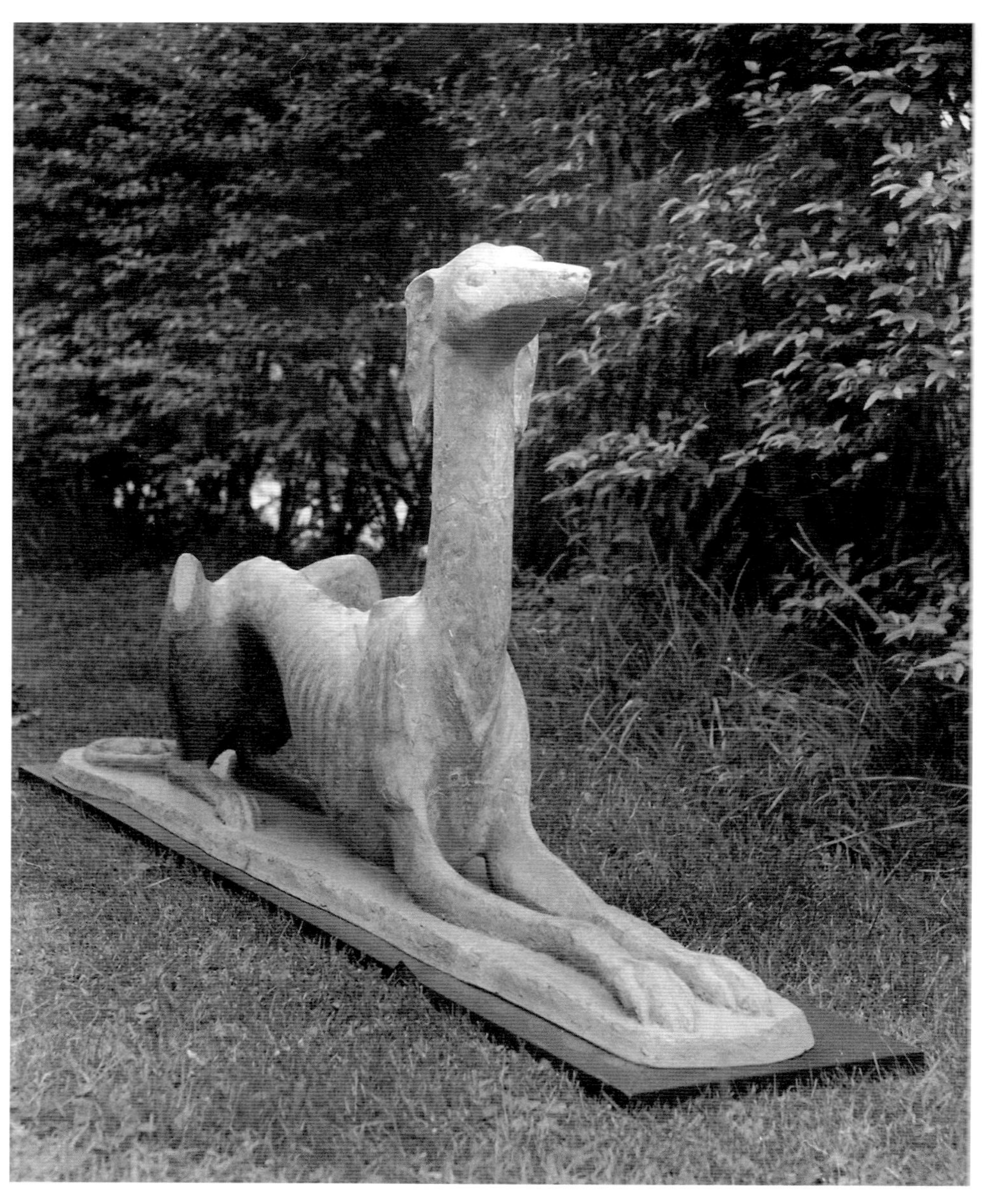

Saluki, 1963.

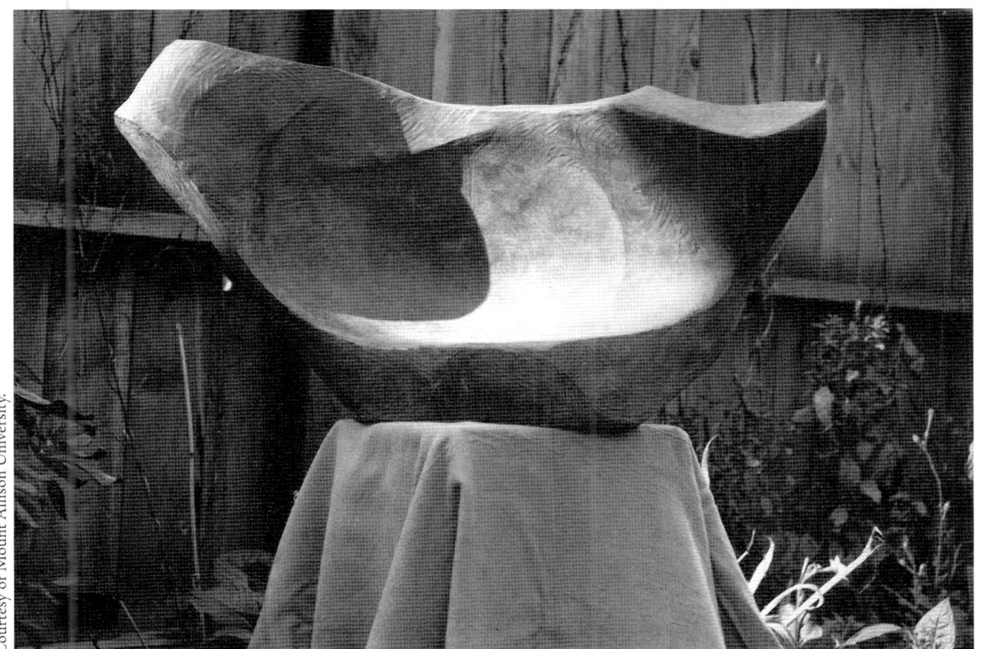

Song 'n the Wind, 1968.

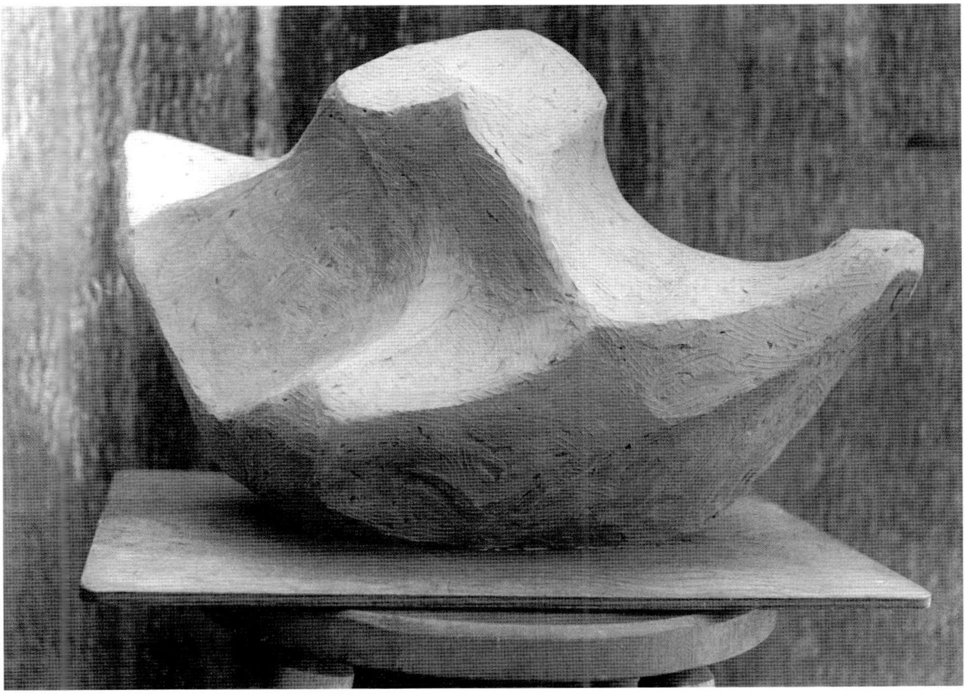

Ship of Earth, 1968.

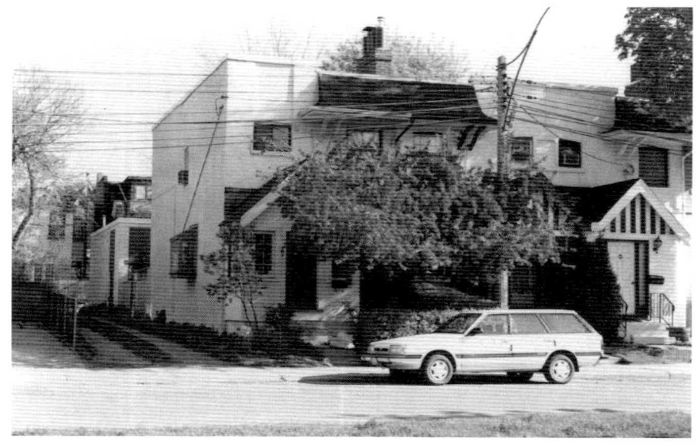

Sixty Birch Avenue, *circa* 1968.

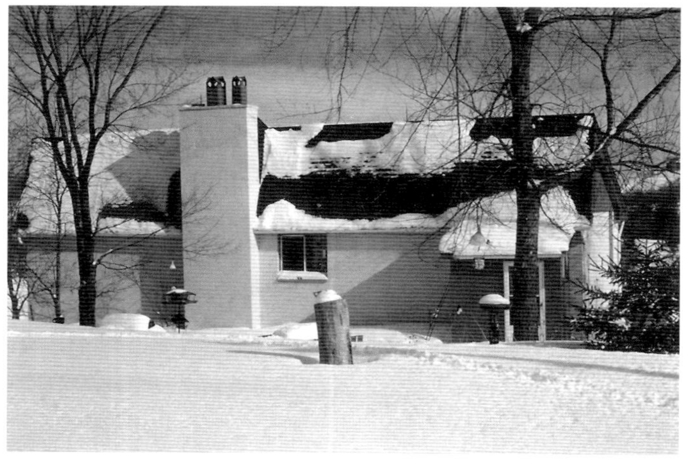

Frances Gage's house, Crosshill, *circa* 1978. "After five years in a tent."

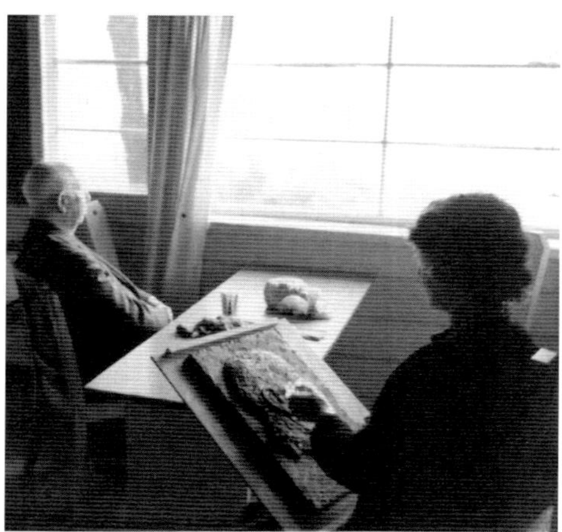

Frances Gage and A.Y. Jackson, Guild Inn, 1967.

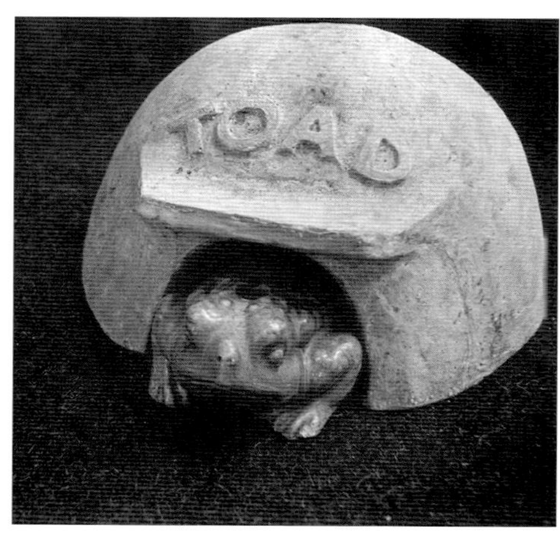

Toad House, 1978.

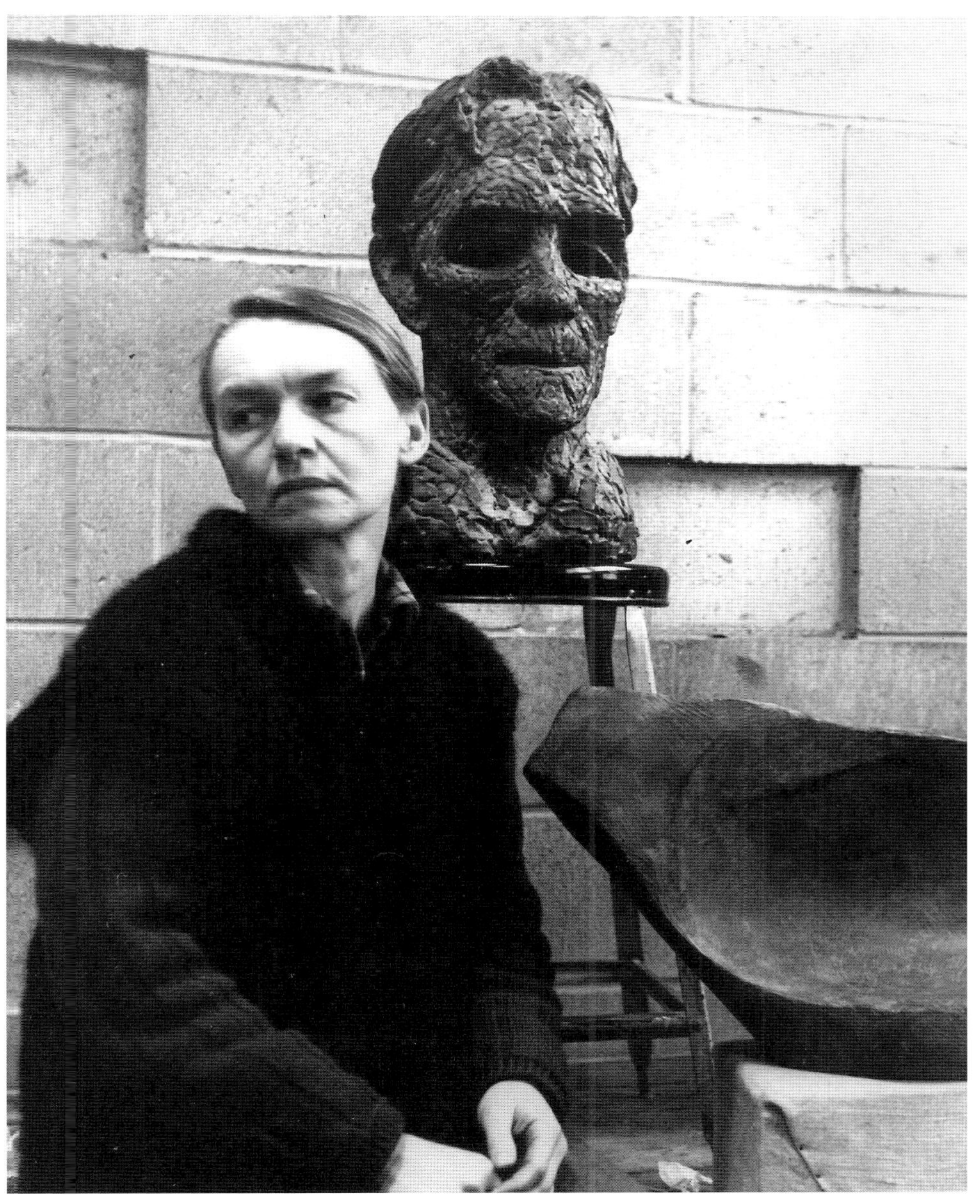

Frances Gage and Frederick Varley, 1967.

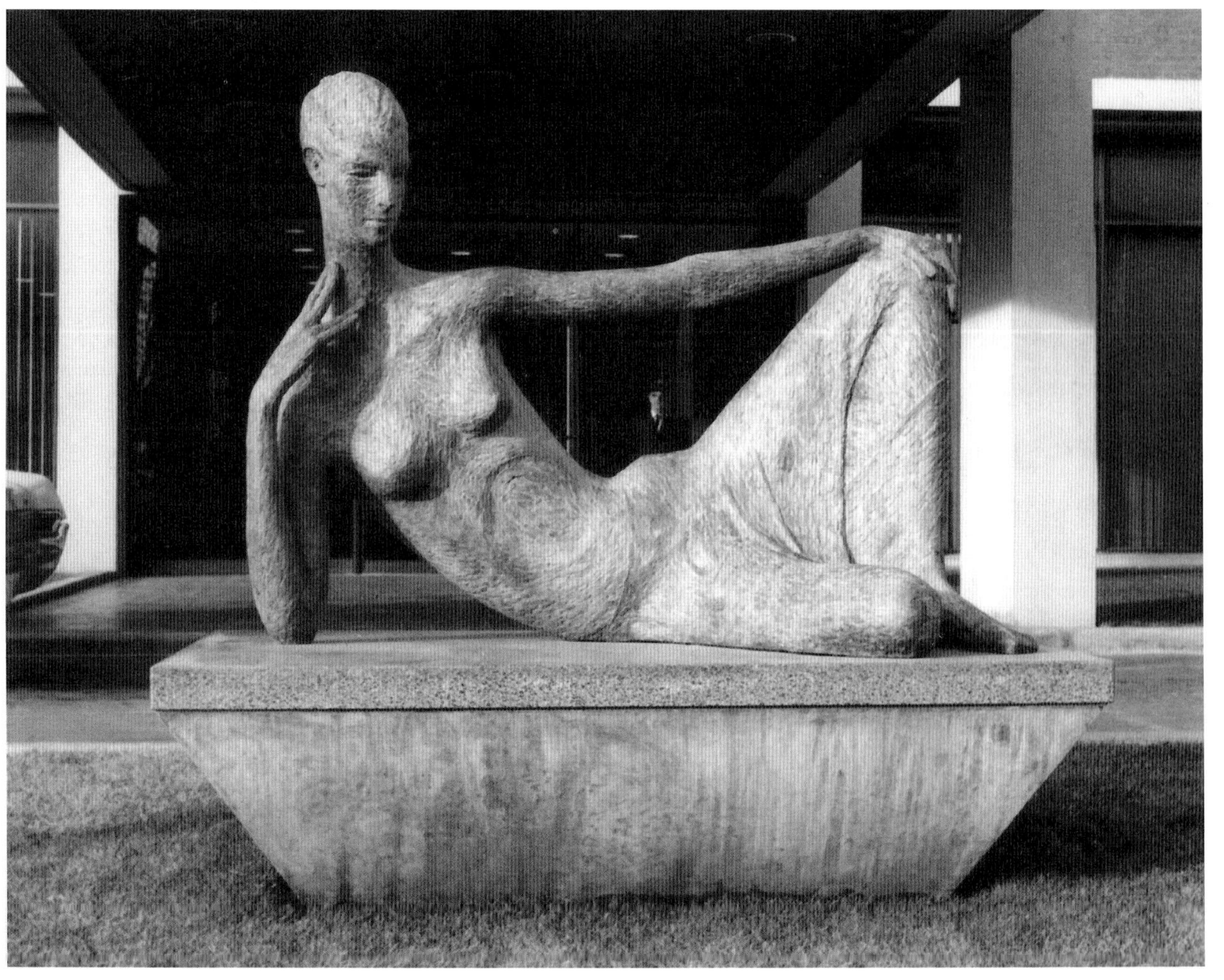

Rosamond, 1968.

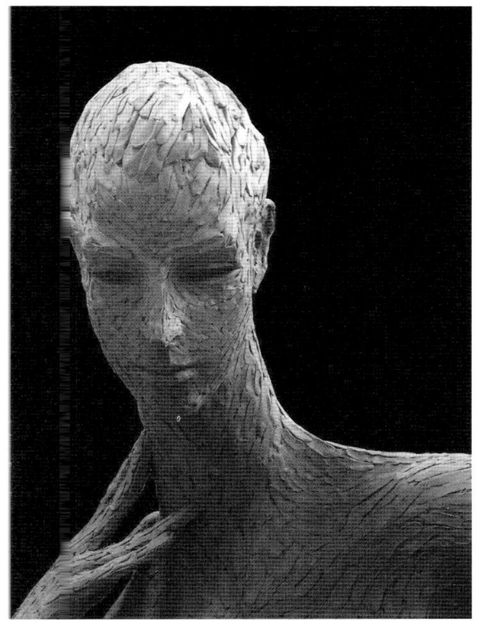

Rosamond (detail), 1968.

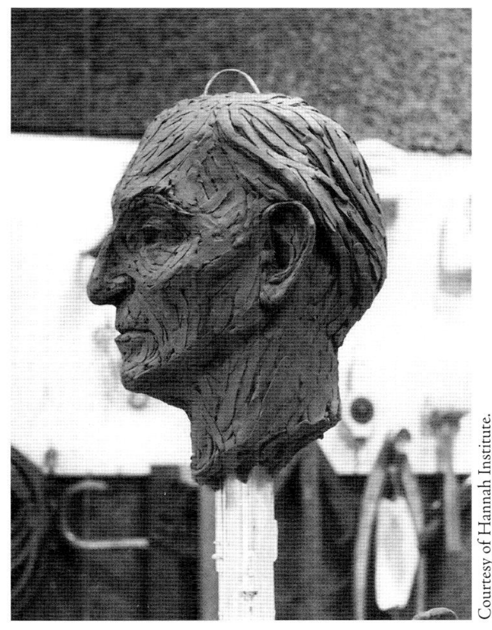

Dr. Jason Hannah, 1976.

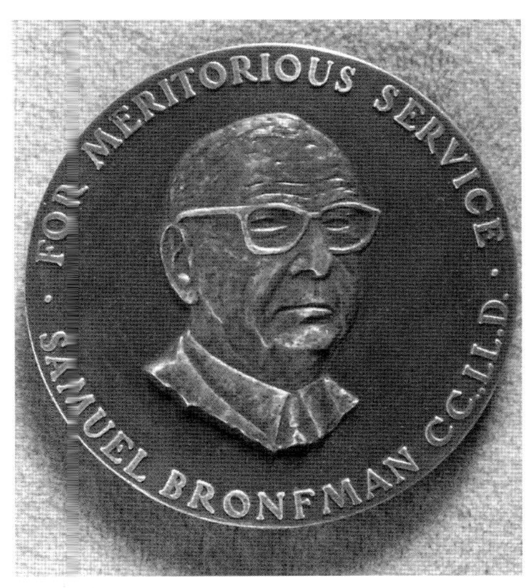

Bronfman medal, 1971.

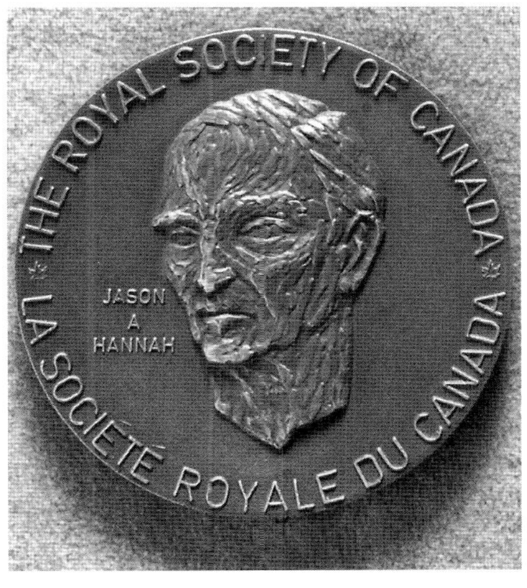

Hannah medal, 1977.

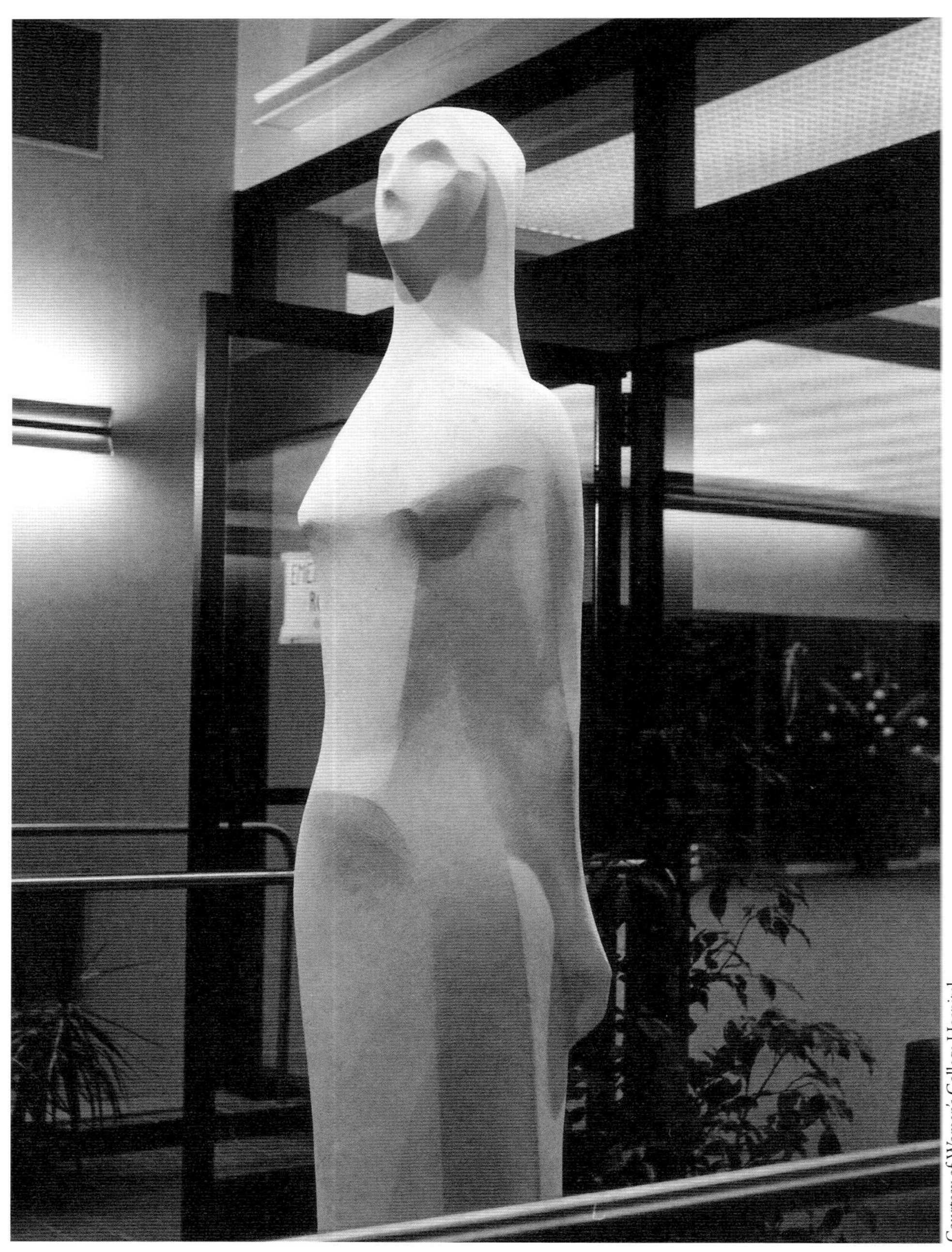

Woman, 1971.

Courtesy of Women's College Hospital.

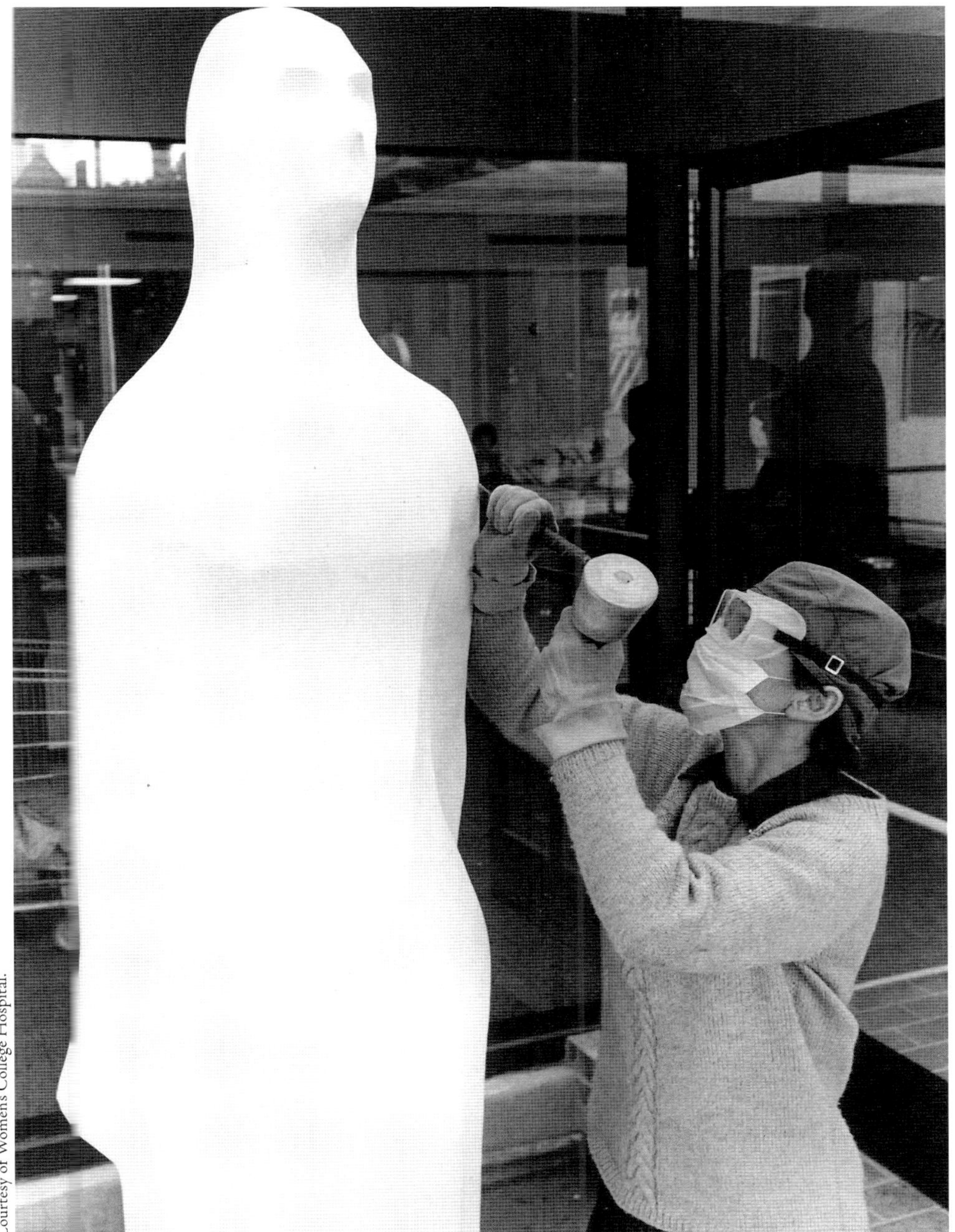

Woman, 1971. "The dust of the marble was like talcum powder, so I wore a mask, and goggles, and my navy hat cover from my days as a Wren."

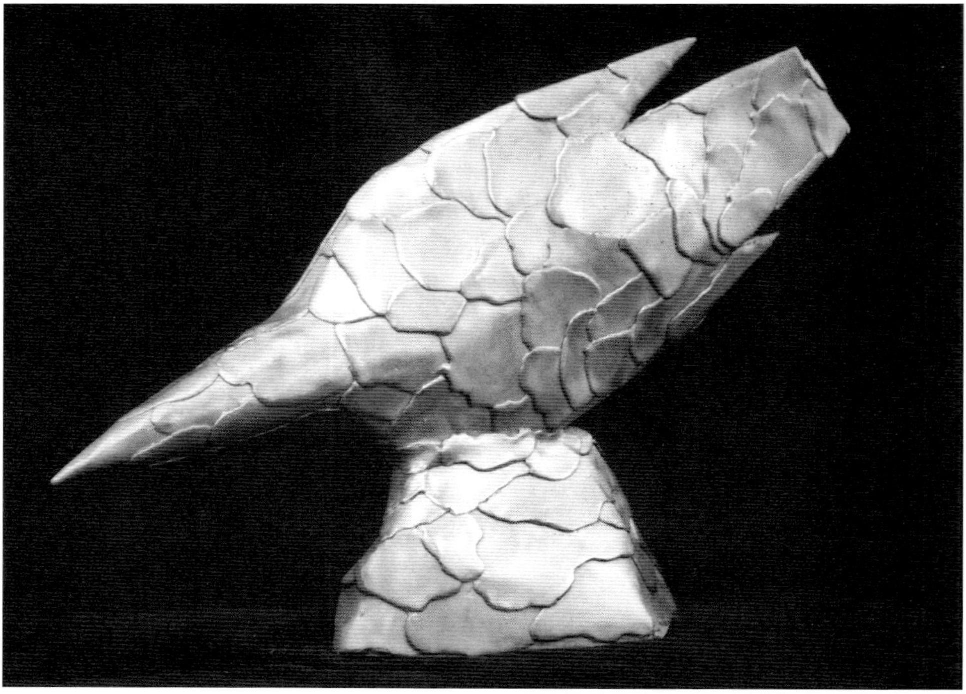

Diving Bird, circa 1980.

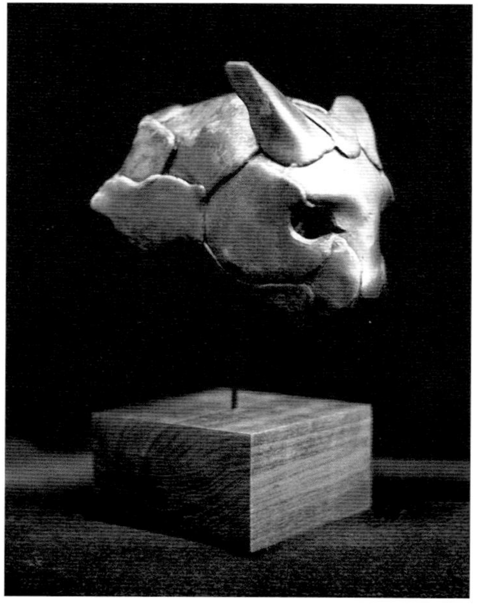

Cat's Head, 1968.

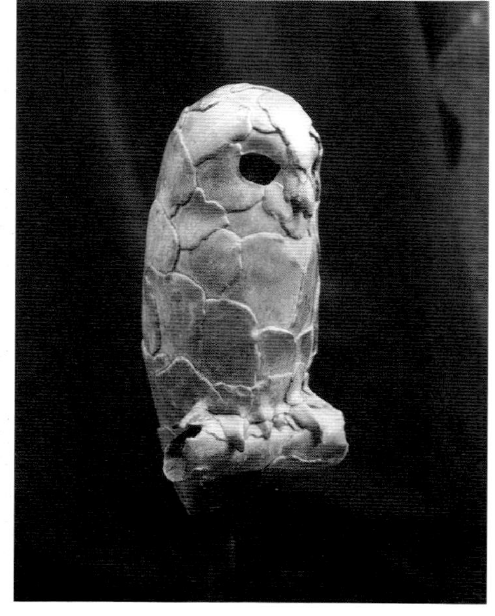

Owl, circa 1971.

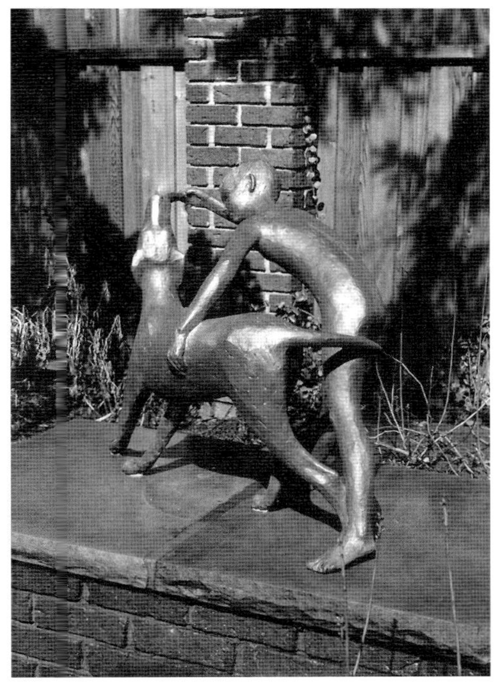

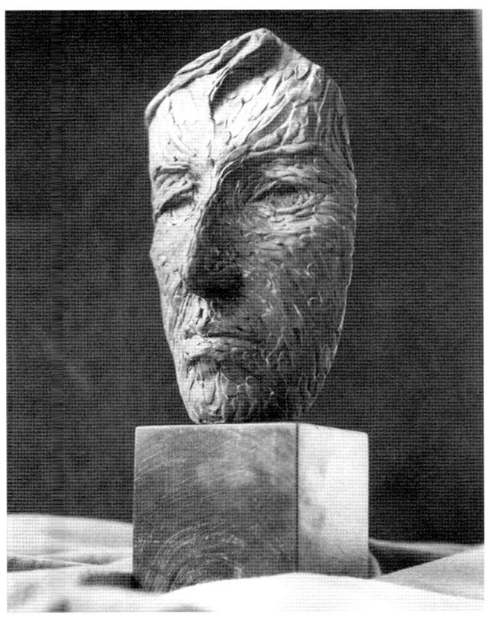

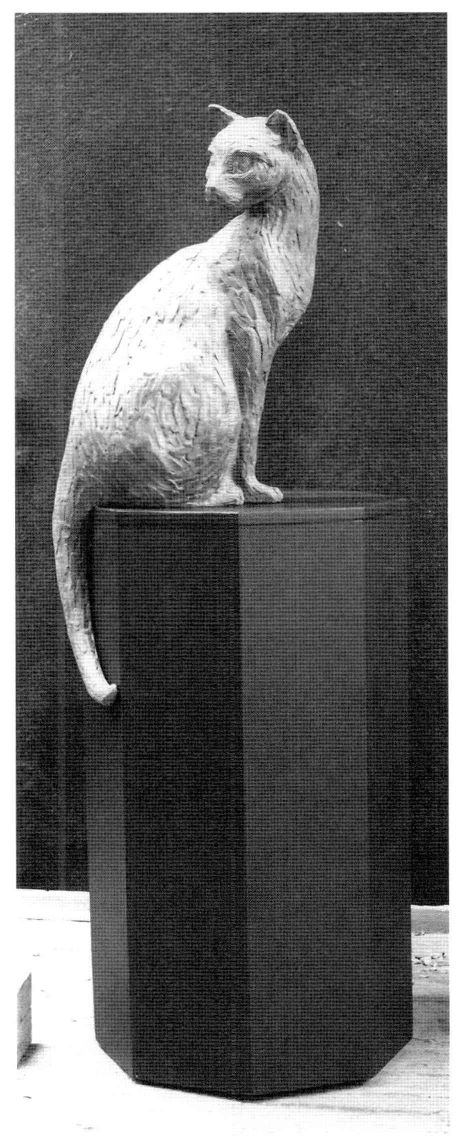

Top left: *Boy and Dog*, 1969.

Bottom left: Frances Gage's mother, 1968.

Right: *Kaspar*, 1973. The wild cat.

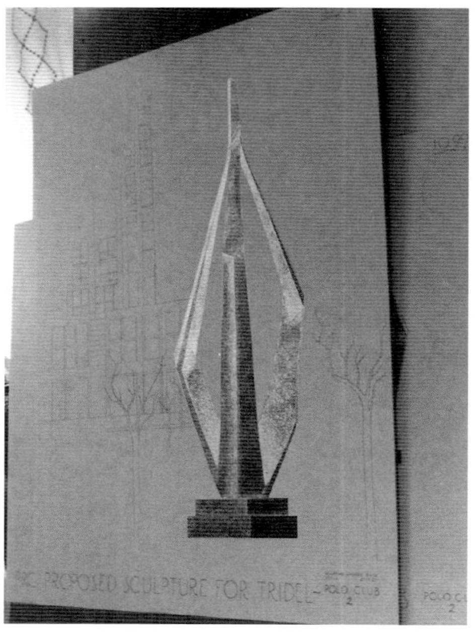

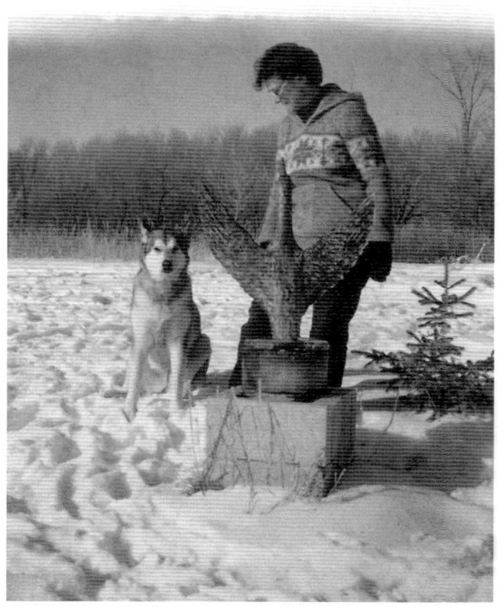

Tridel proposal, 1985. "A very nice piece, best thing I ever did, and the architect thought it was super, but Tridel shot me down."

Frances, Mindy, and *Loon*. Crosshill, *circa* 1980.

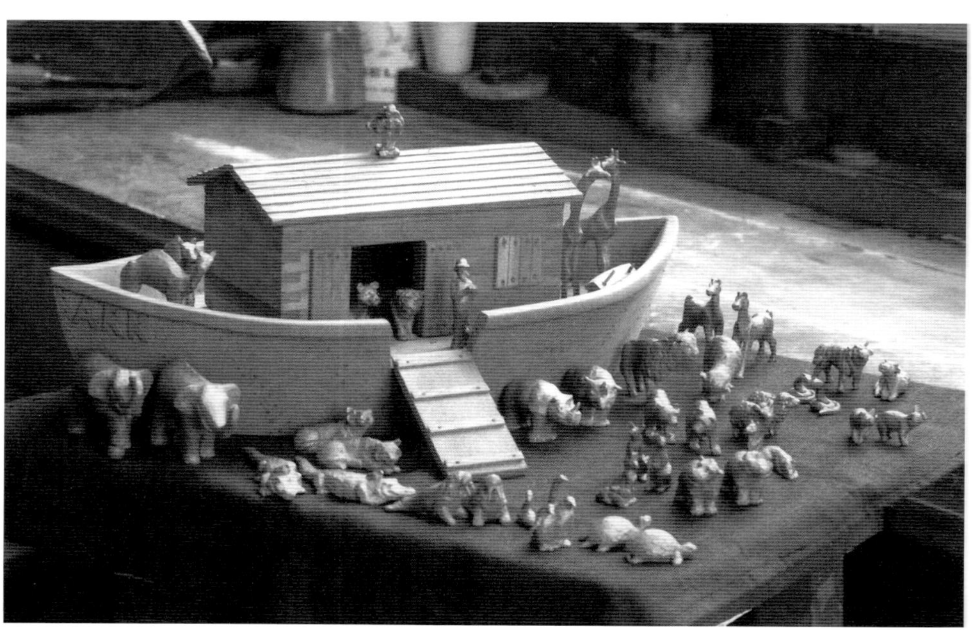

Noah's Ark, circa 1981.

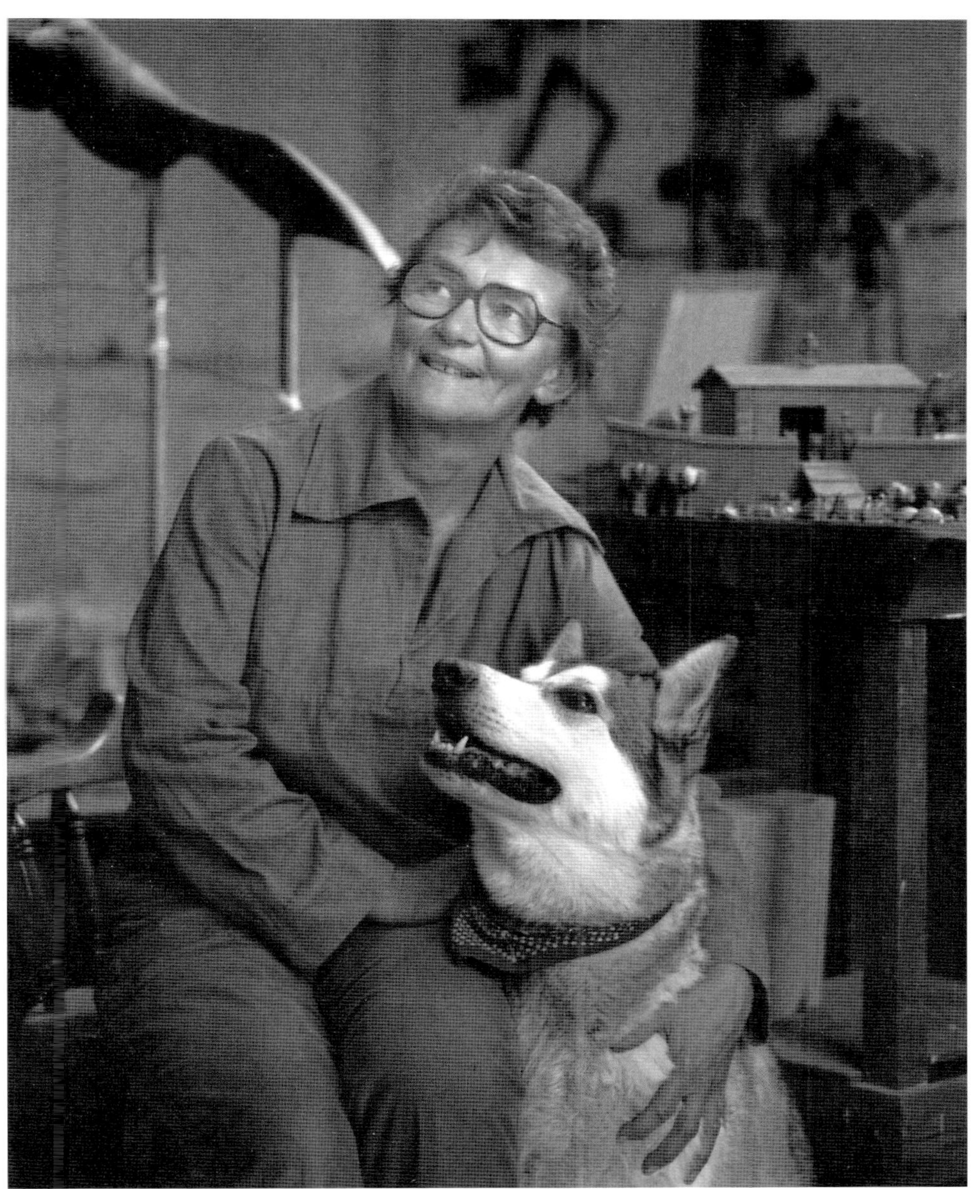

Frances Gage, *circa* 1985.

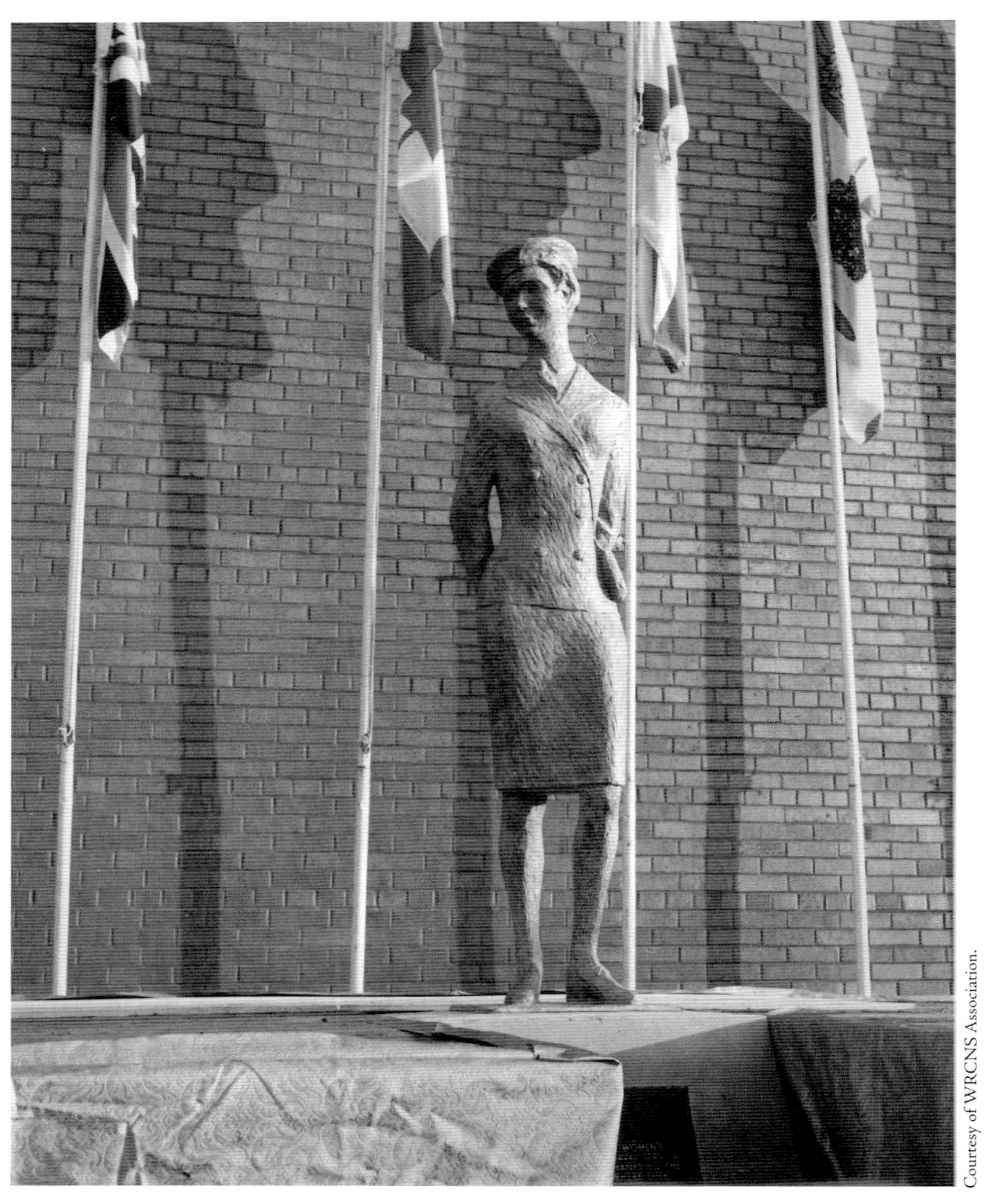

Jenny, 1972.

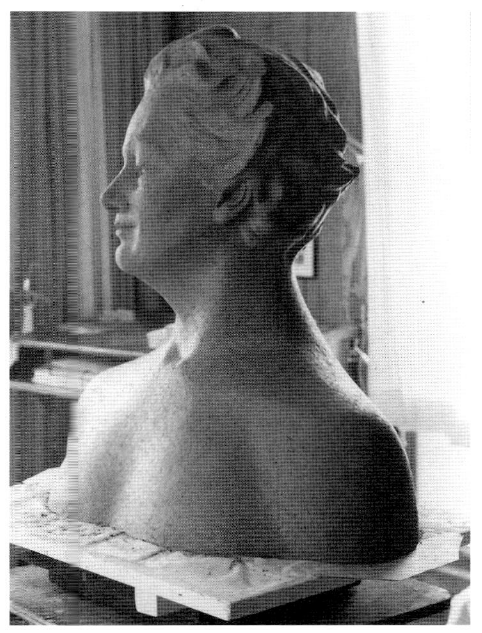

Senator Nancy Ruth, 1994.

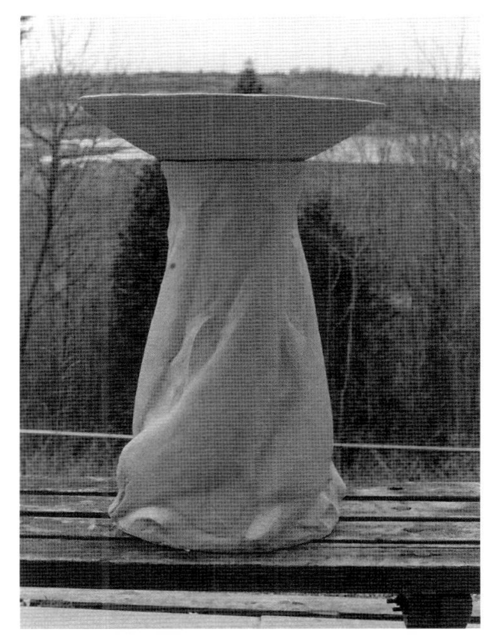

Dolphin fountain, 1995.

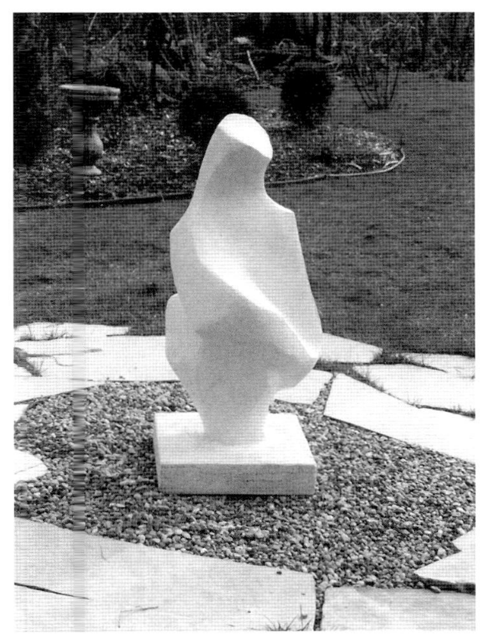

D'Artagnan, 2000.

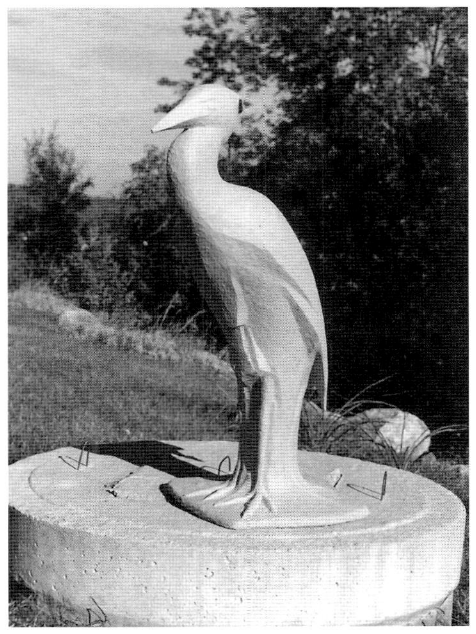

Heron, circa 1995.

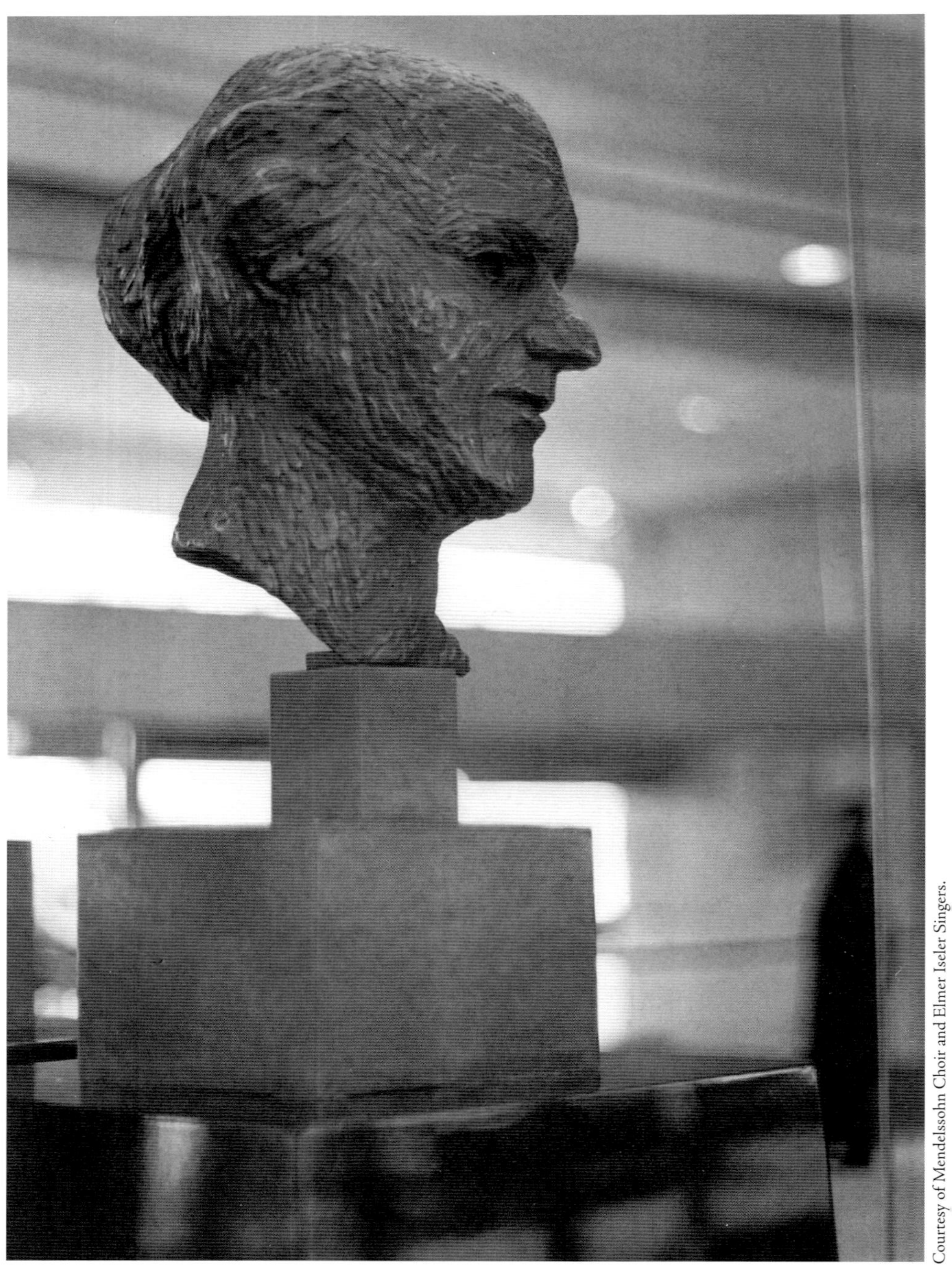

Elmer Iseler, circa 1989.

Now the lane, or road, was hers, officially. "On July 9, 1973, after what seemed like centuries of bureaucratic foot-dragging, I became legally liable for my Crosshill property, though I was still living in a tent." She put up a Private Road sign, as required by the township, and tackled the lane. "Road work," she groaned, "with wheelbarrow and shovel. Exhausted. Slept like a log, with some alcoholic help."

But a Private Road sign was an invitation to Attila. He tore it down. Frances put up another one, and he tore that down, too. Frances might have shrugged, muttered "Okay, I can take a hint," and done without the sign. But the township insisted that the lane be clearly marked as private, so that if anyone got hurt on it the township wouldn't be sued. Strange attitude. The lane and the surrounding twenty-five acres were legally Frances's property; if anyone got sued it would be her. But then, who can fathom the bureaucratic mind?

One evening in that summer of 1973, Frances talked to her friends about Attila. In contrast to Attila and his frightening activities, it was so quiet and peaceful sitting around the fire in front of her tent, steaks sizzling on the grill, the pleasant atmosphere marred by the subject of the conversation.

"Attila's destruction of my Private Road signs had annoyed the township," said Frances. "The signs were erected on their direct orders, and here was Attila tearing them down whenever he felt like it. It made the township look bad; it made them seem weak and ineffective. They should have charged him, but they were afraid of him. Everyone was afraid of him. I mean, this was a guy who opened fire on people!"

Not a pleasant topic of conversation on a summer evening. "Farther down the lane," said Frances, "I could see the police cruiser slowly driving by at dusk. 'Police at dusk.' Sounds romantic, if it weren't for that word *police*. But they kept checking on me."

In addition to the lane, there was the path that led through the woods to the Beans' property. "The path that continued from my house, or tent at this time, into the woods, that was the path that I walked a lot. And also the snowmobile club went through there. I allowed them to, thus, in a very real sense, they patrolled the path. For them, it was like paying the Mafia for protection. It was in their self-interest. If they didn't treat the path well, or gave me a hard time in any way, I would have put a big boulder right in the middle of the path. They got the message. I felt like Don Francesca, La Mafiosa, making them an offer they couldn't refuse."

Attila was bad enough, but to put it as charitably as possible, the problems he created were periodic; the difficulties Frances encountered in her lane were ongoing ones of hallucinating proportions. The lane was simply — if *simply* is quite the right word — eight hundred metres of dirt, covered lightly with gravel.

Heavy rains were always a disaster. "I barely got out of the lane in my car. You'd think if they expected me to maintain the lane, they would have provided me with a lane that was maintainable. I don't think they ever intended it to be a road of any kind. Until I came along. Then it was considered 'a road', and they had a resident maintainer — me — who was bound by law to look after it." She tossed a shovel into her wheelbarrow. "Roadwork," she grated through clenched teeth, and sloshed off down the lane.

Later she tried digging narrow trenches down each side of the lane, in child-like faith that the rain water would go that way, instead of just lying there in the middle of the road. In the end, the trenches just made it easier for the water to rush down to the middle of the road. And lie there.

At just about any given time you would meet (a) a determined Frances on her way to roadwork, or (b) an exhausted Frances returning from roadwork. Lane-wise, to be worry-free was a dream.

At these times, it must have passed through her mind how handy it would have been to be married, just for six months of the year; to have a convenient man to whom she could hand a shovel. "See you next week, when you're finished!"

Within two years of her arrival, Frances had reluctantly come to view Crosshill as a mixed blessing. There was the utter bliss of the fields, friends, animals, and birds; there were her gardens, and the long wonderful walks in the woods — these were indisputable joys. Yet, everywhere she looked in those early years, she saw problems: The attacks of Attila, the backbreaking roadwork on her lane, the groundhog damage, the winter storms.

As in any life, however, there were positive aspects, too. Frances was concerned over access to water; there was no municipal supply to the wilderness that was her property. There was, however, a local dentist who was known as a talented dowser who could find water anywhere. Frances called him, and he came out one day and found water in four areas. "Ultimately he decided where there should be a well, and we had it drilled. Right at the top of a hill. A new well close to an old one. They went down to a depth of twenty metres, and — *voilà!* — there was enough water for a good-sized town! Beautiful water!"

There was always the paradox posed by the Crosshill winter. For a season that brought so many difficulties for Frances, it's surprising that it charmed her so much. Two days before Christmas, 1973, she arrived at Crosshill. "Stuck briefly in lane, walked in, cold — temperature was zero — dinner alone, out to ski, late wind fantastic, drifts piling up." The next day she wrote: "Skiing, and a long, long walk — or wallow, really — snow thigh-deep. Had David and Fran Bean for dinner; gorgeous cold evening."

She paused, remembering. "It was … wonderful." And as night settled over the snow-covered hills of her land, there may have been tears on her cheeks.

During the early months of 1974, she devoted her time to sculpture; small works, uncommissioned, ones that appealed to her, often placing them in galleries and retail outlets. But when spring came, it was time to put aside all things artistic and get back to planting trees. Frances said — and it's right there in her diary; she must have been experiencing a gothic moment — "Planted oaks, and scythed the long grass in a thunderstorm, in the dark of the moon …"

Scythed? Thunderstorm? *In the dark of the moon?!* It sounds like something out of a second-class romance novel: There! You can see her! Frances atop the hill, swept by the driving rain, a black cape swirling around her, wielding the scythe, illuminated by the flashes of lightning in the stormy night, and all the neighbours' children hiding, trembling, beneath the bedclothes as the Phantom Sculptor Of Crosshill walks abroad in the dark of the moon …

In summer 1974, for one brief moment, "construction" began on Frances's house. Then abruptly stopped, because they were about to lay the foundation with the kitchen door facing south instead of north. "I don't like to think what would have happened if I hadn't been there at the time." Later, the foundations were poured correctly, and Frances celebrated her fiftieth birthday sitting on the cement next to her birthday cake.

In the final months of 1974 — two and a half years after her arrival at Crosshill, when she had stood in the middle of her new property and seen nothing but broad fields and trees — she still saw broad fields and trees, and not much else. Four months before, the foundations of her house had been poured. The walls and roof were up, but the wind blew through the empty interior. In September, Frances had received the windows, only to find they were the wrong size. "I mean, you have a certain opening in the wall," said Frances, as if explaining something to a small child, "you want to put a window in there, so you measure, the contractor orders them, the windows arrive … and they're the wrong size?"

In November the big north window had been boarded up. More exasperation for Frances, a condition which was rapidly becoming chronic. "The workers … *sheesh!* They all departed to go hunting, so they just boarded it up instead of putting the window in. The Mennonites go hunting in October, so everything else gets forgotten," recalled Frances. "I was pretty upset by that, because if the window had been in, the house would have been more winter-proof. But instead, it was just a piece of plywood board tacked over this big hole in the wall. And it was that way all winter."

Like a good environmentalist, she cut down trees, but planted them, too. "Planted three chestnuts, one was a year old, the other two were two years old. I brought them from Toronto. The squirrels kept planting them in my alley at Birch Avenue, so I took them out to the country."

At the end of a rewarding day on the land, she would gaze through her trees, across her vast estate, gaze to the west "until the sun fell below the yardarm," or between the branches of a pine tree, or whatever, then pour herself a liberal scotch. If she couldn't see the sun through the thick foliage, she would shrug, and mutter, "Oh, it must be below the yardarm by now," and have a double scotch anyway.

"In the winter it was a 'slotch'; I'd pour scotch into a glass filled with snow. Sort of a grown-up Slushy. They didn't sell *that* to the kids down at the 7-11."

Tree-planting, tree-cutting, and continual sculpting brought on a recurrence of her carpal tunnel syndrome. Frances shrugged, forcing herself to look upon it as an occupational hazard one had to accept, then get on with one's life.

In her Birch Avenue studio, while she was putting the finishing touches to a bronze figure, she said, "Now here's an interesting effect. Cat pee lends a wonderful patina to a bronze piece. You take the wet kitty litter, and pour hot water on it, and let it set for awhile. Then you spray the fluid onto a bronze, and you get a lovely blue-green. That's a new trade secret, so don't tell anyone."

The passing months saw Frances celebrating the planting of the final trees in the program organized by the Department of Natural Resources. It had begun the year before, with students doing the work. The number of trees planted on Frances's property was ten thousand pine, three thousand spruce, and five hundred black walnut. The students got little help from Frances, who was suffering what was by now a chronic bad back from shovelling gravel in her lane. She was barely able to make the trip to the hospital to visit her father who was prostrate with bladder cancer. Happily, he survived this ordeal, the operation was successful, and he was shortly thereafter released and returned home.

She was at Crosshill on Christmas Day for lunch, though the meal was marred by the usual winter irritations: (a) "After lunch I left Crosshill in a blizzard" and (b) "Goddamn snowmobiles all over my property." These were indiscriminate snowmobilers. Her Mafia-like agreement regarding her path was with a snowmobile club, a more considerate group.

In addition, from the very beginning there were the hunters. "Work on my trees was always a dangerous occupation during hunting season," said Frances. "There were hunters all around. They seem to think it's their right to shoot anywhere they want to in the world. I remember one time, I had taken my father's rifle, it was a .22, and I was lying on the ground outside my tent, shooting at a tin can that I had set on a fence post situated on my eastern property line. I was testing, to get the sights right — I'm a pretty good shot — and I looked over into my neighbour's property, and there was a hunter, standing as if crucified. He thought I was shooting at him! Maybe I was, subconsciously. After that, I think the word must have got around: That crazy old lady's a crack shot! They're probably still telling tall tales in a bar somewhere in Pittsburgh, or maybe Minnesota: 'Hey George, did I ever tell you about that maniac up in Ontario, Canada? Man, lemme tell ya, that's dangerous country. I mean, there I am, minding my own business, bagging a couple of deer, when suddenly this old bat opens up with an assault rifle, AK-47 it was, three hundred rounds a minute. I'll show you the hole in my jacket. Flesh wound. Lucky I survived,' he'd probably say, and let someone order him a double scotch."

The past year had seen some sales of sculpture: The big one was the garden piece for the Heintzmans (4,500 dollars), which eventually was donated to the Mount Pleasant Cemetery sculpture garden. A slow year by past standards, but improved by the bliss she found daily in her Crosshill paradise.

From the top of her hill she paused and looked out over her acres. "A snowy start, but a heavenly day. Pruned apple trees!" she exclaimed with delight, as if given a precious gift. "Wonderful to have the time outdoors."

And the rest of the gorgeous day stretched ahead of her. "Went for a three-hour walk. When I went for a walk in my woods, I'd look at the birds. If the red-tails (hawks) were nesting, they'd follow me, screaming, until I got out of the way. There were so many wonderful birds. And wild flowers, and wild garlic. Just a beautiful stretch of bush. This was along the path that eventually led to the Beans. About a kilometre; nice walk, ending with a huge hill, whichever way. Up or down a big hill at the Beans' end and the same at my end. Lots of exercise. Not much fun in wet or snowy weather, but I was well-equipped, well-dressed."

And then a nice supper. "Ordered Chinese food from the Chinese restaurant in St. Clements, a town about eight to ten kilometres east of Crosshill."

The next day, she was back in the woods. Her woods. "Walked all day among my trees."

In late summer one year, Frances sat down and did some figuring. "By my calculations, my dog Mindemoya has slain around a hundred and eight groundhogs, certainly over a hundred. And those were the ones I counted. Mindy probably left a lot somewhere else."

Frances was mesmerized by Mindy's world-class ability to dispatch groundhogs. "It's been one a day, average, over a five-month period. Every time I buried one I dug the hole for the next one. The garden was mostly sand so it was easy. When Mindy caught one she would circle around the yard, proudly showing me what she'd done. Then I hid behind a bush and watched where she buried it. Later, I would go and dig it up and bury it where I wanted them buried. Some of them were so big I had to go and get a wheelbarrow. Sometimes they ran to three or four kilos, maybe fifty centimetres long. I got a recipe for cooking them, but I just couldn't do it. They have glands under their forearms and glands around the tail, and you'd have to cut those out, and you'd have to skin them, and, *ecch*...."

Defending her garden was difficult enough, but trying to guard the trees against the groundhogs was simply naïve. There were just too many trees. And too many groundhogs.

"Once, in late winter I got up at 5:00 a.m. in Toronto to go to Crosshill and install tree guards." Frances had bought thousands of them. They were plastic with holes in them to let the air through. "By the time I left Birch Avenue it was minus twenty-five degrees Celsius. There was a blizzard all morning; by noon it was thirty-three below zero. Worst blizzard I'd ever seen." She was not likely to forget what conditions were like at Crosshill. "We had winds on my hill. I mean, thirty-three below zero, and a howling snowstorm blowing parallel to the ground. It was pointless to try putting on tree guards. Even the groundhogs stayed home."

Some years later the groundhog problem became a thing of the past with the coming of the coyotes. "It just seemed that one year the coyotes appeared, and the next year they left. No fanfare; just quietly arrived, cleaned up the groundhogs, then just as silently departed. Nature has her own way of handling things. When it came to dispatching ground-hogs, Mindy was pretty efficient, but the coyotes were professionals."

Throughout the early years, and the unavoidable emphasis on mundane Crosshill activities — building, planting, roadwork, and the numberless municipal considerations to be addressed — Frances's sculpting was forced into almost a secondary role. She had worked on a number of sculptures — the garden piece for the Heintzmans for example — and there were a few smaller, relatively minor pieces produced, but her output was considerably less than previous years. Rarely was she heard to remark on the progress of this or that project; more often it was "lovely walk in my woods," or "tended my garden," or "so beautiful on my hill at dusk," or "saw a deer outside my window." All uttered in a tone suffused with joy. And so often the association was personal, possessive, proprietary: My woods, my garden, my hill. Her life revolved more and more around the satisfaction of daily tasks, rather than artistic pursuits.

She was becoming more a farmer, and less a sculptor.

Frances's references to the pleasure she gained from the walks in her woods always carried a profound delight in ownership. It was never just her woods; it was always *her* woods," "*my* woods," with the subtle inflections in her voice always there. These references, coloured by the delicate change of tone in the words, appeared like some operatic leitmotiv in every remark regarding her Crosshill property.

But as pleasant as these walks were, she couldn't walk everywhere. She was conducting sculpture classes in Guelph, forty-odd kilometres to the east, and wood carving classes at her Birch Avenue studio in Toronto, over 150 kilometres away. A car was mandatory.

"Early March, and a fantastic storm was building. I drove down to the road at 7:00 a.m. The road was often impassable during and after a storm. I had to get the car out while I could. Coming back, if the storm was as bad as it usually was, I'd leave the car at a friend's place in the village, and walk in to my lane and home. I kept snowshoes in my car at all times!"

After a violent storm she would join her neighbour David Bean in the lane, cutting up the trees that had fallen; otherwise they couldn't get the cars through.

Winter on the freeway to Toronto was not much fun either. "A couple of days before Christmas," Frances recalled, "I was on the freeway, and had a flat tire. Very interesting situation. Subzero temperatures, cars and trucks zipping by at 130 kilometres per hour about five centimetres away from my door handle. When I got out to change the tire — fortunately I was wearing a man's long underwear, the ones with the trapdoor in back — the wind from a truck going by blew my door right up against the fender. Bang went the hinges. I had a rope in the car, so I pulled the door closed as much as I could, attached the handle of the door to the passenger seat, and limped into Guelph to the car dealer, where they shut it for me. 'Come back tomorrow,' they said, 'and we'll see if we can fix the hinges.'" — *See if we can?* she thought. *What happens if you can't? Do I have to buy a new car?* — "Years later, some smart politician got the law changed so you weren't allowed to change a tire on the freeway. Probably saved a lot of lives; I know more than one person who was hit by a car while changing a tire on the freeway. But after the law came into effect, you had to get a tow truck. Whichever way you turn, a car costs money. The only escape is to leave the car at home and walk. On the freeway, if you didn't have the money for a tow, your alternative was flappity-flappity-flap along the hundred-kilometre-per-hour lane to the nearest exit ramp, and hope that at the end of that ramp there was a repair shop."

While Frances was living dangerously on the freeway, others were at risk, too. The medical facilities were busy as always. In March, two months before his eightieth birthday, Frances's father was back in hospital again, this time for a prostate operation.

At the same time, Frances's long-time friend Edith Williams, the vet, was admitted to St. Johns Hospital in north Toronto, a rehab centre. The problem was an ongoing one, and alcohol-related.

"Edith had those bouts for most of her adult life," said Frances. "She moved to Burlington Crescent where she could walk back and forth to her clinic on St. Clair Avenue. She would come home and have a glass of skim milk with gin in it. Very sad."

But Edith Williams was not alone.

Alcoholism was no stranger to Frances's family. Father, brother, sister — all were familiar with beverage alcohol to a detrimental degree. And not to put too fine a point on it, Frances herself was becoming a fair hand at social drinking. Though perhaps the term "social," implying group drinking, is not quite correct; her life was both rural and artistic, and both tended to be solitary pursuits.

"I was very much a lone drinker," she said. "But I never drove my car when I was drunk. I got blotto when I got home."

She frequently visited her sister Barbara, who lived in Grand Bend, a small town on Lake Huron about sixty kilometres northeast of Sarnia. "Drinking with Barbara," said Frances. "It's only around forty minutes by car from Crosshill. We were drinking buddies."

Sometimes the results were disastrous. Returning one afternoon from Grand Bend, Frances was involved in an accident. "I smashed my car coming from Stratford. The car wasn't a total write-off, but close. Barbara and I had been drinking all night. Most of my problems came when I was hung over, rather than when I was drunk, because I never drove when I was drunk. This time, I was coming out onto the highway and didn't look well enough, and I was bashed by a taxi. No one was injured, just the car."

On top of all that local alcoholic brouhaha, her sister, too, was involved in her share of automobile accidents. "Barbara hit the deputy reeve with her car while she was impaired. Just a little bump. She was really mad about it. He, too, understandably, was furious. So he charged her."

As usual, Frances found her sister's problems depressing, which in turn frustrated her, affected her work, and the frustration became anger, which had a further negative influence on her sculpture. "Why should I be so irritated?" she exclaimed. "It's not my fault! Almost all of Barbara's difficulties were self-inflicted."

These incidents, or accidents, all alcohol-related, seemed to occur more frequently. Her father occasionally came to visit; he loved Crosshill. By the time he left it was always a "lost evening." Her sister Barbara phoned often, almost always in the middle of drinking, to rant about one thing or another. These calls left Frances deeply depressed. Terrible thoughts filled her mind: "Happened like that all the time. Black thoughts … that I was no good, that my work was not worth anything, or the work wasn't going well. That sort of thing. Terrible, terrible depression."

In this, as in many of her frequent periods of depression she banished the bleakness the old-fashioned way: Work. "Put tree guards on five hundred walnut trees, and shovelled manure for Fran Bean. There was simply too much for Fran alone."

By the end of 1976, Frances's house was virtually complete in its basic structure — five tent-years after she had first arrived in Crosshill — but it still lacked some fundamental utilities. "In December, though there was a terrible storm, I still drove into Kitchener to the Beans' home. Kitchener was the Big City, relatively speaking, and I could shop for things I couldn't get in the village of Crosshill. I'd also have dinner with Fran and David, and do my laundry, and have a bath. Yes, a bath; I was still living in my tent in the summer, and on a cot in the Beans' living room in winter. My house wasn't finished — at least, it didn't have any plumbing in it. In the summertime, I used to put a child's wading pool out behind the studio. In the sun, the water would get nice and lukewarm, and I'd have a bath."

By year's end, while her house was indeed on the threshold of being livable, there was still much to be done.

"Ceiling men," said Frances. "That's all they were doing, installing the ceiling, and it took five days."

Then, finally, she was able to say: "Ceiling done!" But one might ask: When does anything to do with house-building ever go smoothly? The ceiling had hardly been completed when it started to rain. Solid rain for four straight days; no break at all. The north wall of Frances's house was soaked. "It was just cement block. It hadn't even been sealed!" The water just came right through, aided by the incredible Crosshill winds that could penetrate steel plate. Frances was familiar with the Crosshill winds. "My tent would half-collapse sometimes, but it was a big tent and I was usually able to save it." ("Usually" is another way of saying "not always," and it makes an interesting picture: A fifty-two-year-old woman, alone, trying to save a large six-person tent from collapsing in hurricane-force winds!)

The fall of that same year, 1976, as with all autumns, saw hunters on Frances's property. "They seem to think they can go anywhere they want." Well, they certainly felt at home on Frances's land. "There were four of them. Four goons with guns and dogs. Dumb hunters. I had to put them off."

But despite the threat of hunters, she still managed to spend time in sculpting: a baby in Kew Gardens in Toronto for the Historical Board; a loon for an anniversary celebration at Tannamakoon, the summer camp where she had been an instructor for so many years; and a head of Dr. Jason Hannah.

"Dr. Hannah started the first prepaid medical plan in the country," explained Frances. "When the Ontario Hospital Insurance Plan (OHIP) took over, he donated money for five (university) chairs in the history of medicine. ("The first Hannah Chair was established at the University of Western Ontario in 1974. Chairs were subsequently instituted at Queen's University in 1975, the University of Toronto in 1976, and McMaster University and the University of Ottawa in 1977." — Associated Medical Services)

"He commissioned me to do a head of him," said Frances. She produced five copies, one for each of the universities. "I also did a medal, because they wanted a medal to be presented each year; the heads went to the various universities. It was a nice job, and I loved him. He was wonderful. He was very ill; I helped him on with his coat once, and he said 'Don't ever do that!' He was quite an independent chap. I went to his house a few times. Beside me on the car seat, I would have the head I was working on, and I'd drive with one hand on the wheel and the other hand on top of the head. I didn't get arrested."

January 1977 brought with it the inevitable blizzards, and now that she had moved into her house, there were difficulties with oil deliveries. The oil truck would get halfway up her lane, then with a shrug have to back out, unable to get through the snow drifts, and Frances would be obliged to have the lane snowblown, to the tune of forty dollars, then schedule another oil delivery, and hope it came before another blizzard brought a replay of the same old game.

But there were the supremely satisfying in-between times: "Super day! Skiing in the morning, right there on my own property, then sleeping in the afternoon, and skiing before dinner. Lovely evening!" But it was still January: "On the twenty-eighth, a blizzard struck just before lunch. Worst one yet." Still, the next day when she looked out —"A fuzzy sun this morning" — there was a contented tone to her voice, a tone of profound pleasure: "My valley below the house is filled with snow!"

But mid-March saw her standing up to her knees in water, gazing despondently at her lane and the cheerless sight of a full "eight hundred damned metres of flooded roadway, and every metre looked like one of those old-fashioned miles we used to measure by a couple of years ago. Two lakes," she said, "with islands, right in the lane! The two lakes were five or six metres wide, and the 'islands' were hills of mud sticking up, each about three metres in diameter."

The lane was bad news for a bad back. But that wasn't enough. She occasionally slept downstairs in the bunk beds used by guests. "In the upper bunk. It gave me a better view out the window. One night I had a nightmare that made me leap out of bed and land on the concrete floor. As I say, I slept in the upper bunk because it was more scenic. And yes, easier to injure myself falling out of." So she was away to the hospital the following morning at eight-thirty. "Compressed fracture; lumbar," said Frances, the medical expert of Crosshill.

From a medical point of view, Frances's isolation at Crosshill might have struck many as inconvenient at best, even potentially life-threatening. This never seemed to cross Frances's mind. Not through bravery or a conscious gamble; she simply didn't think about it, and might have been surprised if you had mentioned it.

Yet there were repeated reminders of what could happen, to such a degree that Frances over the years became fairly knowledgeable in matters of pathology. Name it, and she'd had it, or was currently suffering from it, or would certainly contract it shortly.

In the summer of 1977, her carpal tunnel affliction resurfaced. Ten years before, her physician had diagnosed the condition, but at that time Frances had been deeply involved with the sculpture *Woman* for Women's College Hospital in Toronto, one of the most exciting and satisfying works of her life, and she had not been prepared to even consider hospitalization and surgery, due to the time it would take from her work. But now, a decade later, the condition had passed beyond a question of choice. "Sometimes," she said, "I would wake up and both hands would be numb." On the twenty-ninth of August, she underwent four hours of bi-lateral carpal tunnel surgery.

For the next few days she was without the use of her hands. A neighbour's son took her shopping, and the same neighbour dressed the affected limbs. Weeks of physiotherapy followed, weeks Frances spent muttering about "nothing getting done." Whether this referred to sculpture or farm chores is hard to say. On a farm there are always things to do, and she was doing them, but was not putting her hand to much in the way of sculpture.

Toward the end of December, Dr. Edith Williams was placed in a nursing home. "She'd had a stroke," said Frances, "and she always had such a terrible temper and wouldn't do any physio, so her right side was paralyzed. She could have improved, but she wouldn't."

But the year ended on an upbeat note for Frances. Friends arrived for a skiing party. "So exciting to know I can actually ski on my own property! Wonderful hills!" Even the presence of unauthorized snowmobiles cavorting on those same hills couldn't dampen her delight. "Though deep down I wanted to open fire and take no prisoners," she muttered darkly.

During these times Frances was still able to produce a number of small sculptures. She made these items, in editions of anywhere from six to fifty, for sale in retail outlets across Ontario and Quebec. She would sometimes cast smaller versions of an element of a larger work, and market them. In the summer of 1976 she had twenty-five copies of a loon made. The loon was part of a larger memorial. Many artists did this. Rodin sold copies of arms, legs, and heads that were part of bigger, more complex works; the author Pierre Berton, among others, did the same thing with much of his literary output.

Despite the backbreaking freight that winter brought, Frances was continually enchanted by a winter day, a snowy vista, the tracks of an animal, the song of a bird.

She looked from her window with delight. "Thin ice over deep snow." The sight would lift her spirits. "I was on top of a hill, an esker, over this wonderful valley where I went every winter on my snowshoes. There was about two metres of snow down there in the winter. I went there every winter morning and pulled up dead pieces of wood for my kindling." Every morning, in her diary, she would note the arrival of the sun, as if it were a living, welcoming presence. "I loved the sun's coming, its moving, over the days."

Slowly the sun would rise to gleam through the thousands of trees planted earlier by the Department of Natural Resources. "At their own expense — well, my taxes, I suppose; yours, too! Thanks a lot! — they'd planted thousands of trees on my property, and it only cost me pennies per tree, for something like ten thousand trees. It was a very good deal." Years later, she would cull the older growth, and send it to a nearby mill.

Spring brought the pleasures of a bright and productive vegetable garden, to the extent the groundhogs permitted. With the season came a gift of a pair of mallard ducks from a friendly vet. Frances, influenced by her love of classical music, named the ducks Tristan und Isolde (without a word of apology to Wagner). She built a pen for the pregnant Isolde, with a large tin pond for her to swim in. "Isolde had twelve ducklings, and they were exquisite, you never saw anything so lovely as a newly-hatched mallard. Once, I filled the tin pond in the duck pen too high, and I got there just in time to see one of the ducklings going down Mindy's throat, and another one of the ducklings was missing. Mindy just ate them. Get the feathers the right way, and down they went."

There was a brief and welcome period in early 1977 that saw no activity from Attila, Frances's neighbour. Sadly, it was a period that ended in summer.

"Road block," recalled Frances. "Big boulders that blocked my road. Incredibly, there seemed no way to stop him. The police had to catch him doing these things. If they had seen him do it, then I could have taken some kind of action, testified or something, but then again I didn't know if I wanted to. I might have got shot! I knew that anything I did would have to be conclusive enough to put him away, otherwise I wouldn't have been able to sleep at night.

"The police were doing the best they could," she continued, "but they couldn't just live there twenty-four hours a day. Sometimes I'd wake in the middle of the night and see a police car going around the lane."

The police presence was reassuring to a degree, but the fact that they couldn't be there all the time made the reassurance a fragile and almost pointless thing. The relatively empty rural setting gave Attila a free hand.

By this time the repeated harassment was beginning to seriously affect her work and her sleep. "You felt so helpless, you know? He was insane — and his wife looked like something out of a Käthe Kollwitz drawing." (Käthe Kollwitz was an early-twentieth-century German artist, whose black-and-white drawings depicted stark, depressing, poverty-stricken working-class people.)

One day Frances returned to her house in Crosshill and found her road blocked by trees, half a dozen large trunks piled across the roadway.

"What could I do? The detectives were still trying to catch him at it. At one point," she said, "he took a gun to the people who were putting up my hydro line, but they were Mennonites, and they wouldn't complain. They wouldn't testify."

And then, at last, two police officers arrived from Elmira. "They had finally caught him," she said. "A young man he didn't like had been standing outside Attila's house on the highway. The young fellow had been chatting with his girlfriend, and Attila went and held him up with a gun. The cops charged him this time. They didn't give him any sentence or anything, as they should have. Anyway, it certainly stopped him. At least he didn't give me any more problems."

By the end of the summer, Frances was asking herself, *Can I manage Crosshill?* Some might have asked, justifiably, "What took you so long to come to that conclusion?" She watched, powerless, as two days of rain washed out her road. Again. It was flooded to a depth of more than half a metre. The problem was that the lane was a couple of metres lower in the middle than it was at either end. "There was nothing I could do but wait for the water to go down." She spent the day working in the ditch, and eventually reached the point of complete exhaustion. She staggered back through the dark and rain, and dropped, aching and resigned, into bed.

"When the heavy rains came — continuous, monotonously continuous — they just washed out the road," said Frances. "There was nothing I could do, but I had to do it anyway; I couldn't just stand there, looking at it. At those times I seemed to spend every waking hour working on the road, ceaselessly, senselessly. Those were the times I would ask myself: Have I bitten off more than I can chew? And I was afraid of the answer."

Meanwhile, back at the farm, it was work. And then more work. "Picked stones in the fields," said Frances. "It's true. Stones. Every year the stones would come up from the effects of the frost, so you had to pick them out of the field, otherwise all the machinery would get ruined. It was a yearly job, both at the Burkharts and the Beans, and pretty backbreaking, too. You had to pick them all up and put them on a stoneboat, then dump them someplace. Every year. Anything up to a couple of kilos you could pick up easily; anything bigger … well, you'd pick up those, too, somehow."

The same frost came back again, almost maliciously relentless — in the middle of June(!). "I mean, June, for Heaven's sake! Think of the effect on the plants!" cried Frances. "Unless you can go out and spray the leaves before the sun comes out, they die. But if you can spritz all the plants, they can survive. My Mennonite neighbour Angeline

Martin came out with that idea. But it has to be done before the sun comes out, otherwise the combination of the sun and the frost kills the plant."

Stones and plants were serious problems, but other problems, though equally serious, had an air of the absurd about them; major difficulties which, when finally resolved, left her laughing. Take steers for example.

"Once, or rather once more," said Frances, "I ended up chasing a steer. What could you do? They were escaping, and we all had to get together and catch them and herd them back to the barn. They were just running down the road. They seemed to have a lovely time when they got out, but I imagine they must have been scared to death, with all the cars and the people running after them, and all the shouting. It happened frequently. A steer would lean up against a fence. They were heavy animals, and … crash! … the fence would collapse, and the steer would trot off down the road. The animal didn't seem to remember what happened the last time it got loose. Each time was a revelation: 'Hey, I'm free! Let's see what's down this road'. When there was only one escapee it was all right; it wasn't hard to round up one guy. But usually every one went. They'd all follow the one that got out. Maybe forty or fifty of them. But mostly they stayed together as a herd, so you could generally gather them all up together."

Early 1979 marked the beginning of what was a unique project for Frances: *Noah's Ark*. It was a singularly complex work. From the initial idea to its completion it spanned over two years.

The idea, and countless sketches, began in February, and continued sporadically until almost the end of 1980. It was during the first months, while in Georgian Bay with the Beans, that she started working on the animals.

Genesis tells us that "Pairs of animals … came to Noah and entered the ark …" From Frances's hand they also came two by two, though for understandable reasons, not in quite the same volume and variety. Frances took a representative sampling of twenty-five animals

— alligators, bears, bison, camels, cats, cows, doves, elephants, geese, giraffes, hippos, horses, lions, monkeys, penguins, pigs, rabbits, rhinos, serpents, sheep, tigers, tortoises, wallabies, walrus, and wolves — and produced twenty-four sculpted pairs (the alligators and doves were done as one carved pair, each alligator with a dove on its back).

"Unlike Noah, it took me a couple of years," said Frances. "I've always been fascinated by Noah's ark, and how they all got in there. Well, you know, they didn't, but anyway … and I love animals. I started with the biggest one and one of the smallest ones — the elephant and the snake. The alligators have the doves on their back because the doves were too small, they would have been lost.

"It was very hard on the eyes," she said. "Many animals were only an inch and a half. It took about two days for the elephant. From the mould, each animal had to be touched up. I had to get the mould marks smoothed off, get rid of the rough edges. I'd make one, then for the second one, I'd just change it slightly, and I'd have two animals, each a bit different. But I couldn't do that with the lions, because I had to take the mane off one of them."

Eddy Martin, a cabinetmaker, made the wooden ark for Frances. "I didn't make any of the arks; I just designed it, and made the animals. Martin produced an edition of five wooden arks. The late Dr. Howard Shanks did a ceramic ark. He was a woodcarving student in one of my classes.

"I sent art brochures to various people, hoping to sell. It was advertising, and I just used the mails. One perseveres. The price of the ark, including the dozens of animals, was seven thousand dollars. It was worth the cost of the mailings. The mails didn't cost much in those days."

By February 1983, in preparation for the project's first public showing, she had assembled one of the completed arks, with all its animals — and Noah himself, notebook in hand as he checked off the animals, two by two. On the nineteenth of February it was displayed at the Alice Peck Gallery in Oakville, Ontario. (Twenty-four years later the final ark and its animals were donated by Frances to the Metro Toronto Zoo.)

On a summer evening, after a day working on the ark, she walked in her woods, brushing away the mosquitoes, and thinking: "If Noah had been blessed with common sense, when the two mosquitoes came to the ark, he would have swatted them!"

At the same time that Frances was working on the ark's animals, she was developing, for her own satisfaction, a flying red-tailed hawk in walnut. This was during one of the periodic flurries of sculpting she engaged in over this year. The hawk was almost complete by August, and she had begun a pigeon for David Bean's secretary, Helga Slavic, whose husband, a racing pigeon fancier, had died. Helga wanted a pigeon for his memorial (Frances's price: seven hundred dollars). "In earlier years, the Beans had sponsored Helga so that she could come to Canada. She became David's secretary, and was his secretary for a long time. Years later, when he was in a nursing home, she was there. She was very faithful to him. Lovely woman."

Frances got a frightening phone call in September, when the Wisnewskis of 50 Prince Arthur Avenue got through to her to report that someone had poured paint on the *Rosamond* sculpture. "I was at Crosshill," said a horrified Frances, "so I went tearing in to Toronto. Fortunately it was just a milkshake, so they could wash it off. If it had been paint, the sculpture would have been ruined. They watch it pretty carefully. There's a bus stop right there, and people seem to like and admire the sculpture."

"Phone's not working," said Frances. It had happened before, with potentially serious effects on her work. "It was a private company, certainly the last private telephone company in the country, I would say. It eventually closed, and Bell took over while I was living in Crosshill. While it was a private company it was awful, because a lot of calls just didn't get through. It was still operating in May 1978. I remember at one point a lady tried to phone me about a project I was doing for her, and she couldn't get through. I don't know what the extent of its service was. I think it was probably just Wellesley Township or something," she said. "How about calling it Crosshill-TelGlobal, with a snappy advertising slogan like 'Today Wellesley Township; Tomorrow, the world!'"

During the summer of 1978, Frances was still devoting some of her time to sculpting, producing a number of small works — a cougar in cherrywood for example, and a portrait of a neighbour's daughter. "I was also casting some toad houses. Toads like shady dark places. I made these toad houses in cement and gave them away. Toads would know it was a toad house because I put the word *Toad* over the door. I never got a toad in my toad house, but other people discovered them in theirs. The toad houses were about thirty-five centimetres round by twenty centimetres high."

There was also a major commission: A portrait of Dr. Gordon Nik-kiforuk, dean of Dentistry at the University of Toronto. This project was particularly gratifying, not only because of the pleasure she gained from the work, but also the six thousand dollars that was added to her bank account.

Frequently, if Frances was not sculpting, she was teaching or talking about sculpture. In October she gave a lecture to 150 attendees at the Elora Mill, for which she was paid 120 dollars (when you're an artist, every little bit helps). "Actually, at one point I almost bought the Elora Mill," said Frances. "I could have got it for fifteen thousand dollars, but I thought I wouldn't have been able to stand the rushing water all the time. Very noisy below the mill."

November 23, 1979, was a sad day for Frances. Dr. Edith Williams died. Frances's friendship with Edith went back to the earliest days of Frances's career, when she worked part-time in Dr. Williams's animal clinic while attending the Ontario College of Art.

On May 22, 1980, Frances's father was once more admitted into hospital; it was still the bladder problem. But this was to be the last time. On the twenty-ninth he suffered a massive stroke, and died on the thirty-first.

Two days before, Frances had taken some asparagus to her father. "But he was his mean old self. He loved asparagus. But not this time, apparently." She sighed painfully. "I tried so hard."

At this time of ultimate loss — both mother and father now dead — Frances's spirit was lower than ever before. But with her father's passing, her depression was touched by an old anger. She had tried so hard, so often, but had failed repeatedly to penetrate his lifetime of selfish indifference, and even at this terrible final moment, it generated once more a bitter resentment.

The end of 1979 brought a welcome gain. On December 11, Frances signed a contract for thinning the trees on her property, a gratifying contract that generated ten thousand dollars in income. The contract was with the Hawkesville sawmill. "They bought the trees through the Department of Natural Resources, but they paid me," Frances explained.

The winter storms that caused so much trouble for Frances indirectly brought a benefit for her sculpture classes. During a blizzard, a great blue heron passed over Frances's property, but not quite high enough. "It killed itself flying into the hydro pole in the storm. I retrieved the bird, took the head, and boiled it with baking soda. It was very beautiful. I already had the skeleton of a fox, and a groundhog, and somebody's cat. I used them for anatomy in my art classes."

The snowstorm that provided her with the heron's skull exacted a heavy price in discomfort and inconvenience. "Horrendous blizzard, hurricane winds! Coming back from Guelph, I managed to get my car into the driveway of John's place, a nursery eight kilometres east of my home. With Mindy, I snowshoed on toward Crosshill and got as far as the Beans' farm. They had tried to get out to feed the steers, but had to give up." Frances stayed over at the Beans' farm, frankly afraid to push on to her home. The following morning a neighbour took her back to her car on his snowmobile (she refrained from ranting about snowmobiles), and she was able, somehow, to drive the car home. It was eighteen degrees below zero Celsius. "When we got inside, Mindy flatly refused to leave the house, which shows what a smart dog she was. Outside, I was literally blown off my feet. It was called the worst blizzard of the century. Winds of over 150 kilometres per hour." She was luckier than many; she only lost a few shingles from her roof.

In preparation for spring, Frances built an "apartment house," and painted it white. It was four feet tall, and was hung from the branch of a nearby tree. "All sorts of apartments," she said, laughing. "A high-rise apartment building for birds." When spring came, so did the tree swallows, to move happily into their nice new apartments.

Their lease was short. For perhaps a week there was a lot of grim territorial activity around Frances's "apartment block." Tree swallows versus starlings. "The starlings were trying to take over from the tree swallows. I went rushing out, banging pie plates to scare them off, but I finally gave up. And the starlings took over the apartments."

Spring brought the starlings, but winter wasn't finished with Frances, and on June 11, frost struck. "In mid-June! I lost two-thirds of my tomatoes, and all the peppers. Lost the rest of the tomatoes the next day. I was seriously thinking of a greenhouse."

The next day was spent gardening, trying to salvage something from the frost disaster. But the following morning brought more frost.

"The hose was frozen, vegetables all gone. Greenhouse would have been great. But (sigh), too little, too late."

In the early part of 1980, Frances was working on the sculpture for the Charles Lake Gundy memorial. During this period she also created memorial works for her own mother and father, a shamrock for Mother, an elm tree for Father.

Charles Gundy was chairman (1967–78) of Wood Gundy, the stock brokerage firm established in 1905 by his father James and his partner George H. Wood. "I saw Mr. Timney at Mount Pleasant

Cemetery," said Frances, "about the arrangements for the installation of the Charles Lake Gundy memorial at the end of this year. The memorial has a loon, a salmon, a Canada goose, and an African assegai — a spear — because those were symbols of his areas of interest. The memorial is at the entrance to the cemetery, right near the office." Frances frowned, an expression touched with sadness. "December 29 was the date of the actual installation of the Gundy memorial. As the artist, I went there. But when I arrived, I found I was alone! Nobody there, nobody came. And yet, somebody had been there, because on the bare plinth there was a single rose. Someone, I didn't know who, had a thought for him. It was so … so inexpressibly sad. The feeling I got was that the wife — she and Gundy were divorced — ordered the memorial, then everybody appeared to just … well, wash their hands of the whole affair."

In the latter part of 1980, Frances celebrated the admittedly qualified success of one of her oldest friends. The Prince Arthur Gallery in Toronto produced a show of Barbara Howard's paintings. "It was a wonderful show, a sellout. She then had a second show, and raised her prices so high that nothing was sold. She was very upset about that."

Crosshill welcomed the fall with the annual hunting problems. Frances saw the hunters as a group designation. We refer to a pride of lions, or a gaggle of geese; Frances endured an exasperation of hunters. "They actually took off my gate for ease of access to my property. Naturally they did not replace it; I had to put it back on myself."

December elbowed its way over the countryside, and one of the first things it did was drop a metre of snow in Frances's lane, effectively blocking it. The township came to her rescue, in a manner of speaking, and scraped the roadway. "Then they sent me a bill. But of course! It was my lane, wasn't it!" she said sweetly, the sweetness barely hiding the angry woman underneath. An anger, in addition, that was not made any sweeter by the waves of snowmobilers who found her property so entertaining, a property clearly posted as private. "Damned snowmobilers," she said, then sighed. "But what can I do about it? Other than open fire."

The twenty-first of December is the winter solstice, and Frances was to celebrate this date for many years. Friends would come, each bearing a candle. Her entire house would be illuminated by candles alone. She would serve up a couple of her justifiably famous award-winning squashes, stuffed with good things, and after everyone had eaten, they might all go out and spend the winter evening carolling. This year, however, was not quite the same. "Carolling lousy," said Frances. "Too cold. Many did not come. But five ladies made it, in the blizzard!"

Yet, for Frances, the year ended well. "Went skiing all over my wonderful, wonderful property!"

On Christmas Eve the following year, Frances did go carolling, together with her neighbours the Whites — father, mother, two children, and Frances. They serenaded the rest of the neighbours. "I don't think the neighbours appreciated it," Frances admitted, "but we tried. I think we were pretty good, too. But at minus twenty-two degrees Celsius, with a wild wind … yes, it was cold. In almost gale-force winds, we walked into the village and sang. And then we walked back home again, bent double against the strong gusts. With neighbours maybe three hundred metres apart, and impassable roads, we arrived home, and fell through the door, exhausted beyond measure. We had done it, and despite the negative response, we, at least, were happy, and wished each other a very merry Christmas! Dickens would have approved, and Scrooge too, and certainly Tiny Tim."

When Christmas Day dawned, however — eight years after she had gained Crosshill, her Paradise — there came over her a wave of depression, and with it the frightening question: Had Paradise become Inferno in disguise?

The joys, the aching happiness, the utter bliss of Crosshill faded with the realization that she was willingly turning her back on her career, on the very life she had begun so many years ago at the Ontario

College of Art, and on the sculptures that provided such satisfaction and a profound depth of meaning to her life.

"I was surrounded by Crosshill, wonderful Crosshill, but I knew I was ruining my life, because I enjoyed the farm too much. I recognized that one of the problems was, truly, Crosshill itself: I was too involved with all the beauty, the rewarding activity, the fields, my friends, animals, birds, the long wonderful walks in the woods, my gardens … instead of working, sculpting. I knew it was also the drinking. So many, so many days lost to alcohol."

She knew, in that sudden yuletide vision, that she would have to change, drastically, fully, and immediately.

But, ah, yes … mice and men, and sculptors, too, and their poor wee plans, as Burns might have said. The subtle temptations of Crosshill effortlessly worked their magic, and when the sun "fell below the yardarm," a double scotch helped. The glorious Crosshill days stretched out before her, and empty resolutions faded with the wondrous dawn.

But the problems remained.

In the spring of 1981, Frances took her sister Barbara on a short holiday to New York City. Barbara had never been there. "I had studied there, so I played the tour guide," said Frances. "We stayed at a hotel right on Central Park, and we saw the opera, and some of the galleries. It was just so nice. For some reason we avoided drinking, which was a miracle. Yet, strangely, Barbara was very sad when we got back."

A few days after their return, Barbara phoned. "She sounded forlorn," said Frances, and felt sad herself. "Lots of depression, and we had such a fine time in New York, too."

It was a depressing spring indeed. On May 29, 1981, Frances's brother's only son, William, was killed in a car accident.

The year was also a bad one for the Beans, Frances's neighbours. "In the fall, Fran Bean learned she had cancer," said Frances, "and she had to have a kidney removed and the bladder, because they were both infected. And that was the beginning of a long and awful story. To see her vitality slowly ebbing, falling daily deeper into her affliction, was unbearable. We had been neighbours, friends, and now, to be a power-less witness, was heartrending."

But in all this bleakness, there must surely have been a heartwarming spark, and there was.

Frances's niece Mary (daughter of sister Barbara) and Simone LeBrun operated a school for handicapped children. "This was a private school," said Frances, "operated by these two ladies, not the government. It was at 41 Roehampton Avenue, east of Yonge Street, one north of Eglinton."

The school is called "Kohai," meaning "junior" in Japanese; senior is "senpai." The relationship between senpai and kohai is one of big brother and little brother, with the implied growth. The senpai's responsibility is to guide and teach the kohai, who will, with time, become the senpai of a future kohai. Each, thus, has a great obligation to those who precede and follow them.

"The teachers take children — autistic, Down syndrome, spastic, and others considered hopeless — and put them back in the workforce. I taught these kids for three years. And I'd get burned out." She slumped in her chair and shook her head. "You know? Those teachers have the children for eight hours a day, often more. And me? I get burned out after half a day a week! I remember one child … I think I spent one whole day teaching her how to hold a chisel."

In mid-May, as the result of a voluntary attempt to stop drinking, she reported happily: "Fifteen days no drinking!"

If this sounds like an old familiar song — same old tune, just different lyrics — you're right. Drinkers who try to stop by themselves have been singing that song since time began. It never works. Frances's happy fifteen drinkless days slid sadly into "… five lost nights. Yep (sigh), there go all those days of no drinking."

Secondary effects appeared. She found frequently that an evening without alcohol left her sleepless. The next day she would be drinking again, and sleep that night. And the deadly cycle would begin again.

Notwithstanding the effects of alcohol, Frances was still producing sculpture. A bronze cat, life-size, 2,400 dollars, went to Debora Johnston, owner of the Now and Then studio in Toronto, where Frances did a number of memorable works in earlier days.

The year 1982 began as Crosshill years always began — blizzards, and temperatures that dropped off the graph. On January 10, it was twenty-seven degrees below zero Celsius, with gales, snow, and whiteouts that made a joke out of travelling by car. This was the story for the entire month. Constant snow and whiteouts, footing impossible, walking a challenge; by comparison, blinding freezing rain became a comparative relief. Temperatures dropped and stayed there. But after ten years of this hellish carry-on, Frances had grown so blasé, that early January saw her casually toddle off for a light lunch with the Whites two kilometres away, then walk back (thanks to snowshoes) to entertain two guests for supper.

But when spring had finally sprung, winter's weather woes gave way to chores, in preparation for next winter. "In mid-March," said Frances, "I had twelve full cords of wood cut for my fireplace." But who cut it, and who stacked it? Twelve cords is a lot of wood: over forty cubic metres; not the kind of thing you do over a weekend, by yourself, at sixty years old.

On the first day of spring, Frances planted tomatoes and herbs and all kinds of good things, but with annual misgivings. It was frustrating to know that, remorselessly, the unpredictable weather would freeze them, wild animals would eat them, and whatever survived would be trampled by hunters.

But the next morning she saw a finch, and a cowbird, and heard a robin sing, and she was happy.

Thoroughgoing pessimists, on the other hand, see spring as merely the brief time that follows winter, and from whose vantage point they can look down the months, and in the distance see the winter yet to come. Pessimists are like that. But for Frances, despite the storm, car, and snow difficulties that every winter brought, there were periods of deep pleasure. On December 21, 1982, Frances celebrated what would be her last winter solstice party at Crosshill. "The parties were so lovely. Often it was bad weather. People would come on snowmobiles or snowshoes. There was one person, Dr. Irene Hain, who would ferry people up and down the lane. She had a really powerful snowmobile. She was a very strong woman; in difficult places she could actually lift the snowmobile and turn it around." For the party, Frances cooked and served a couple of the enormous squashes she grew, stuffing them with all manner of meats and spices. "They were spectacular! I'd have one cooking while scooping out another for the oven. This night, someone brought a bottle of scotch, but three or four guests sat downstairs and drank it all, and I never had a chance! The evening lasted from six o'clock till the food was all gone, perhaps midnight or something like that. The rooms — big high ceilings — were lit entirely by candles; the whole house. I had to watch them, of course. Everyone would bring a candle." She sighed. "It was such a nice place," she said, almost crying at the thought of it all.

Christmas was a time of contentment. To a certain degree, at least. Frances was always an enthusiastic caroller; she had the voice for it. "Off to the hospital to sing. Isn't that nice! We were singing carols at the Kitchener-Waterloo hospital. There were some people there that we knew, so we sang to them out in the hall. The carols were received very well by the other patients."

In early 1983, Frances placed her seed order for the coming season. She did this every year; squash, carrots, flowers, the lot. Squash especially. "I grew great big squashes, some of them running over ten kilos. I don't like to brag, but I did win awards for them, you know." Harking back to her solstice celebrations, she said "I'd cut them open and take out the seeds, and stuff them with sausage, spices, sardines and pickles, and put them in the oven. I'd serve them just like that at the table."

Then, from the sublime to the ridiculous, mid-February would see her snowshoeing around the swamp below her house; Mindy was not too keen about pushing through over a metre of snow, while Frances performed her annual swamp check. "I'd walk down with the dog and identify those trees that I would haul up for kindling. It was a lovely low area, very, very beautiful. It was a morning routine for me, on snowshoes."

Her cat was smart enough to seek a quiet spot behind a curtain in the house during these daily winter jaunts to the swamp. Sadly, he would never have to do it again. Kaspar, her cat of many years, did not live to see another summer. He died an old and beloved cat, in early March, deeply mourned.

In April she drove to Kitchener to do a little shopping for a lunch she was giving for her sister Marion and brother-in-law Charles Johnson. "It was in a tiny little park among my pine trees. It was where there was an opening in the pines, and it was just so … so quiet and secluded that nobody would ever know you were there. There was a little path through, and I kept some chairs there. It was lovely. It was near my house, but it was so secluded, quite lovely." And once again Crosshill was reaching out to her, banishing her thoughts of Birch Avenue, art, and sculpture … reaching out to her, stroking her, offering her beauty, and peace.

When you're on the threshold of sixty, as Frances was in 1983, little injuries become big injuries, and stay big longer. A simple moth put Frances out of action for months. "I had invited some neighbours for dinner. While I was preparing the meal, I spotted a moth, and went rushing after it, tripped, and broke my ankle. For more than a week it was just agony. Finally, I went along to the hospital (after a week of "agony"?). Dr. McTavish put my leg in a cast. All because of a moth! By the eighth of August I had been in a cast for three weeks, still suffering the broken leg … well, all right, broken ankle. It was the worst possible time, too. A long hot dry period caused the town to issue an order restricting water use. So there I was, hardly able to move. A couple of neighbours were supposed to water my garden, but they didn't, and I had to sit there in a cast, all because of a damned moth, and watch my beautiful garden die."

The difficulties and discomfort caused by the ankle sent Frances into a period of depression, and not a little downright anger at the frustrating limitations placed upon her. "By a moth, for heaven's sake." Sculpture suffered, as did all the daily activities that brought her so much pleasure. Little hills of irritation became mountains of resentment. "Damned newspaper, or rather the work involved in getting it. I had to walk almost a kilometre to my gate." (She had been doing this for years without complaint.)

And with the depression came a return to alcohol, and the end of another attempt to stop drinking.

Frances had planned to attend the Medallic Arts Exhibition in Florence, Italy, in the fall of 1983. Her brother Bob and sister Barbara heard about it, and decided they wanted to go, too. "So there we were," said Frances, "the three of us, in Florence, theoretically to attend the exhibition and gain technical knowledge and be artistically uplifted by the medal work on display. Oh, it was a terrible trip, terrible trip. Bob and Barbara were both into the sauce. Well, all three of us were, actually, though Barb and Bob were into it a little more than I was."

The day after their arrival in Florence, Barbara and Frances went for a walk. "We came back to the hotel to find Bob sloshed."

Two days later the exhibition opened, but Frances was the victim of Montezuma's Revenge. The change in food and water had a disastrous effect. "I was sick as a dog," she moaned. But they managed to get Bob off to Pisa to see the leaning tower. Later the same afternoon Barbara left for Venice. Frances remained in Florence and spent the day in a small park, near a toilet, suffering. "A lovely Danish lady helped me out, bought biscuits, cheese, mineral water, and a tiny bottle of scotch." Later the following day Frances was somewhat better, and was able to attend some of the exhibits.

The exhibition ended (and not a moment too soon, in Frances's view), and after a couple of days of tourism, the three visitors left for Rome and the plane to Toronto.

For days after the group's return to Ontario, Barbara was on what Frances referred to as "a rampage," fuelled by alcohol. "She'd make telephone calls when she'd had a few drinks, raving, making no sense at all. I told her, 'Barb, get some help!' Barbara sneered: 'Go throw a rock in your own lake,' she said."

In April of 1984, Frances started each day with the tortured expression "Bad night." Every evening became more tortured than the one before. "By this time alcohol was beginning to play a large part in my life. Very large. I wasn't waiting for the sun to go down below the yardarm anymore."

She was still annoyed when hunters invaded her property. Thanks to alcohol, she just didn't see them as often.

One day she was gazing out her window, pleased by the broad sweep of her grass, though it was a bit yellow in patches, when she suddenly realized the grass a short distance from her house was on fire. She ran outside, but quickly saw she would not be able to extinguish it herself, so rushed back in and called the nearby Linwood firemen. Afterward they reported the usual cause: Hunters, their cigarettes, and a strong wind.

The period from spring through to mid-August was a terrible time for Frances. Unable, apparently, to do anything about her alcohol problems, in addition she had to stand helpless as her old friend Fran Bean slowly and painfully died of cancer. Heavily sedated against the pain, Fran Bean died on August 13, 1984.

Earlier that year was the beginning of the end of Frances's life at Crosshill. But, as time would tell, only the beginning; the end was still some distance down the road.

She had decided to leave Crosshill.

"I was so profoundly depressed over that decision. I'd thought about it for some time, but couldn't face it until now." Apparently she still couldn't face it. Even though the last few years had shown her the subtle negative effect Crosshill had on her work, and though she stood up now and boldly stated her intention to leave, and on some upper level of her brain meant every single word … the upper level was just superstructure; the powerful lower levels still ran the show. Having made her intentions clear, she then filed them away, and life went on. Not until a buyer emerged with the promise to purchase would she feel the wrenching fact of it, and recognize, at last, that Paradise was truly lost.

In June, Frances's Multiple Listing Service on her Crosshill property expired without generating any prospective buyers. She did not lose any sleep over this; with the exception of Fran's death, and her recognition of her own relentless dependence on alcohol, she continued to enjoy her Crosshill life. Beyond the drinker's pseudo-concern over a perceived alcohol problem ("Yep, must do something about it. Definitely have to cut down on the drinking. Tomorrow."), her life there continued as before, all-encompassing, filled with activity, wonder, joy, and satisfaction.

And sculpture, too. At least activities that were sculpture-related. Fanshawe College (the Ontario Provincial Institute of Trades), the site of her first major work, *Discovery of the Hands* (1964), contacted her to report the sculpture was deteriorating. Nobody had looked after it, it was cratered, and many pieces were simply falling off. "Someone had drawn up an estimate for having it cast in bronze," recalled Frances. "It would have cost around twenty-five thousand dollars (1984 dollars)." She sighed. "A lot of money."

In December, any trip to or from Frances's Crosshill property made snowshoes mandatory. "I had to snowshoe to the swamp because the snow was too deep to walk in. It was well over a metre deep in some places. I lost a snowshoe once — slipped off my foot — and of course, your leg goes right down. Over a metre down, actually. I finally had to roll over on my back, and put my snowshoe on with my leg up in the air, then roll back over and get on my feet. I was, of course, doing this sober; I couldn't have done it any other way. I would have still been there."

December ended, and January 1985 began, with little change in overall conditions. "Twenty-five-acre rink, that's my property. All sheathed in ice. The lane has been blown. This time the township didn't do it and then send me a bill; I hired someone else. Either way, I pay."

January and February were not nice months at Crosshill, and just in case Frances had forgotten, the two months reminded her, repeatedly. "Storm of the decade. Called blower for whenever. Screaming wind. Drifts of snow over two metres … power out, so I was off to the Beans in deep, heavy, wet snow. Get skis … lane blown. Waste of time. Lane full again within the hour … terrible trip in to my house, snow wild, Mindy floundered, David White made a trail for us … gales, terrible storm, snow, sleet, winds of seventy kilometres per hour …"

Welcome to 1985, Frances.

In April, Frances was very excited about a presentation she was putting together for Toronto's Tridel Group, builders of shopping plazas, industrial complexes, and condominiums. "They had a wonderful place for the sculpture, and I made a presentation to them, a very nice free-form piece that the architect thought was super, but Tridel shot me down anyway." *Hmph.* "Damned Tridel. It was one of the best things I ever did. But (sigh) some people have no taste. It was a beautiful piece.

"I was really mad about my presentation to Tridel. I had to take it out by dogsled to get it to the car, then take it to the post office for shipment. I included a proposal to produce the finished piece in stainless steel. It was a lot of work, and I worked all night. It was a very nice piece. I was prepared, of course," said Frances, preparing herself, "to accept the idea of not winning." (Translation: "I was *not* prepared, under *any* circumstances, damn it, to accept even the mere *thought* of not winning.")

"It made me mad. I had more taste, I think. I guess I was just angry at what they chose. I don't even remember what it was, which just goes to show what their choice was worth. I mean, I worked my butt off on the presentation I submitted. Worked all night." — Kicks chair — "Couple of nights." — Glares out window — "Worked all night."

Anyway, who needs Tridel, right? The following month the City of Toronto arranged for Frances to design a small park to display three or four of Loring and Wyle's sculptures, among which was Loring's striking *Harvester*. At the entrance to the park, there are two small busts facing each other, one of Loring by Wyle and one of Wyle by Loring. The little park, about one hundred by eighty metres, and shaded by tall trees, is at the corner of Mount Pleasant and St. Clair avenues, in view of The Girls' old church. Happily, in these days of vandalism as a career choice, the little park and its pleasant sculptures still stand, proudly overseen by the neighbouring houses, affording the passerby a restful moment away from the noise and traffic of the day.

Frances seemed to be doing a lot of plain and fancy beefing at this time, either through her natural dislike of things that were unfair or unnecessarily second class, or — as in the case of Tridel — through the veiled suggestion, or perhaps what she perceived as a suggestion, that her work was not acceptable, was not up to professional standards.

There was another reason to complain: poachers had invaded her property. This annoyed her, as did any unauthorized use of her land. But the question that arises here is: What was poachable?! Groundhogs? Red-tailed hawks? Hunters? Well, if someone had wanted to poach hunters, Frances would have gone along with that, would have helped in fact. But what outraged her was this: The poachers were motorized. Frances felt this was grossly unfair. Whatever animal they were poaching didn't stand a chance. "One of the poachers I encountered was after foxes, and when I complained, he said 'But what good are they?' And I said 'What good are you?!' And that certainly shat him up. Shat is the past tense of shut. But in the old days the poachers went after the animals on foot; poacher and poachee had an equal chance."

Contests were another source that generated a lot of good old-fashioned complaining from Frances. She claimed she never won any. Some might shrug and say she was a poor loser, and in a sense they would be right; Frances would have much preferred to win contests. But what often grated on her ego was the quality of the winning entry, and the not-so-subtly implied view that her work was inferior to, as she would say, "that horrible piece of untalented garbage."

In the summer of 1985, Frances had spent considerable time on an entry in a contest. "It was for a piece in a garden someplace in Toronto. I can't remember who was behind the contest. Could have been the City. Or it could have been an architect. Neither are noted for their good taste," she said scornfully. "The contest 'judges' didn't like it. Judges! I decided right then that I was finished with contests. From now on, if anyone wants something of mine they can come and buy it."

And there were some who sought Frances's services, and no contest was involved. She had done a lot of restoration work for the Ontario Historical Society, so when the province needed repairs done to the equestrian statue of King Edward VII, which is prominently located in the park that surrounds the legislative buildings in Toronto, they naturally turned to Frances.

There seems to be a common genetic flaw among thieves and vandals, some powerful twist in their DNA that draws them to steal bits and pieces from the city's public sculptures. Over a period of thirty years, Frances must have earned more than fifty thousand dollars in repairs and replacements to scores of statues in the city's parks.

The statue of King Edward had been vandalized. On a dark night in the summer of 1984, the thieves had struck! King Edward had been powerless to defend himself. In a matter of moments the vandals had made off with his sword. Frances was called in. It was an expensive theft: her repairs to the statue, the remaking and restoring of the sword, cost the Ontario taxpayer 1,600 dollars.

King Edward and his horse seemed to be a favourite target. Two years before the sword affair, a university student had painted the horse's testicles red, probably as a fraternity requirement. As Frances tells the story, "It must have been a terrible job to clean the statue. After all, you couldn't take the bronze horse back to the shop, you'd have to clean the testicles right there in the middle of Queen's Park! Hilarious by day, and even more so at night, under lights!"

There was one other thing. "The testicle painter," said Frances, "was my nephew."

Early April saw Frances the victim of a strange and serious medical condition. She had been experiencing a bleeding problem, the cause of which the Kitchener hospital appeared unable to diagnose. "So this idiot doctor thought he'd poke around anyway, and find out what it was. And, unknown to anyone at the time, in the course of probing around with his scalpel, he hit an artery. Then they sent me home, and because the area was frozen, I didn't know anything was wrong until I began to hemorrhage severely. I phoned the hospital and told them what was happening, and they said 'Come in right away!' Right away, indeed; I got stuck behind a cattle truck, and it took me an hour to get to Kitchener. I left my car in the parking lot, got in the main door, and collapsed. They got me on a gurney, and as they were rushing me down the hall someone said 'We're losing her!' Though I couldn't talk, I said, in my mind, 'No, you're not.' I imagined the newspaper headline: 'Tough girl sculptor defies death! Beautiful, blond, five-foot-two, famous Canadian sculptor survives against all odds!'"

"That surgeon was supposed to be very good," said Frances, "and he was — at hitting arteries. But whoever said he was a good surgeon simply wasn't paying attention; he was a disaster. Afterward, he shook my hand (!). 'You're a wonderful patient!' he said. I sure was; I was the very best: I didn't sue him."

Frances's situation in Crosshill was now settled, at least to the extent that she was prepared to sell, and return to Birch Avenue and the world of business. In the late summer, she went abroad for a holiday with David Bean and his daughter Margaret. Frances's expenses were ostensibly "paid for" by a bronze of David's late wife, Fran.

The announced reason for the trip was to see the Salzburg Festival, but was undoubtedly also a form of withdrawal from trauma: Frances's loss of Crosshill, and David's loss of his wife after her long and agonizing battle with cancer.

The trip was not the happiest of times, certainly not for Frances. For her it seemed an endless catalogue of noise and senseless aggressive action. In addition there was her medical difficulty.

"I was still bleeding." Incredibly, Frances had embarked on the trip while still suffering the mysterious and as yet undiagnosed bleeding. "Despite the surgeon's messing around inside me, and the bleeding he caused, they still hadn't determined the cause of the original bleeding problem, so I bled all over Europe."

Lucerne: "Little sleep. Noise, fights outside. Wild parties everywhere."

Verona: "Big parties everywhere, lots of beer, a real nightmare."

Austria: "Kids playing with cars and motorcycles, late."

Return to Salzburg: "Incredible traffic noise. To the Belvedere to see works by Gustav Klimt and Egon Schiele."

Vienna: "Margaret got us a room on a street filled with trams, buses, cars, and prostitutes."

The return to Canada on the thirtieth of August was a welcome end.

In Toronto, after a visit to Women's College Hospital, and an examination by Dr. Richardson, the bleeding problem was finally diagnosed as ulcerative colitis, a fairly common affliction. "There's a lot of pain connected with it," Frances remembered. "There were great ulcers in my gut, bleeding, which was what I was doing all over Europe." (At some point in all this, an observer would have to wonder: "Where did she get all this blood?!" And, not incidentally, how was she still able to cavort all over Europe for two weeks?)

By the middle of February 1986, the Crosshill winter had shown itself to be at least as bad as usual. "Here it is, February eighth," said Frances, "and my lane has just been blown for the fifth time this winter."

And the winter went on and on. February 20 saw Frances's lane cleared by the snowblower for the eighth time. "That's the third blowing in twelve days!" she cried. "At forty dollars a time!"

The next day, she watched three centimetres of snow fall. "A mere three centimetres, and it blocked my lane. The wild winds create huge drifts."

Frances suffered from a number of allergies: garlic, for example, made her physically ill. But the most serious allergy was her reaction to a wasp sting. "With a wasp sting allergy, you finally get to the point where you can't breathe. You swell up and it affects your chest, and without anything being done, it affects you terminally. The first time I noticed it — the allergy — I was up at Tannamakoon, my summer camp. I was stung, and I didn't understand what was happening. The glands under my arm swelled up, and I broke out in a rash, and then started to smother. Fortunately, they were able to get a doctor who was out fishing on the lake." Later, I visited a doctor I knew, Dr. Jancelewitz, an expert on wasps, and he gave me a series of immunization shots. I carry epinephrine in the season, and I'm not troubled by wasps anymore. Still hurts when they sting, though."

Early summer, and Frances was off to the Sunnybrook eye clinic for her second operation for cataracts. The right eye this time; the left had been done back in the seventies. After the operation, she returned to Crosshill. "Walked for miles in my forest, by myself, bored and depressed. There were weeks of recuperation where I had to cut down on my activities."

Toward the end of August, her eye had improved to the point that enabled her to work on a bronze wolf (four thousand dollars) for her friend Rosamond Wisniewski. "When she died, the wolf eventually went to the sculpture park in Guelph."

After the Wellesley Fair in September, there was simply no talking to Frances. She had submitted four of her giant squashes in the vegetable category. From the standpoint of the effect on Frances's ego, it was foolish of the judges to award her a first prize. But to give her four prizes, one for each squash, was sheer madness. But there she was, strutting around, the Big-Time Horticulturist, with blue ribbons for two firsts, another ribbon for a second-place prize, and the final squash took a third-place prize.

April 24, 1987, marked the end of Crosshill.

Her friends Sue Beal and Gary Oulton purchased the property. "Sue was the daughter of Ken Beal, a friend who was a preacher. She herself was a vet. She and her partner Gary wanted to buy my house at Crosshill as early as 1975." Not much chance of that; by then Frances was so enamoured of Crosshill she would never have let it go. "And now, twelve years later, they finally did buy it. Then, shortly after, they split up. That made me very sick, because I thought Crosshill was perfect for them, and they were perfect for Crosshill. The people to whom they then sold the property — their name was Downey — were the ones who raised emus. At that point, emus were very popular. The Downeys got about three thousand dollars for a breeding pair, and they sold the eggs and the meat. An emu drumstick was about the size of your leg. It was one of those popular things, like chinchillas, and then like so many fads, it passed."

Shortly before she left Crosshill, her neighbours got together and planted a tree, an English oak, and next to it a memorial stone to Frances's memory. "They thought it would be a nice thing to do before I was dead." She was surprised and deeply moved by the gesture. Her neighbour Aaron Gerber used his front-end loader to move a huge boulder — "Couple of tons it must have been" — to a point by the memorial tree. The neighbours then put a little brass plaque on it: "Erected by so-and-so-and-so."

When she left Crosshill, she looked across the land that had been hers for almost sixteen years. "Some of the walnuts that had been planted back in early 1974 were bearing fruit."

"Today is September 28, 1987. Finally moved. Left Crosshill at four-thirty in awful sorrow. Terrible, terrible day." At the moment of leaving, she was terrified by the thought: *Am I doing the right thing? Wait … wait!* But the tears came and blurred the last sight of her home.

With her departure came the physical end of Crosshill, but not the psychological end; that was to last forever, illustrating the depth of Crosshill's effect on her. It's hard to determine what it was about the place — after all, it was just a tract of land; dirt, stones; the province is full of them. And consider the negative aspects: For a woman "of a certain age," living alone, the winters were appalling. Her roads and lanes fought her with relentless determination, and won. Wildlife of all kinds preyed upon her at will, and continually. Neighbours were often not neighbourly. With almost all of her sculpture work carried on in the Toronto area, travelling was often onerous. All these negatives were made worse by the endless series of medical difficulties she supported through all the months of her Crosshill years. And always in the background was the grim and growing shadow of alcohol dependency.

Yet, decades later, her memories of Crosshill still lived, as bright, as deep, as vibrant as ever. Crosshill never died.

In her heart, she never left.

| 9 |

THE MAGNET OF MAMMON

FROM CROSSHILL TO BIRCH AVENUE. From the sublime to … well, perhaps not the ridiculous, but for Frances it was depressingly similar. She had arranged for extensive renovations to be done in advance of her arrival so that, theoretically, she could walk in and get on with her life. But things are rarely that simple.

Hugh Conover, one of her woodcarving students, had been signed up as the contractor. "He was supposed to have the renovations to the Birch Avenue house finished when I moved in," said Frances. "He started the day I moved in. It was a terrible mess, just a nightmare. It was a very old house, and I was changing almost everything. I thought Hugh would do what he said he was going to do, but I guess contractors are notorious, aren't they! You can imagine: plaster all over the place, walls coming down. All my stuff had to be put down in the basement. I slept on my workbench in the studio. I had no bed. The house was all torn up. The dining room and kitchen were a shambles, so I had to forget about having meals there, but I had a hotplate in the studio, and I went to the Rosedale Diner a lot." For years the Rosedale Diner was Frances's second kitchen. It was a short five-minute walk from her house, and in winter or summer, she would frequently let the diner replace her scanty culinary skills. In addition to meals, the diner served as a break from problems, both social and sculptural, and in many instances helped her to retain her sanity.

Frances had hardly settled in at Birch Avenue when her dog Mindy died. Among all the dogs that shared Frances's life, Mindemoya (Mindy) was arguably her favourite, remembered vividly over the decades. With immeasurable sadness, Frances returned the dog's ashes to Crosshill where the animal had spent so many happy years terrorizing the groundhogs. The weather — cold, rainy, miserable — was a dismal echo of Frances's mood.

But her depression was gradually absorbed in other activities, and a few months later Frances picked up her new dog, Thisbe, so named from the mythological story of Pyramus and Thisbe.

She was still being treated for her bleeding problem, and it affected her work. And yet, Frances still managed to produce sculpture, which was, after all, one of the major reasons for her return to Birch Avenue and the working world. Her friend Debora Johnston — former student, owner of the Now and Then Studio and, on more than one occasion, valuable client — was once more a customer, commissioning two bronze dogs: a large saluki ($3,900) and an Afghan hound ($3,700). This was in June: a nice way to start her renewed life in Toronto.

In April 1988, Frances was given the job of teaching sculpture at the Canadian Opera Company. "It was teaching sculpture to the makeup people and the wig-makers, so they would know their anatomy. I think the costume designers and seamstresses probably benefited, too. They were very good; they grasped principles and methods quickly. It was an interesting departure from my usual classes. I did it for about two or three years. This was the same opera company that opened the new opera house in Toronto almost two decades later. They were going to open one in 1988, too. They finally got there. They were working toward it for so long. In 1988 their premises were in the O'Keefe Centre on Front Street."

Matters did, indeed, seem very positive for Frances. Her work instructing at the opera school was going well, and in September she celebrated the start of her twenty-third year of teaching the Guelph classes. "I began those classes back in 1965, and continued them for about thirty years."

In early December, Frances mailed her winter solstice invitations. Twenty-six people made their way through the snow, down the alley between Frances's house and that of the gypsy junk dealer, past the tiny garden patio at the rear of 60 Birch Avenue, to the sculptor's studio behind the house. "To have enough room, I held the solstice party in the studio. The room was eight by twelve metres, with a high ceiling. I was still trying to stop drinking, but solstice was solstice, so we had wine and cheese, and coffee and tea, lots of finger food, and we just stood around and played Christmas carols. Everyone brought a candle. It was at Crosshill that I started the bringing of a candle. It was so wonderful, like something out of Dickens's *Christmas Carol*. I expected old Fezziwig to pop in any minute, dancing a merry reel. The night was cold, and people arrived with wide grins, blowing on their hands, their cheeks rosy. It was just so lovely!"

In March 1989, Frances revisited Crosshill for the last time. "Beautiful day, walked a lot, cooked dinner for David Bean. Since Fran died, he was alone, and not eating well."

She walked to the western edge of David's property, to the start of the path that led through the woods toward her former twenty-five acres. Standing in the trees, she could not see her house. But she could feel it; both she and the house, reaching out to each other. She turned away, knowing if she stayed any longer she would simply stand there, crying, like a foolish old woman. "I wanted so much to run down the path, run and see my house again. Yet, at the same time, I just couldn't bring myself to do it. I guess it's true: You can't go home again. It wasn't mine anymore. It wouldn't have been the same."

Back at Birch Avenue, Frances had the opportunity to submit an entry in a juried show, but declined brusquely. "I will not be juried. I don't like juried shows, with supposedly professional judges telling you 'Yes, you're good enough' or 'No, you're not'. Me? Sixty-odd years old, and this 'judge,' who's younger than my nephew, is saying I'm not good enough? No. That annoys me very much." She stomped off and had a mid-afternoon drink, and thus suffered another "lost evening."

Her choice of liquor was generally scotch. "I got the biggest I could afford. On an evening I might sit in my little chair before the fire, and drink half the bottle, until I fell off the chair." More than one artist has claimed that drinking brings inspiration. More often it produces garbage. But at least the drinking artist was active, he was doing something. Problem drinkers do nothing. They just sit, and drink.

This year, 1991, was probably the most painful, and at the same time most significant year of her life. On the fourth of March she attended her first Alcoholics Anonymous meeting. "Having to admit to an incurable illness — alcohol — in front of a bunch of strangers, is a shock, something like a self-psychoanalysis. And then to sit down and conduct a fearless inventory with an addictions counsellor. I had a very good counsellor, who finally died from lung cancer," said Frances, "because she couldn't stop smoking. I talked to her every week, and after I moved away from the city, east to the town of Roseneath, I still phoned her regularly. She was a great help. What else can I say? She was a great help. But it was the soul-searching I found difficult. I felt as if I were sort of naked on an autopsy table."

But AA isn't a magic wand; no beneficent gesture, no light touch and — *voilà!* — you're cured. Less than a week after her first AA meeting Frances attended her sister Barbara's birthday party, "… and slipped … drank … lovely party …" and easily fell back into her old alcoholic habits.

There were then days of not drinking, followed almost inevitably by lapses, "lost" afternoons, "bad" nights. Then, on March 31, she went for a nice long walk, returned home, lost the afternoon — who knows where it went? — and then had an accident.

"Bad fall," said Frances. "I guess. I honestly don't know. Blacked out completely. That was the worst one I'd ever had. I drank until I passed out, and ended up on the floor in a puddle of blood, and I didn't know what had happened, or how. I broke my nose. Blackened my eyes." She shook her head in dismay. "Really great, that I could do that to myself. I told the people at the hospital that I'd fallen off a ladder while watering the plants. I heard the nurse tell the doctor 'She's been beaten.' And I, of course, could neither confirm nor deny that. I just lied about it. That's the sorry story of it, you know. You lie. But, well, anything could have happened; maybe the nurse was right!"

Three days later she had an accident in the nearby park. "Another accident!" she exclaimed. "I was really getting fed up! A big dog, a retriever, just hit me behind my knees and knocked me down. I think football referees call it 'clipping'. Broke my wrist. And I was already covered in stitches from the damage I'd done to myself before!"

A few days later she was back in hospital "having the stitches removed from the first accident, removing the cast on my arm from the second accident, and getting my knee checked. Yeah, my knee; as a further dividend from the series of accidents, I had twisted my knee. This happened when I was knocked down by the dog, but I wasn't really aware of it at the time, because *everything* hurt! One of the tendons was damaged. March and April was a bad time."

The bad times were not made any better by alcohol. In her daybook she would all too frequently remark "Dry day," implying there were other days that were not.

AA was there for her, and she attended regular meetings. There was a group at the Ontario Institute for Studies in Education (OISE) at Bloor and Bedford Road in downtown Toronto, less than two kilometres from her Birch Avenue home. She would walk there for the 7:30 a.m. meetings. It was a relatively small group, sometimes four or five persons, though frequently as many as fifteen. "The group was quite varied," said Frances. "There were men, women, different nationalities. We'd sit around a table, and someone would choose a topic that dealt with some aspect of alcoholism, and we would all discuss it. There were no strangers at that table; we were all immigrants from the same terrifying country, and we never wanted to return. We were there to help each other."

Late summer brought voices from the past, the distant past, in the death on August 20 of Frances's old friend, confidant, and instructor from OCA days, Will Ogilvie. At the same time Frances learned, sadly, of Frieda Fraser's slow decline into Alzheimer's.

The present, however, brought better news. Frances was commissioned to produce a bronze head of the noted singer/composer/conductor Elmer Iseler for the foyer of Roy Thomson Hall in Toronto.

"Elmer Iseler was a wonderful man," said Frances. "He was a singer, a tenor I believe, in the Mendelssohn Choir under Sir Ernest MacMillan, and then eventually took over the choir.

"He would tramp down my lane to the studio in the back when he came to pose. His wife Jessie would be with him. He was an excellent model; never moved. He would sit with a music score in his hand, completely lost in the music. I could almost see the music rising around him; I'm sure he could. I always felt I got something more, because he wasn't posing.

"He was quite bald, with long white hair in back that his wife would blow dry before a performance.

"He loved cats. In their home in Caledon Hills, they had thirty of them," said Frances, stroking her own cat.

After one of the AA meetings at OISE, Frances went to the Arts and Letters Club in Toronto for lunch, had a drink, and ended up suffering "a bad night with liquor."

The following day she was seized by a momentary feeling of remorse and self-disgust. The sensation lasted for only a few seconds, but it was enough. She took the half-empty bottle of scotch and poured it down the drain. "Oh it hurt, it really hurt," she remembered. "I kept thinking how wonderful it was. Can't remember the brand; I always got the same kind. Good stuff. Glenfiddich? Still, the action was yet another start of being dry."

The twenty-first of December was once more the winter solstice and Frances held her annual party. "Nice evening. Wine $346, food $226." Nice evening, but more sauce than sustenance.

On May 17, Frances voluntarily admitted herself into the Donwoods medical facility. "It's for addictions," said Frances, "not specifically for alcoholics, but I went there as a day patient. I went every day for three months. They were very thorough, gave me a big medical, all sorts of lectures about diets and things like that. I got the impression they were very negative about AA; it seemed to me that they considered it a kind of cult. In my own mind, so far as AA is concerned, there's too much emphasis on the God stuff. That's something I had to deal with. I get kind of cross with the bunch at some of the meetings. My most successful meetings were at OISE in Toronto at 7:30 in the morning. We had Jews, Muslims, and everything under the sun, so of course they didn't say the Lord's Prayer. There were none in that outfit who preached. I'm adamant about that. When I told my friend Barbara Howard that I was very worried about the God stuff, she said 'Well, remember, She's Black, She's Jewish, and She's homosexual.'"

Frances would sometimes take a break from alcohol problems by spending a day in the park, at Cottingham Public School, just down the street from her home. Every year, sitting in the park, she would do cartoons, sell them, and donate the money to the school. Some days were better than others. "Cartooning in the rain today," she said. "Still, the rain didn't bother me, and it didn't bother the kids. I did cartoons of the children and dogs and all that sort of thing."

Frances had returned to Birch Avenue at the beginning of 1988. She would remain there for six long years, getting back into the sculpture business and reaching out to the other artistic and financial opportunities the Big City offered. But her efforts were half-hearted. She had come to realize that the amenities of the city did not offset the deeply-felt loss of Crosshill. She saw, and accepted the fact, that she was a country woman. The wonders and the joys of Crosshill far outweighed what she viewed as the spurious benefits of a noisy, dirty, crowded, indifferent city. She hated Toronto. She hated the cement under her feet, longed for earth and clean country air. Though she was, herself, in business, she was contemptuous of the blind business orientation of the city. In a good mood she might have told you that Toronto wasn't too bad, but she would have been kidding you, and kidding herself. In the final years at Birch Avenue she had developed a pathological dislike for all things urban, fuelled by her memories of Crosshill. She began looking, seriously, at the real estate section of the newspaper.

"A neighbour brought me an ad for a place near Roseneath, a small town on the south shore of Rice Lake, about 130 kilometres east of Toronto. There was a brief period of indecision — it was a third of an acre (visions of Crosshill's glorious wooded acres rose for a heartbreaking moment in her mind), but it went right down to the lake. The price was around $200,000. But it was rural. Country. The lake was at her doorstep. There was farmland around her, broad spaces, blue skies. And peace.

On the twenty-seventh of September she bought it.

There was Roseneath on one hand, and $200,000 going out, but she still had the house on Birch Avenue, and no buyers.

Finally, one evening toward the end of November, a prospective buyer arrived. "It was an awful night," said Frances. "She said she would buy the house, but … she was drunk!" Frances could understand the drunkenness; she had lived in that wild country for years. But she also knew from experience how unreliable drunks can be.

Nevertheless, the woman did buy it. On the last day of November the Birch Avenue house changed hands for a little over half a million dollars, and two weeks later the house at Roseneath became the home of Frances Gage.

Birch Avenue was history, Crosshill a beautiful memory. Frances found herself again the mistress of a "rural estate."

But it wasn't the same. It would never be the same.

It would never be Crosshill.

| 10 |

A KIND OF VICTORY

FRANCES'S ROSENEATH HOME overlooked the south shore of Rice Lake, and from the start she was enchanted by the lake and its bird population. "When I first arrived, I looked out across the lake. It was mostly frozen over then, but there were a few open areas. It looked so beautiful." Mornings were magic. "Often there would be mist on the water, and as the sun rose, its light would be softened and diffused. I would take my small boat and row out, and sit drifting all alone on the lake, surrounded by the mist, alone in the splendid light of the rising sun."

In her walks around the area, she noticed that swans were nesting along the lake's shore. "One morning, I saw a heron and a loon on the lake. So lovely. Ospreys flew right up to my window; I could almost touch them. They sometimes had prey in their talons."

Clinging to memories of Crosshill, she instituted her first winter solstice party in her new home. She prepared the invitations, and delivered them by hand. To her vast satisfaction, it was one of her most successful solstice parties. "Thirty-one people came. Sundown was at 4:38. I served sandwiches. Super party, the neighbours loved it." She insisted that everyone bring a candle, an important part of the solstice tradition she had begun so many years ago in Crosshill. Her insistence on candles brought a happy response: "There were eighty-three candles!"

It didn't take Frances long to realize that the move from Birch Avenue denied her whatever positive aspects the city could offer, but gave her nothing even remotely resembling Crosshill. A lose-lose situation. "As early as two years after moving to Roseneath, I was already beginning to think of relocating to Cobourg, a town on Lake Ontario, twenty-five kilometres south of Roseneath." Cobourg offered more: It was the county's major town — close to 20,000 population — and certainly the artistic centre of the area. It had a somewhat rural non-big-city flavour, but more of the city's advantages. "Before I even moved to Cobourg, their art gallery was planning a show of my work."

She also found, to her dismay, that as she was still teaching classes in Toronto, she was faced with a three-hour return trip for each class. When those trips occurred in winter, as they did when she first arrived in Roseneath, they were not only onerously time-consuming, but potentially dangerous.

"Once, returning from a class, maybe nine-thirty or ten at night, I was driving along one of the secondary highways. What had started as 'wind; snow flurries' rapidly became a dangerous storm. Conditions were very icy, and suddenly I lost control on one of the curves. I ended up going north in the southbound lane. Interesting situation. Fortunately — if I can use that term! — on that particular stretch of road, it was fairly flat country, so I didn't go into a ditch. I just found myself going the wrong way. Very scary. And coming back, my windshield wipers' rubbers were torn right off because it was freezing so fast. So I had to get back to Roseneath with no windshield wipers, driving with my head out the window — in the freezing rain! Nice; makes your hair curl.

"I realized that it was simply impossible, and the classes would have to end. It broke my heart," she said. "I'd been conducting those classes for thirty years, and had enjoyed every minute. They were wonderful years."

She began to wonder if she really needed the city any longer. She knew she didn't want it; never did. But in Roseneath she had felt the lack of big city amenities. Little things grated on her nerves. No sched-uled garbage pick-up at the sidewalk. Indeed, no sidewalk. "In winter the slope of my driveway seemed like a forty-five-degree skating rink. Solid ice. Not a car in the country could drive up it. I watched some try, and had to laugh as the vehicle began to skid, then slide slowly back to the road."

And so her eyes turned south to Cobourg.

"On December 21, 1997, I had a great winter solstice party, the last one in Roseneath, and the best ever. Forty-six people came, and all brought candles."

By the end of 1998, Frances had sold her Roseneath house, moved to Cobourg, and settled into her new home on Ball's Lane, a few hundred metres from the town centre. Almost immediately she began construc-tion of a studio at the rear of the premises, an addition that was com-pleted in mid-May of 1999.

In mid-December of 1999, Frances was sued by the new owner of her former home in Roseneath. Merry Christmas, Frances, and wel-come to Cobourg! The reason for the legal action? The well had run dry. It's difficult to understand how Frances could be held responsible for this, but the senseless suit went on for six months. The following March, Frances finally won. "I had explained that it did run dry once," she said, "and during the legal proceedings the man who bought the house said he was aware of that. So his wife, who had initiated the suit, possibly wasn't very happy with him as well as with me. It was a lengthy affair, and while I eventually won, it still cost me eight hundred dollars. Doesn't seem fair, does it? She sues, she loses, I win, but I lose eight hundred dollars!"

The end of 1999 saw Frances still very depressed over the pointless legal action, a condition that was not improved by the passage of the winter solstice with no carolling and no solstice party.

Then, on February 3, 2000, there was the Sister Barbara Fiasco. "My sister Barbara had phoned the Cobourg police and told them I had a gun and was going to commit suicide. I had this lovely rifle of my dad's; a lovely little .22. I'd had it for years, and scared the life out of hunters with it. But Barbara phoned the Cobourg police. She was in her cups, I guess. Maybe she was feeling suicidal and she transferred the feeling onto me. I was understandably very upset about the gun affair, not only on my own account, but more for Barbara. I mean, the phone call to the police was crazy.

"I had looked into the matter of gun registry," said Frances. "Seems laughable to be obliged to register a .22, doesn't it? AK-47s, submachine guns, okay, we sure want to know who's got those, but a .22?! I found that to register a gun I had to go to the post office and get a form, then pay a lot of money, and then tell them every time I took the gun out of the house, and every time I brought it back. It was ridiculous. In the end I just took the gun apart and gave it to one of my nephews."

In October 2000, Frances was admitted to Toronto's Mount Sinai Hospital for knee surgery (left knee, lateral miniscus), followed by weeks of physio, a walker, and home care until the end of November. And in January 2001, the other knee was done. Physio for these knees was a painful experience. "I had physio twice a day. They gave me two Tylenol 3s an hour before the physio, otherwise I'd have gone screaming up the wall. At the end of that period I was hooked. I shook for a day when I got back home. I mean, two Tylenol 3s twice a day, for two weeks."

To banish a period of depression, at the end of September 2002, she took a brief trip to east Africa. The strangeness of the trip fascinated her. "There was such a different atmosphere. Living in a tent was nothing new for me, but to wake at 3:00 a.m. and hear lions outside. There was none of that at Crosshill!" The next day she saw lions and elephants, on a ridge, motionless against the sky. Above, vultures circled slowly. Before she left for home, she went down to the seashore and gazed out across the Indian Ocean. She fancied she could see, in the distance across the unending expanse, the coast of India. "The Indian Ocean! Sinbad's sea of a thousand-and-one nights! I swam in it. The sand was so white, the waters warm."

A week after she returned, in mid-October, she took a solitary walk along Lake Ontario, less than a kilometre south of her home. She strolled along the shore, a world away from the Indian Ocean's thousand-and-one stories. She felt again the insupportable sense of loneliness, of sadness. It was as if her heart knew what was about to come.

On December 7, 2002, Barbara Howard, her close and well-loved friend of more than fifty years, died in hospital. She had suffered a broken hip. Admitted to hospital in Peterborough in early December, she underwent surgery. While under the anesthetic, her heart suddenly stopped, and she was gone.

Her husband Richard was shattered. "He was a poet, and she was his muse," said Frances. "When she died, his whole life seemed to go with her, and he was never the same again." Less than an hour after Barbara's death, Richard phoned Frances, and whatever hold she had on her emotions was swept away in a heartbeat when he said, "Promise me, Frances, promise me you won't drink."

That his thoughts were of her at such a traumatic moment, when he had lost all that ever mattered, was more than Frances could bear. A few weeks later, still as deeply affected as Richard himself, she found herself on the eve of the winter solstice, lonelier than ever, no carolling, no candles, her oldest friend gone forever. In sadness, and with a profound sense of loss, of Barbara and indeed herself, she returned to her old crutch in times of stress, and began drinking again.

But one or two lost nights do not a drunkard make. At least not an irreclaimable one. AA, as always, stood up for her, and through regular meetings she started the long road back. Yet, from this year on, carolling was just a memory of times past. The winter solstice became simply another day in the calendar, the candles set to one side, forgotten, unlit.

EPILOGUE

SAD ENDING? WELL, SAD, YES, but sad *ending*, no. Frances had encountered these depressions before, and recognized them for what they were: Evanescent states; painful, but passing. She recognized them, rejected them, and got on with her life.

And it had been, and still was, a life worth getting on with. She'd experienced the good and the bad; the very good and the very bad. She'd been raised to Heaven itself by the production of a successful sculpture, and she'd lived below, in the darkest corner of hell, with alcohol. She'd gained a paradise in Crosshill, and suffered its irreparable loss. Over the years, her own body seemed to fight her every inch of the way, laying treacherous medical pitfalls in her path, yet that same body carried her through them all.

Her later life's debilitating dependence on alcohol could be seen as the major tragedy of her life. But her problem, the one that defined her life, was not primarily alcohol; that was admittedly serious, but it was another issue, an issue over which she had at least some control. Her real tragedy was the conflict between Crosshill and the City, over which she had no control at all. She loved the country, but it was detrimental to her work; she hated the city, but that was where the work was.

Crosshill was her Catch-22.

Was her life a positive one? By any yardstick, we have to say yes. But it came at a price.

"Other women will tell me how lucky I am, how wonderful it must be to have a life like mine: A successful artist; fame, wealth." Frances smiled, remembering the past fifty years, remembering the frozen hands in Tom Thomson's shack, and how difficult it was to pay the ten dollars a month rent. She also remembered the five years it took to build her Crosshill house because she didn't have the money to pay the builder; remembering the times — so many times — when she simply didn't have the money she needed, for *anything*. To these women she would say, "You all want what I've got, which is the life I've created for myself — by sacrificing what *you've* got."

Giving up Crosshill was undoubtedly a major, if not *the* major loss of her life.

Crosshill and alcohol: twin tragedies. But she knew this, and accepted the first, and conquered the second, and saw her life through realistic eyes. She had devoted her life to art, and was successful; she had met her problems, and surmounted most of them, eventually. In later life she was still trying to solve some of them, while creating enduring works of art.

Tragedies they may have been, and in the case of Crosshill, certainly were, but failures? No, not failures. She didn't fail in her life's aims. Over the half-century of her artistic life she did what she wanted to do: spent a life in art, as a sculptor, and enjoyed notable success.

But decades later, Crosshill was still able to reach out a distant tentative hand, and touch her heart, and bring the tears of loss.

Still, to think she spent all her time dreaming of Crosshill would be absurd. All her artistic life, Frances was active. A sculptor does not create art, and market it, by sitting on her hands. She was, in addition, almost always faced with what she would feel was an "interfering" host of medical problems. These were often difficult to deal with in Crosshill. And she suffered these ailments while at the same time battling the elements and losing, but returning repeatedly to fight, and lose again.

Throughout all her years, despite the multitude of problems that threatened her work, she continued to produce beautiful, lasting, works of art.

The terms "failure" and "tragedy" now seem grossly inappropriate.

She was able, in these later years, to look out her window and see, not a narrow provincial street, but a broad boulevard, a brilliantly illuminated thoroughfare of accomplishment.

I have dropped by her house this day to check a couple of points in this book that I feel need clarification. I fight my way past Steena, her boisterous dog — we have become old friends over the years — and walk around to Frances's backyard.

She has decided to install a sculpture garden among the trees. Graceful bronze forms are already pushing the trees into the background. Free-forms, memorials to friends; it is growing daily as new sculptures are added.

I see her talking to the two workmen who are doing the heavy lifting. The three of them are laughing uproariously over something Frances has just said.

I stand, unnoticed for a moment, and smile. Frances Gage, the eighty-four-year-old retired sculptor? Is she sitting in a chair in a darkened room, passing her years looking out the window, watching the world go by? "It is to laugh," she would have said in her best French from her days in Paris. She has been busy producing miniatures of Woman, one of her major sculptures, and is planning another large project.

I had been hoping to visit her the previous Friday, but no, she had something going on then — probably signing on as quarterback for the local football team.

Don't laugh. It could happen.

BIBLIOGRAPHY

American Naval Fighting Ships, Dictionary of (www.hazegray.org/danfs).

Arnason, H.H. *History of Modern Art: Painting-Sculpture-Architecture Photography*. New York: Harry N. Abrams, 1968.

Art Students League News 26, 7 (November 1973).

Bazin, Germain. *The History of World Sculpture*. Lamplight Publishing, 1968.

Benton, Thomas Hart. Conference of Canadian Artists. Kingston: Queen's University (1941).

———. CBC interview (June 26, 1941).

Bittner, Herbert. *Kaethe Kollwitz: Drawings*. New York: Sagamore Press, 1959.

Bobak, Molly Lamb. *Wild Flowers of Canada*. Toronto: The Pagurian Corporation, 1983.

Boxer, Rosemary. "Sculpture, Bravo!" *Toronto Telegram* (June 1961).

Brent, Paul. "Our $10B hangover." *National Post* (July 2, 2005).

"Canadian sculptor's problems …" *Kitchener Record* (November 17, 1967).

Capp, Al. *A Collection of Quotable Quotes*. Bicester: Aura Books Advanced Marketing (UK), 2004.

Carter, Dorette. Interview (April 27, 2005).

"Collip sculptor tells …" *London Free Press* (August 1965).

Cuevas-Carmichael, Elizabeth. Foreword, *John Hovannes: Memorial Exhibition* (catalogue). New York: Art Students League, 1973.

"Douglas Duncan …" *Globe and Mail* (August 1969).

Farmer, J. David. "Overcoming All Obstacles: The Women of the Académie Julian." (*www.californiaartclub.org/newsletter/articles/article_julian1. shtml*) (2000)

"Field is narrowing …" *Ottawa Citizen* (May 1946).

Filey, Mike. *Toronto Sketches 7*. Toronto: Dundurn Press, 2003.

Francis, Roy. "Jenny the Wren …" *Galt Evening Reporter* (October 10, 1972).

Gage, Frances. *Wood Sculpture*. Toronto: Ministry of Community and Social Services, 1974.

Hoffman, Malvina. *Sculpture Inside and Out*. New York: W.W. Norton, 1939.

Houterman, H. (*www.unithistories.com*).

Jackson, A.Y. *A Painter's Country*. Toronto: Clarke, Irwin, 1958.

Jarrassé, Dominique. *Rodin: A Passion for Movement*. Paris: Éditions Pierre Terrail, 2001.

John Hovannes: Memorial Exhibition (catalogue). New York: Art Students League, 1973.

Kitman, Marvin. *A Collection of Quotable Quotes*. Bicester: Aura Books Advanced Marketing (UK), 2004.

Kritzwiser, Kay. "The Silent Lady of Pears Avenue." *Globe and Mail* (June 20, 1964).

———. "Sculpture goes back …" *Globe and Mail* (September 29, 1970).

Larsen, Wayne. *A.Y. Jackson: A Love for the Land*. Montreal: XYZ Publishing, 2003.

"London garden …" *London Free Press* (July 1961).

MacKenzie, Susan. "Wren sculptor …" *Kitchener Record* (May 12, 1972).

Mays, John Bentley. *Emerald City: Toronto Visited*. Toronto: Viking, 1994.

McCarthy, Pearl. "Frances Gage carries on …" *Globe and Mail* (May 11, 1957).

"Music's grand …" *Toronto Star* (October 1971).

Newlands, Anne. *Canadian Art: From its Beginnings to 2000*. Toronto: Firefly Books, 2000.

Nicoll, Jessica. *To Be Modern: The Origins of Marguerite and William Zorach's Creative Partnership, 1911–1922*. (*www.exitfive.com/zorach*).

Norman, P. Edward. *Sculpture in Wood*. London: Alec Tiranti, 1969.

"One goes abroad …" *Toronto Telegram* (April 1968).

Parmelee, Helen. "Paint brush …" *Toronto Telegram* (October 27, 1960).

Quantrell, Jim. "Canada's Wrens …" *Cambridge Reporter* (November 18, 1987).

Rilke, Rainer Maria. *Auguste Rodin*. Introduction by William Gass. New York: Archipelago Books, 2004.

Sisler, Rebecca, RCA. *The Girls*. Toronto: Clarke, Irwin, 1972.

———. *Passionate Spirits: A History of the Royal Canadian Academy of Arts, 1880–1980*. Toronto: Clarke, Irwin, 1980.

"Six cousins serving ..." *Simcoe Reformer* (October 19, 1944).

Sokoloff, Heather. "AA's model ..." *National Post* (June 30, 2005).

Spilsbury, J., ed. *Cobourg: Early Days and Modern Times*. Cobourg: Cobourg Book Committee, 1981.

"Sponsor smitten ..." *Stratford Times* (June 1965).

Stinson, Scott. "Hunting for clues ..." *National Post* (June 30, 2005).

Sutton, Joan. "The world of ..." *Toronto Star* (October 11, 1973).

"The joys of woodcarving." *Globe and Mail* (1965).

Tippett, Maria. *Stormy Weather: F.H. Varley, A Biography*. Toronto: McClelland and Stewart, 1998.

———. *Bill Reid: The Making of an Indian*. Toronto: Random House, 2003.

Town, Harold, and David P. Silcox. *Tom Thomson: The Silence and the Storm*. Toronto: Firefly Books, 2001.

"University acquires unique piece ..." *Guelph Daily Mercury* (March 1, 1968).

Williamson, Marnie. Interview (August 4, 2005).

"Workshop valuable ..." *Peterborough Review* (February 1968).

Wright, Gerald. "Fight over site ..." *Kitchener Record* (October 10, 1972).

Zorach, William. *Art is My Life*. Cleveland: World Publishing Company, 1967.

INDEX